William Shakespeare's
The Merchant of Venice

Wiliam Shakespeare's *The Merchant of Venice* (1600) is one of his most contro-versial and disturbing plays, bringing us the unforgettable Shylock and his pound of flesh.

Taking the form of a sourcebook, this guide offers:

- extensive introductory comment on the contexts, critical history and production of the play, from early performances to the present
- annotated extracts from key contextual documents, reviews, critical works and the text itself
- cross-references between documents and sections of the guide, in order to suggest links between texts, contexts and criticism
- suggestions for further reading.

Part of the *Routledge Guides to Literature* series, this volume is essential reading for all those beginning detailed study of *The Merchant of Venice* and seeking not only a guide to the play, but a way through the wealth of contextual and critical material that surrounds Shakespeare's text.

S. P. Cerasano is the Edgar W. B. Fairchild Professor of Literature at Colgate University, Hamilton, New York and co editor with Marion Wynne-Davies of *Renaissance Drama by Women* (1996).

Routledge Guides to Literature*

Editorial Advisory Board: Richard Bradford (University of Ulster at Coleraine), Jan Jedrzejewski (University of Ulster at Coleraine), Duncan Wu (St. Catherine's College, University of Oxford)

Routledge Guides to Literature offer clear introductions to the most widely studied authors and literary texts.

Each book engages with texts, contexts and criticism, highlighting the range of critical views and contextual factors that need to be taken into consideration in advanced studies of literary works. The series encourages informed but independent readings of texts by ranging as widely as possible across the contextual and critical issues relevant to the works examined and highlighting areas of debate as well as those of critical consensus. Alongside general guides to texts and authors, the series includes "sourcebooks", which allow access to reprinted contextual and critical materials as well as annotated extracts of primary text.

Available in this series:

* Some books in this series were originally published in the Routledge Literary Sourcebooks series, edited by Duncan Wu, or the Complete Critical Guide to English Literature series, edited by Richard Bradford and Jan Jedrzejewski.

William Shakespeare's
The Merchant of Venice
A Sourcebook

Edited by S. P. Cerasano

Routledge
Taylor & Francis Group

LONDON AND NEW YORK

First published 2004 by Routledge
11 New Fetter Lane, London EC4P 4EE

Simultaneously published in the USA and Canada
by Routledge
29 West 35th Street, New York, NY 10001

Routledge is an imprint of the Taylor & Francis Group

Selection and editorial material © 2004 S. P. Cerasano

This volume first published as *A Routledge Literary Sourcebook on William Shakespeare's
The Merchant of Venice*

Typeset in Sabon and Gill Sans by RefineCatch Limited, Bungay, Suffolk
Printed and bound in Great Britain by TJ International Ltd, Padstow, Cornwall

British Library Cataloguing in Publication Data
A catalogue record for this book is available from the British Library

Library of Congress Cataloging in Publication Data
A Routledge literary sourcebook on William Shakespeare's
The Merchant of Venice / edited by S. P. Cerasano
     p. cm.—(Routledge literary sourcebooks)
Includes bibliographical references and index.
1. Shakespeare, William, 1564–1616. Merchant of Venice.   2. Venice
(Italy)—In literature.   3. Jews in literature.   4. Comedy. I. Cerasano, S. P.
II. Series.
PR2825 R68 2003
822.3'3—dc21   2003011942

ISBN 0–415–24051–4 (hbk)
ISBN 0–415–24052–2 (pbk)

Contents

2: Interpretations

The Work in Performance   97

3: Key Passages

4: Further Reading

Illustrations

Annotation and Footnotes

Annotation is a key feature of this series. Both the original notes from reprinted texts and new annotations by the editor appear at the bottom of the relevant page. The reprinted notes are prefaced by the author's name in square brackets, e.g. [Robinson's note].

Acknowledgements

I would like to thank the officers and staffs of the Folger Shakespeare Library, the British Library, the Shakespeare Birthplace Trust and the Colgate University Library for assistance in the preparation of this volume. The editorial staff at Routledge, particularly Liz Thompson, deserve warm thanks as well, as does Duncan Wu, the series editor. Additionally, the administrative officers of Colgate University, along with the staff of Case Library, have supported my research in a wide variety of ways. In this, Jack Dovidio (Dean and Provost), Chris Vecsey (Director, Humanities Division) and George Hudson (Chair, Department of English) are especially to be thanked. The Colgate University Research Council provided a Garrison Fellowship that assisted me in completing the research necessary for the preparation of this volume. The London Goodenough Trust (now Goodenough College) supported this research in many tangible and intangible ways. Family, friends and colleagues – both here at home, and in many distant places – have readily offered conversation, advice and encouragement.

The following illustrations (in order of appearance) have been reproduced with the kind permission of those institutions cited:

1. THE FOLGER SHAKESPEARE LIBRARY, for engraving of 'A View of Venice' from *Civitates Orbis Terrarum* by Georg Braun and Frans Hogenberg (1593), D12 B75 Cage fo., n.p. Reprinted by permission of the Folger Shakespeare Library, Washington, DC.

2. THE BRITISH LIBRARY, for engraving of 'A Street Procession from St Mark's, Venice' from Giacomo Franco, *Habiti d'huomini et donne Venetiane* (1609), C.48.h.11, fol. 8. Reprinted by permission of the British Library, London.

3. THE BRITISH LIBRARY, for engraving of 'Venetian Carnival' from Giacomo Franco, *Habiti d'huomini et donne Venetiane* (1609), C.48.h.11, fol. 17. Reprinted by permission of the British Library, London.

4. THE BRITISH LIBRARY, for engraving of 'Venetian Boat Pageant' from Giacomo Franco, *Habiti d'huomini et donne Venetiane* (1609), C.48.h.11, fol. 30. Reprinted by permission of the British Library, London.

5. THE FOLGER SHAKESPEARE LIBRARY, for engraving of 'The Third Act showing the Rialto Bridge' (n.d.) by Birket Foster, Art file V459, no. 24. Reprinted by permission of the Folger Shakespeare Library, Washington, DC.

6. THE FOLGER SHAKESPEARE LIBRARY, for engraving of 'The Rialto, Venice' (1830) by Samuel Prout, Art file V459, no. 13. Reprinted by permission of the Folger Shakespeare Library, Washington, DC.

7. THE FOLGER SHAKESPEARE LIBRARY, for ink drawing of 'Shylock' (n.d.) by Sir John Tenniel, Art Box T311, no 2. By permission of the Folger Shakespeare Library, Washington, DC.

8. THE SHAKESPEARE BIRTHPLACE TRUST, for photograph of Royal Shakespeare Company performance at the Royal Shakespeare Theatre, 1981, with David Suchet (Shylock), showing the trial scene (IV.i), taken from the Thomas Holte Theatre Photographic Collection. Reprinted by permission of the Shakespeare Birthplace Trust.

9. THE SHAKESPEARE BIRTHPLACE TRUST, for photograph of Royal Shakespeare Company performance at the Other Place, 1978, showing Shylock (Patrick Stewart) and his scales, taken by Joe Cocks Studio. Reprinted by permission of the Shakespeare Birthplace Trust.

10. THE FOLGER SHAKESPEARE LIBRARY, for photograph of title page from the first quarto of *The Merchant of Venice* (1600), printed in London, STC 22296, copy 1. Reprinted by permission of the Folger Shakespeare Library, Washington, DC.

Introduction

Although it has become clichéd to say that Shakespeare is a playwright for all time it is clearly the case that some of his plays seem to enjoy a certain immortality on the stage. *The Merchant of Venice* is one of these. During the last sixty years the play has enjoyed over forty major productions in England and America alone. Within the last century it has been translated into forty-seven languages, including Arabic, Bengali, Korean, Turkish, Serbian, Urdu and Zulu. Additionally, it has found a place in the psychoanalytic analyses of Sigmund Freud and in the commentaries of prominent social and legal historians. No less importantly, *The Merchant* has been the inspiration for films – both silent and spoken – along with operas, orchestral music, novels, one-act plays, full-length dramatic adaptations and sequels.

The reasons for the play's enormous popularity are numerous; and, in fact, *The Merchant* is so complex and controversial a play that some critics have debated over its very nature. Not surprisingly, they frequently offer contradictory interpretations. Is the play exclusively a romantic comedy; or, as Nicholas Rowe argued in 1709, does it contain elements of the tragic? Is Shylock a victim or a villain? Are the lovers simple romantics or anti-Semitic narcissists? Is Bassanio a well-intentioned suitor, or a social-climbing seeker after 'the golden fleece' (his own metaphor for describing Portia)? Is the play a plea for the tolerance of religious difference, or a condemnation of usury and, by implication, of the Jews who were associated with this particular practice by some of Shakespeare's contemporaries? Does the play celebrate the carnival of life, or warn of the dangers of a society that has become so thoroughly enslaved by economic motives that it has allowed commercial interests to supplant humane values?

In fact, Shakespeare was no stranger to moneylending, or to the necessity of making money. Therefore, the perils hinted at in *Hamlet*, when the king's advisor Polonious delivers his well-known adage, were those with which Shakespeare would have been well acquainted: 'Neither a borrower, nor a lender be.' Interestingly, however, it is not in *Hamlet* but in *The Merchant of Venice* that this warning is played out to its fullest. Nor would it be overstating the case to say that *The Merchant* is more consumed by issues relating to mercantilism and its attendant ills than any of Shakespeare's other plays. As I suggest through the materials that I have assembled for this collection, these interests were embedded in the very nature of Shakespeare's theatrical world. In a variety of ways the play would have been commodified both by and within the theatrical environment. For example, as a dramatist William Shakespeare would have sold his play to the acting company that performed it. In turn, the actors 'sold' the play to the spectators who paid to see it performed; and Shakespeare, along with the other shareholders in the company, would then have collected a percentage of the profits on each performance. Later on, if a printer made the play available to the reading public he too would have profited financially from the play; and in this last phase of economic production the players might also have benefited in a roundabout way from the play's printing. Readers who were intrigued by reading a play might be encouraged to visit the playhouse and see the play performed.

The Merchant of Venice was first printed in 1600, although it was probably performed earlier. (Editors differ in their estimates of the play's first performance.) This is the phase of Shakespeare's career that comes shortly after the early comedies, such as Love's Labour's Lost and The Taming of the Shrew, and his earliest cycle of history plays, the first Henriad (Henry VI Parts 1, 2 and 3). As might be expected The Merchant shares similarities with other Shakespearean plays that were written during this era. Like The Two Gentlemen of Verona and Romeo and Juliet – which were written near to it, chronologically speaking – The Merchant is set in Italy and is concerned with subjects related to love, loyalty and friendship. Similar to Richard II (1595), Shakespeare uses The Merchant to raise issues related to choice and the consequences of making choices (both wise choices and foolish ones). Like The Two Gentlemen of Verona, The Merchant includes a disguised heroine. Not only this, but similar to Love's Labour's Lost, The Merchant ends with uneasy characters on stage, and unanswered questions hanging in the air.

By the time that The Merchant was completed Shakespeare had demonstrated that he could write comedies with clear-cut resolutions, such as The Comedy of Errors (1588–94) and A Midsummer Night's Dream (1595–6). Yet other early comedies leave the audience feeling more unsettled. It is to this latter type of play that The Merchant of Venice belongs. This is not only because the final movement finds Antonio – the 'merchant' of the play's title – alone (or at least 'uncoupled') while the other characters are happily married; but also because, for so many Western readers and critics, a post-Holocaust sensibility requires that audiences question whether Antonio's 'punishments' really fit Shylock's 'crimes'. (Shylock is the moneylender with whom Antonio signs a bond at the outset of the play. When Antonio defaults on payment Shylock seeks a pound of his flesh. Then, in the last moments of a trial scene, Antonio is saved by Portia, a wealthy lady of Belmont, and Antonio pronounces sentence on Shylock for seeking his life.) Of course, none of the controversies presented in the play is simple. But although it is easier for an audience to interact with a play that utilises well-defined situations, precisely drawn characters and a neat conclusion, it is because of its difficult oppositions that generations of audiences and readers return to The Merchant of Venice time and again.

In many ways this sourcebook is intended both for those who are being introduced to the play for the first time and for those who are returning to it. In an attempt to explore some of the ways in which *The Merchant of Venice* has intrigued professional critics and lay readers alike, the material collected herein focuses on a variety of areas that intersect under the following rubrics: mercantile society and the commodification of human relationships; the character of Shylock and his position in the play relative to the Belmont community; and the historical context created by the play's Venetian setting. In so doing, this Sourcebook underscores the many facets of mercantilism and the knotty issues associated with them. Concurrently, it also attempts to bring these concepts squarely together with the actual ways in which the theatre of Shakespeare's time functioned. The poetry of *The Merchant of Venice* is replete with images of borrowing, buying and cashing in, testimony that the 'merchant' of its title – Antonio, not Shylock – is very much at the centre of the play. Given this, it is wholly understandable that Freud described the choices made by Portia's suitors as 'investments'. After all, we – as readers and spectators – are encouraged by Shakespeare to 'profit' from looking carefully at the play's socio-economic contexts.

This book is divided into four major sections entitled 'Contexts', 'Interpretations', 'Key Passages' and 'Further Reading'. The opening section ('Contexts') contains three subsections – 'Contextual Overview', 'Chronology' and 'Historical Contexts'. The first subsection provides an overview of major socio-political contexts related to the play; it also highlights the shaping influences of economic issues within the play. The second subsection surveys Shakespeare's professional life in the 'capitalist playhouse'. The second subsection presents contemporary thinking regarding the history and mythology of Venice, as well as material relating to the commercialism of the social and theatrical culture in which Shakespeare and his fellow actors were immersed. As a whole, the 'Contexts' section of the book demonstrates the many ways in which the commercial forces operating within London and the early modern theatre influenced Shakespeare's career, the plays written for the contemporary playhouses and the text of *The Merchant of Venice*.

The second major section of the book ('Interpretations') offers a combination of critical commentaries on the play, mostly twentieth century in origin, and performance-related sources that address aspects of the play in performance.

The third major section of the book ('Key Passages') presents extracts from the play, but not the entire play text. Rather, the selection of passages collected here is intended to provide a strong overview of the play within the areas of interest that I have outlined above. In order to assist readers I have provided copious annotations that gloss unfamiliar words, interpret difficult passages within the text or provide supplementary information. (The specifics regarding textual presentation are provided in the introduction to 'Key Passages'.)

The final section of the book offers a list of recommended editions that present the full text of the play, together with a selection of 'Further Reading' listing historical and critical sources supplementary to those excerpts reproduced in this collection.

All in all then, this sourcebook is a toolkit for beginning (or renewing) work on *The Merchant of Venice*. It does not pretend to be more than an overview.

However, if it assists readers in exploring the complexity of the text and under-standing the fascination that continues to surround this play, then the primary goals of the book will have been met.

1

Contexts

Contextual Overview

Introduction

Shakespeare set many of his plays in foreign places; yet few settings are as central to an understanding of a play as Venice is to *The Merchant of Venice*. The central division in the play between Venice and the mythical country location called Belmont defines, to a significant degree, the attitudes and ideas that are explored in *Merchant*; and in the course of the play Shakespeare is clearly harkening back to a former era in which Venice was known throughout Western Europe for its political sophistication, its forward-looking legal system and its colossal mercantile success. Although the heyday of Venice had passed by the time that Shakespeare wrote *The Merchant of Venice*, the Venetian setting allowed him to shroud his play in a vivid, exotic mythology that uniquely captured his concerns about commercialism, commodification and the future of English society as it became increasingly capitalist in its orientation. Moreover, the theatrical setting in which Shakespeare wrote and performed was blatantly commercial in its orientation and, in this, the play's commercial setting mirrored the commodification of culture that was at the centre of the theatre as a business. Therefore, an understanding of Venice's complex mythology provides an important portal into the world of *The Merchant of Venice*.

Venice: Myth and Reality

In 1593 Georg Braun and Franz Hogenberg published their collection of maps entitled *Civitates Orbis Terrarum* (*The Towns of the World*). One of these was an engraving of Venice (see Figure 1). According to Braun and Hogenberg, Venice was a complicated, isolated world, wholly surrounded by water. Consequently, when one sees Braun and Hogenberg's map for the first time it is difficult to decide precisely where to look first. The inlets and waterways appear to be endless labyrinths, the bits of land seem crammed with buildings and cultivated gardens (many of them quite grand), and the intriguing complexity (which is the city) is surrounded by every kind of sailing vessel imaginable. In fact, Venice

Figure I 'A View of Venice' from Civitates Orbis Terrarum by Georg Braun and Frans Hogenberg (1593).

seems more a sophisticated little world afloat on the sea than the more provincial 'town' that Braun and Hogenberg evoked by the title of their collection; and in this way sixteenth-century Venice must have seemed quite a bit like England.

In examining Venice from Braun and Hogenberg's perspective it appears that they were 'standing' on some point south of the city, looking north at the gem that some of their contemporaries referred to as 'La Serenissima', 'Her Serene Highness'. Yet any other map of Italy makes it clear that there really was no other place located directly south of the city on which one could easily stand. Like other mapmakers of the period, however, Braun and Hogenberg weren't interested in the sort of mechanical accuracy that seems important when we consult a map. Instead, getting it 'mostly right' was just fine, as long as a mapmaker also evoked the sight and smell – in other words, the 'sense' – of a place. As a result Braun and Hogenberg probably would have 'stood' – literally and metaphorically – in many different places as they created their version of Venice. Some of these places doubtless included the streets and marketplaces that served as the commercial venues for that mercantilism which was the hallmark of Venetian culture. At other times they probably glided into the lagoons and along the many canals where goods from all over the world seemed continually to come and go. At still other times they must have stood in various places on the Continent, listening to travellers' stories of exotic courtesans or Carnival festivities (see Figures 2, 3 and 4). Or they stood at the elbows of courtiers who told tales of Venetian political and military glory. Or, in forming yet another perspective, they must have found themselves on some hillside in the vast East, looking over their shoulders westward at a Venice that was known along the trade routes as the gateway to Western Europe. For Braun and Hogenberg, as well as for most of Shakespeare's contemporaries, these many perspectives *about* Venice finally *were* Venice. Venice was as much a place in the imagination as it was in reality.

The English saw the Venetians as a people to be emulated and as a mirror in which they could see themselves. They revered Venetian accomplishments and looked to Venice as a state upon which they hoped to model their own aspirations. As Jan Morris highlights in an essay entitled 'Islanders' from *The World of Venice* (**pp. 32–4**), like Venice, England was a country surrounded by water that enjoyed a strong maritime culture. Like Venice, England was a mercantile nation that depended upon foreign trade. In Venice, the merchants acquired tremendous economic and political importance, in many ways threatening the power of the established aristocracy. So too did the merchants in England. In Venice, as in London, the outward show of wealth was obvious. The Venetian doges (the rulers of the city) rode in golden barges; the English monarchs enjoyed elaborately painted royal barges. London culture was a combination of the homebred and the exotic; so was Venice. Furthermore, the strong base of England's nationalism suggests that the English felt that they were in a pre-eminent position among nations – economically, politically and militarily – although modern historians note that this perception was probably erroneous in all three areas. Similar to the Venetians, English citizens felt that they had a foreordained destiny, as well as a venerable past.

However, Venice differed from England in significant ways, and Venetian

Figure 2 'A Street Procession from St Mark's, Venice' from Giacomo Franco, *Habiti d'huomini et donne Venetiane* (1609).

Figure 3 'Venetian Carnival' from Giacomo Franco, *Habiti d'huomini et donne Venetiane* (1609).

culture was even maligned by some Protestants who thought that the culture had become subservient to the profit motive. As the gateway to trade with the Orient, Venice enjoyed well-established links with foreign mercantile powers that the English could only envy. This gave the Venetians access to a variety and a quality of goods that were unique amongst the European trading centres. The Rialto, or central business district of Venice, was well stocked with goods from Germany and Flanders, Constantinople and Alexandria. Given its geographical and political position Venice also learned of intellectual and aesthetic fashions from the East more rapidly than did other Europeans nations. As a result, the printing trade thrived in Venice, not only by disseminating new ideas in books but by printing music, an art for which the Venetian printers were widely esteemed. As a fiscal state Venice exported artistic delicacies for which its craftsmen were well known, including glassware, silk and intricate jewellery. The Venetian artisans became purveyors of exquisite mirrors and buttons, delicate feathers and made-to-order goods. Nor were commerce and governance separate entities. The

Venetian doge was chosen by the leaders of the local business community, whereas the English monarch was determined by inheritance (or, more precariously, by the outcome of civil war for the throne). Consequently, at least in Venetian terms, commerce reigned supreme.[1]

Mercantile Culture

To the Venetians, their city was one in which 'Christian commerce' was both promoted and protected by Divine favour. Consequently, the city had many saints who watched over its well-being. These included St Mark who, in association with the well-known Venetian winged lion, protected the city militarily. St Nicholas, the patron saint of sailors, protected Venetian trade and calmed the waters to ensure safe passage on the seas.[2] From the eleventh century onwards Venetian citizens gathered together each spring on Ascension Day to perform an elaborate series of ceremonies that were meant to ensure the continued good fortune of the Venetian sailors and, by extension, the good fortune of the merchants who owned and financed the ships. The spectacle featured an elaborate water procession with thousands of decorated boats, of all kinds, which were rowed out into the main lagoon alongside a larger, more impressive vessel in which the Doge sat prominently displayed (see Figure 4). Once at the centre of the lagoon, sacred music was performed, prayers for the protection of the Venetians were recited, and the Doge cast a gold ring into the water. The ceremony, a powerful metaphor for Venetian supremacy, came to be known as 'Lo Sposalizio', 'the wedding of Venice to the sea'.[3]

The concept of exchange – of goods, money and people, all on the move – was at the basis of Venetian mercantile culture and the stories that were told about Venice by foreign travellers; and while Divine influences might intervene in the lives of merchants, governmental intrusion into business affairs was also common. As a result, many elements of business operation were carefully regulated by the state. For example, strict rules guarded against the overloading of cargo and the manner in which it was stowed. In aid of this, each ship bore a mark in the shape of a Christian cross (either painted or carved from plates of iron) on its side to indicate where the water line should ideally fall. Thus, perhaps not coincidentally, every Venetian boat displayed the sign of both government regulation and Christian commerce on its side.

But perhaps more than in any other arena of Venetian life, profit and religion were reflected in the psychology of the merchants. Frequently, they started new account books by penning, at the top of the first page, a common adage: 'In the

1   Jean-Claude Hocquet, 'Venice' in *The Rise of the Fiscal State in Europe, c. 1200–1815*, ed. Richard Bonney (Oxford: Oxford University Press, 1999), pp. 382–415.
2   Garry Wills, *Venice: Lion City* (New York: Simon & Schuster, 2001), pp. 27–36, 240–5.
3   For a fuller description of this ritual see Edward Muir, *Civic Ritual in Renaissance Venice* (Princeton, NJ: Princeton University Press, 1981), pp. 118–24. A recording of 'Lo Sposalizio', directed by Robert King and performed by the King's Consort (Hyperion CDA67048), attempts to create the musical background of this ceremony.

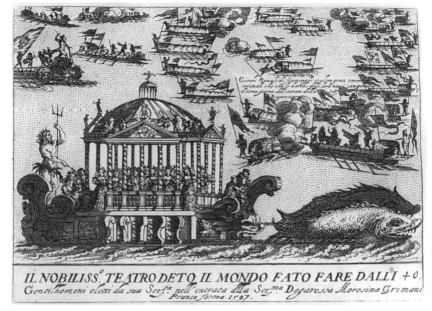

Figure 4 'Venetian Boat Pageant' from Giacomo Franco, *Habiti d'huomini et donne Venetiane* (1609).

name of God and good profit.' And from good profit honour was thought to follow. As one merchant instructed his son when he was leaving the family firm in his hands: 'Make two ducats out of one, if you can, so that you may feel the profit and honour of it, and I peace of mind.'[4] Occasionally, church spokesmen criticised merchants for what they saw as avarice. Yet Alberto Tenenti explains in his essay 'The Merchant and the Banker' (**pp. 40–2**), that although the earnings of the merchant-capitalists were constantly jeopardised by forces beyond their control, they eventually prevailed, attaining social pre-eminence despite the prejudices of theologians and social critics. As Daniel Price – one of the chaplains to King James and Prince Henry – argues in his sermon before the London Company of Merchants in 1607, merchants exemplified the Christian virtues of charity and holiness. Taking the sermon's lesson from Matthew 13:45–6, 'the king of heaven is like to a merchant'. Further, in Price's interpretation the merchant exemplifies industriousness and is to be praised for being a venturer. He concludes: 'Our marchant seeketh good pearles [. . .] & surely manie great wonders hath God made known vnto man, in precious pearles' (**p. 40**).

The all-consuming mercantile culture that defined Venice was felt in the language of bonds, contracts, property transfers and other commercial arrangements, as well as in Venetian literature and thinking more generally. In *The*

---

4   As quoted by Ugo Tucci, 'The Psychology of the Venetian Merchant in the Sixteenth Century' in *Renaissance Venice*, ed. J. R. Hale (Totowa, NJ: Rowman and Littlefield, 1973), p. 359.

Decameron, a collection of tales by the Renaissance writer Giovanni Boccaccio, the phrase 'bad fortune', for example, refers as often to a loss of profit as it does to a broader sense of ill luck.[5] Likewise, many words, phrases and images in Shakespeare's *The Merchant of Venice* bear connotations that relate directly or indirectly to commerce and consumer culture. In addition to employing predictable words such as 'ships', 'price', 'commodity' and 'merchandise', the vocabulary of the play is steeped in references to 'money' (which is used fourteen times as 'money' and five times in the plural as 'moneys') and in vocabulary associated with the exchange of funds. One finds 'borrow' and its variations used in unusual, inventive ways, as in 'he borrow'd a box of the ear' (Act 1, Scene 2, lines 64–5). Similarly, the word 'purchase' is used in its customary sense of 'buying', although unusual things are purchased in the play, including 'merit', 'slaves' and 'the semblance of my [Portia's] soul'. 'Purse' is used both as a noun, to refer to the bag in which coins are kept, and as a verb when Shylock promises to 'purse the ducats straight' (Act 1, Scene 3, line 135). Some words are also used both in a commercial and a non-commercial sense, as 'tender', which appears both in the sense of 'delicate' and 'to offer in payment'. 'Interest' is perverted by Antonio, Shylock complains, who condemns 'my [Shylock's] well-won thrift/which he calls interest' (Act 1, Scene 3, lines 11–12). 'Ducat' or 'ducats' is found in every scene of the play, used thirty-two times in all; and it is superseded in use only by the word 'bond' or 'bonds' which, used only in the first four acts, appears forty times, more than in any of Shakespeare's other plays. In fact, 'bond' is used so frequently in *The Merchant of Venice*, and so infrequently in other Shakespeare plays (in any sense, literal or metaphorical) that it seems a word that Shakespeare associated especially with this particular play. Moreover, one specific phrase commonly found in Elizabethan property deeds – 'to have and to hold' – echoes through both the language of the lovers and the language of borrowers and lenders. As such, the commercial diction of the play is emphasised in order to represent and suggest the many kinds of 'trafficking' that occur in the play.

Within this context, the practice of usury – that is, lending money while charging exceedingly high interest – becomes important. In Act 1, Scene 3 of *The Merchant of Venice*, Shylock and Antonio debate whether it is moral to loan money for profit (**pp. 150–7**); and when Antonio defaults upon the bond he has signed (in Act 4, Scene 1) the subject is again raised. Throughout the play, Shakespeare and his contemporaries would have been conversant with the opinions of Christian churchmen, such as Thomas Wilson, who wrote *A Discourse upon Usury* (1572), arguing that it was against the principles of Christianity to loan money for profit. In the view of Wilson, and other commentators of the time, a good Christian should loan money to those in need without charging interest. In this way, those in need would be treated with mercy and aided by charity, rather than being subject to further persecution. Wilson states that usury is a form of theft, whereas 'To lende freely is a kynde of liberalitie and bountifulnes' (**p. 42**).

---

5   See, for example, the gulling of Andreuccio from *The Decameron* in *Merchant Writers of the Italian Renaissance*, ed. Vittore Branca (New York: Marsilio Publishers, 1999), pp. 3–15, in which a man starts out to invest in a horse and ends up 'investing in a ring'.

Later on, the eminent lawyer and statesman Sir Francis Bacon pointed out that usury was an activity that was necessary for the wheels of the commercial market to turn. Bacon advocated charging interest on loans, even though he was clearly uncomfortable with the practice: 'it is the canker and ruin of many men's estates; which in process of time breeds a public poverty' (p. 45). However, even though Wilson and others acknowledged that moneylending could, from another viewpoint, be considered simply a commercial service (as long as lenders restricted themselves to the 10 per cent allowable under English law), they were wary of its more sinister implications. Moreover, as Wilson admits, the practice was associated almost exclusively with Jews. Thus, the connection between the abuses of usury and Jewish moneylenders was well established at the time that *The Merchant* was written.

Jews in Venice and London

The Venetians would have been familiar figures in early modern London where they came to maintain their contacts with the wool trade and to conduct other kinds of business. Additionally, Venetian ambassadors were frequently in residence at the English Court, and it is through their diplomatic correspondence that so many eyewitness accounts of Elizabethan Court performances (particularly of the masque) have been preserved. However, it is unclear as to precisely how Shakespeare could have been so well informed about the particular place of merchants and moneylenders in Venetian society. In the absence of information that would suggest that Shakespeare had travelled to Italy, we are forced to believe that he created Antonio from a combination of the Venetian merchants that he knew or had heard about in London. Along the same lines, he probably created Shylock from a combination of the tales of Jewish moneylenders told by travellers who had been to Venice, together with whatever he had heard about the Jewish community resident in London in the 1590s.

In accordance with a new governmental edict formulated by the Council of Ten (Venice's chief governing body) and published in 1516, the Jews who lived in Venice were ordered to live in a 'small, isolated area of the city that had once been the site of a foundry'. (The Italian word for 'foundry' is 'ghetto' although Howells (p. 36) notes that it is also derived from the Hebrew word for 'congregation'. Today the word has come to mean a segregated area within a city, occupied by a specific ethnic group.) The area – which encompassed some of the last available land, a scarcity in Venice – was located near to prisons. The 1516 edict marked a turning point in relations between the Jews and the Republic. Up to then 'Jewish merchants and moneylenders had been allowed to do business in the city without being granted rights of permanent residence.'[6] Moreover, the Jews had to deal with other penalties whilst living in the ghetto, as William Dean Howells details:

6   Francesca Brandes, ed., *Venice and Environs: Jewish Itineraries* (New York: Marsilio Publishers, 1997).

'They were obliged to pay their landlords a third more rent than Christians paid; the ghetto was walled in, and its gates were kept by Christian guards, who every day opened them at dawn and closed them at dark, and who were paid by the Jews' (p. 36).

There were other, ongoing penalties exacted against Jews as well: although Venice had 'a consortium of merchants from every nation', only Jews were excluded from it. Moreover, 'they were not allowed to trade with the Levant but had to make use of a Venetian intermediary, and while Jews on the *terrafirma* [i.e. in mainland Italy] could practise any kind of business, those who were members of the "German nation" of Venice, so as not to harm the other inhabitants of the place, had to limit themselves to dealing in second-hand clothes – besides, of course, the practice of usury.'[7] The Jews were also required to wear badges and caps in order that they could be easily identified. These restrictions – whether geographical or trade related – had the effect of separating the Jews of Venice from the Christian businessmen. In order to trade on the Rialto Shylock would have had to walk halfway across Venice, from the area around the Campo del Ghetto Nuovo, located in the district now known as Cannareggio, across the Grand Canal south and east, crossing the area called Santa Croce. In so doing he would have travelled through narrow, labyrinthine streets that were the only venues before the more modern walkways were constructed. The distance was not great, covering roughly one kilometre, or a walk of some fifteen minutes; but the ghetto was clearly a 'distance' – in Venetian terms – from the Rialto.[8]

For the members of Shakespeare's audience, Jews and Jewish customs would have been as foreign and as exotic as the setting of *The Merchant of Venice*. Because the Jews had been expelled from England by Edward I in 1290 'there remained in London only the *Domus Conversorum* or House of Convertites, occasional sojourners from abroad, and individual men of some distinction who had, as Christians, taken their place in English society'.[9] As Peter Berek points out in his essay entitled 'The Jew as Renaissance Man', Jews were 'more available to the English as concepts than as persons, more vivid as sites of speculation than as doers of deeds'. However, concurrently, the Marrano (or converted Jew) 'played a series of roles, all of which were associated with social and economic innovation and change'. Thus, the process of associating 'innovation and change with Jewishness provided Elizabethan Englishmen with a way of acknowledging the mixed feelings they aroused of allure and anxiety' (p. 37). This anxiety came to be felt in a palpable way, according to literary critics and historians, who see it at the root of the anti-Semitism that emerged during the 1590s, both in the more generalised social attitudes and specific events. For example, in tracing the history of anti-Semitism in England some historians and literary scholars have tradition-ally pointed to the trial and execution in 1593 of Doctor Roderigo Lopez, a

---

7   Tucci, 'Psychology of the Venetian Merchant', p. 365. Those of the 'German nation of Venice' were German merchants who had settled within Venice.
8   The Rialto is not precisely at the geographical centre of Venice, but it is very close to claiming this position.
9   C. J. Sisson, 'A Colony of Jews in Shakespeare's London', *Essays and Studies*, 23 (1938), 38–51.

Spanish Jew who, it was alleged, had participated in a plot to poison Queen Elizabeth I.[10] (Lopez was one of the Queen's physicians at this time and a convert to Christianity.) Lopez's trial attracted an enormous amount of attention, and his execution is thought to have become a *cause célèbre*. Yet, even if the use of the Lopez trial as evidence of anti-Semitism is open to controversy, the allegations of participating in usurious practices – the outgrowth of such anxieties – also found a broader expression in the charges of usury levelled against Jews during the period even though usury was, as Berek notes, a 'common and legal business practice' (**p. 37**). Furthermore, 'the ancient prejudice against Jews in England was based not only on religious differences, which made them a race accused, but also on commercial jealousy, which recognized in them inconvenient competitors'.[11]

The Commercial Playhouse

Just as *The Merchant of Venice* showcases a commercial world, so did the playhouse environment in which Shakespeare wrote and performed his plays; and the early modern theatre in which Shakespeare worked was substantially different from its earlier counterpart, particularly in commercial terms. For the first time playhouses were expensive, purpose-built structures in which capitalists 'ventured' substantial amounts of money, and then waited for their investments to be returned, very much the same as those merchants who invested in ships and then waited for them to return home. Thus, the 'venturing', 'risking' and 'profiteering' – topics that pervade the text of *The Merchant of Venice* – were central to the theatre business of the 1590s when *The Merchant* first appeared on stage.

As the Chronology (**pp. 22–6**) suggests, the commercial world in which the playhouses came to thrive was established shortly after Shakespeare's birth, in 1567, when the Red Lion playhouse was constructed in London as a space in which plays were to be performed. Less than ten years later, in 1576, James Burbage (a joiner by trade) and his brother in law, a grocer named John Brayne, constructed a playhouse in Shoreditch called the Theatre, in the north-east sector of the city, near to the road in which much traffic moved in and out of London. Thus, the Theatre came to attract not only resident Londoners but those who were visiting the city from the north of England. Before long, the Theatre had become so successful that Henry Lanham, a groom of the Queen's Chamber, invested his money in another playhouse, constructed nearby. This, called the

---

10 For a discussion of the Lopez trial and Christopher Marlowe's *The Jew of Malta*, see the edition of the play edited by Richard Van Fossen (Lincoln, Nebr.: University of Nebraska Press, 1964), pp. xii–xiii and the edition of the play prepared more recently by Nigel Bawcutt (Manchester: Manchester University Press, 1978), pp. 1 and 49, n. 4. The Lopez trial is also the focus of David S. Katz, *The Jews in the History of England, 1485–1850* (Oxford: Oxford University Press, 1994), pp. 49–106. The view that Lopez was persecuted because he was a Jew has been disputed by Stephen Orgel because, he notes, Lopez's Jewish ancestry was unknown to the general public (see his essay, 'Imagining Shylock' in *Imagining Shakespeare* (New York and London: Palgrave, 2003), pp. 144–62).
11 Sisson, 'A Colony of Jews', p. 39.

Curtain (1577), an allusion to the edges or 'curtains' of the city, functioned as one of the earliest venues for Shakespeare's plays, which were also performed at the Theatre. Apparently, these investments returned significant enough profits that more investors were encouraged to follow suit. The construction of additional playhouses soon followed in other parts of the greater London area. These included a playhouse at Newington Butts, south of the River Thames, as well as the Swan, built by a goldsmith (Francis Langley). Both were constructed in 1577. Then, a decade later, a dyer named Philip Henslowe built the Rose Theatre, on the South Bank, across the river from St Paul's Cathedral.[12] By the time that Shakespeare began his professional career there were five playhouses in London, all of which were owned by men who did not apparently make their livings by writing or performing in plays. They were a new class of investors who were willing to risk their money on a new kind of investment. They collected returns on rent from these buildings and, in some cases, from receiving a share of the profits from the performances staged in their theatres. This pattern – of investors who were principally financiers, and not artisans – was to continue through to the end of Shakespeare's life. Shakespeare and his fellow actors (the Lord Chamberlain's Men, later the King's Men) eventually constructed and owned two large public playhouses (the first and second Globe) and another, smaller private playhouse in the Blackfriars, even though virtually all of the other London playhouses were constructed by private investors who held no other obvious association with theatre as an art. By 1614, at which time Shakespeare had left London and returned to Stratford for retirement, large public playhouses, such as the Theatre, Curtain, Swan and Rose had been joined by the Globe, the Fortune, the Red Bull and the Hope. To be sure, not all of these playhouses survived as glorious successes; however, theatre was considered a good enough risk for many investors to involve themselves in theatre as a business.[13]

In some ways the playhouses and companies with which Shakespeare was associated throughout his career were the most commodified in the business. Although James Burbage and Henry Lanham owned the playhouses which provided the performance space rented by the acting companies to which Shakespeare belonged, the companies formed a consortium of shareholders to purchase scripts (or 'playbooks', as they were called), costumes and other necessities. In the 1590s the fee for each share seems to have been £50 per actor, or an initial investment of £600 that was contributed by a group of twelve adult players.[14] As time passed, however, individual shares became more costly to purchase. In addition, in 1599, when Shakespeare's company decided to construct the first Globe Theatre the project required that the players purchase shares in the new theatre. Consequently, by 1600, Shakespeare would have owned a share both in the

---

12 Information relating to specific playhouses of the period and their owners can be found in E. K. Chambers, *The Elizabethan Stage* (Oxford: Clarendon Press, 1923), vol. 2.
13 For more information on theatre as a business, see William Ingram, *A London Life in the Brazen Age: Francis Langley, 1548–1602* (Cambridge, Mass.: Harvard University Press, 1978) and *The Business of Playing* (Ithaca, NY: Cornell University Press, 1992).
14 The sum of £50 in 1590 is equivalent to roughly £7800 (or $12,850) today. In 1590, the average schoolmaster was earning £20 ($33) per year.

company and in the playhouse in which he performed. Given changing historical events, occasionally players left the company and were replaced by others; and many incoming players assumed similar financial responsibilities to Shakespeare and the original shareholders. Therefore, despite these changes in personnel, the Globe and the Lord Chamberlain's/King's Men were uniquely 'commercial creatures', investing in their own enterprise on every level and also 'bound' to each other financially. Sharing financial responsibility, 'venturing' and 'risking' were part and parcel of being a member of the company. Moreover, Shakespeare, like other actors, had personal experience of being a landowner, a taxpayer and a recipient of fees for performing at Court upon special occasions. (See specific entries in the Chronology, **pp. 22–6**, relating to Shakespeare's personal affairs.) And, along with his fellow players, he borrowed money and lent money. Therefore, he would have been thoroughly immersed in the financial world to which *The Merchant* alludes. As a playwright he 'ventured' by performing before the public; as an actor he 'risked' an investment in a play and all of the trappings of performance, hoping to return a profit from this investment; as a private citizen in London and Stratford-upon-Avon he participated in many aspects of the growing commercial world of early modern England.

Shakespeare's Play and the Theatre: Risking, Venturing and Exchanging

Whether or not Shakespeare had ever travelled to Venice, he had certainly become aware of the degree to which London and other European trading centres created a frenzy of commodification. And clearly, a key issue raised in *The Merchant of Venice* has to do with the degree to which this influences society and social relations. Have merchants (and potentially others) become so caught up in their businesses that commodities and people have become interchangeable? The flesh-bond plot of *The Merchant* helps to illustrate, in concrete terms, the 'interchange-ability' of money and human flesh, as well as the eeriness of the perils therein; and three thousand ducats would have been recognised as a phenomenal sum of money by Shakespeare's audiences.[15] Further, the flesh-bond underscores the depth of Shylock's anger and the extreme manner through which he hopes to exact this revenge if Antonio defaults on the bond.

Consequently, the language of bonds and shareholders, exchange and credit, value and patronage reverberates both within the play and within the commercial setting of the Elizabethan theatrical world in which the play was performed. Just as the spectators 'exchange' their entrance fees to purchase a commodity (entertainment), there are several incidents echoing practices of gift exchange within the play. The caskets used in the marriage lottery would have reminded Elizabethan audiences of the wedding caskets that were exchanged upon marriage. The gold ring that was cast by the Venetian doge into the sea during the city's annual

---

15 In today's terms the gold ducat was worth approximately £2.36–2.43 (or $3.90–4.00). ∎

'wedding of Venice to the sea' returns, in Shakespeare's play, in the form of the gold rings exchanged between Portia, Nerissa and their spouses. (Interestingly, Portia's ring, once 'lost', is restored to her at the end of the play whereas, sadly, Shylock's ring – given to him by his late wife when he was a bachelor – is lost for ever. See Act 3, Scene 1, lines 95–7.)

Nor should the implications of 'exchange', in its broadest sense, be overlooked in terms of the love plot of the play. Portia – the wealthy heiress pursued by many men – is ultimately 'exchanged' by her dead father to her husband Bassanio, and through marriage Portia 'exchanges' her status as a single young woman for that of a more substantial, married woman. Additionally, within the play Portia behaves in both traditional and non-traditional ways, depending upon the circumstances. The ideal woman, as Edwin Sandys wrote in 'Sermon Sixteen' (1585), should be 'honest and modest', which, in the common parlance of the time, meant that she should be 'chaste, silent, and obedient'. As Sandys also emphasises, no person (male or female) should be married without the consent of his or her parents, and to do so was dishonourable. If one marries without parental consent, 'it is not he [God] that coupleth and joineth them together: their estate is base and not honourable in his sight' (p. 49). Alongside these attitudes were those expressed by Juan Luis Vives, the Spanish philosopher, who suggested that women should be educated so that they could be better wives and mothers. For Vives, learning shapes virtue, regardless of the sex of the learner (pp. 49–51).[16] Vives's commentary is interesting in light of the way in which Portia disguises herself as a doctor of law, using her learning in order to interpret Shylock's bond in a way that liberates Antonio, Bassanio's friend. Of course, it is Portia's male disguise that gives her learning a voice in the Venetian courtroom; however, through these means, and in other ways, she too participates in, and contributes to, the many 'exchanges' of the play. In allowing Bassanio to offer her money in order to pay off Antonio's bond she becomes a patron (even, some might argue, a 'merchant') in her own right. Then, in the final scene of the play, she assumes the role of the humorous lady of Belmont who taunts her husband when he arrives home without his wedding ring. However, in returning Bassanio's ring to him she passes it first to Antonio, who then hands it on to Bassanio. In the most obvious sense, Portia exchanges vows a second time in this gesture, but this time it is in the presence of Antonio, the foremost merchant of the play, who stands in to witness the vows as a surrogate father to Bassanio and as a stand-in for Portia's dead father. Thus, whilst she acts in her own womanly dress, Portia's 'exchanges' are those that are acceptable to the traditionalists such as Vives and Sandys; yet concurrently, in disguise she becomes, however temporarily, a participant in the 'exchange' of mercy and justice which

---

16 For more information on Elizabethan marriages, see Anne Laurence, *Women in England, 1500–1760* (London: Weidenfeld & Nicolson, 1994), pp. 41–60. Like Edwin Sandys, Antonia Fraser makes much of 'wife sought for wealth' in Chapter 1 of *The Weaker Vessel* (New York: Random House, 1994), pp. 9–25. Her successive chapters – 'Affection is False' (Ch. 2) and 'Crown to Her Husband' (Ch. 3) – characterise the lives of particular women as they lived in English society according to the tenets and strictures articulated by Sandys and Vives.

the characters from Belmont execute when Shylock attempts to take his pound of flesh from Antonio. Critics who point out the similarity between Portia and Antonio, such as Lynda E. Boose (**pp. 86–8**), are quick to note that there is an exchange at the heart of the marriage between Portia and Bassanio that is different, though related to that between Antonio and Bassanio. Portia offers increased wealth (the 'breeding of money') in exchange for money; but she also offers 'generation', or the breeding of children and lineage. In this way, the central exchanges of the play mirror each other within the commercial context of the play.

Finally, then, the commercial world of *The Merchant of Venice* depends upon a complex web of financial obligation and exchange, as did the historical world of Shakespeare's playhouse. Antonio ventures his wealth for Bassanio as Shakespeare and his fellow players ventured their wealth in putting together a production that they presented. Additionally, the theme of patronage is applicable to both settings. Portia comes to serve as a patroness of sorts, first by giving Bassanio the money that he needs to free Antonio from Shylock's bond and, later, by welcoming Antonio into her house. (By extension she also becomes the financial patroness of Nerissa and Gratiano, of Lorenzo and Jessica, and of the play as a whole.) Likewise, the spectators within the Elizabethan playhouse served as patrons of the theatre in paying their entrance fees, and they were welcomed into the playhouse by the players who entertained them. Moreover, each playing company of the period enjoyed the political patronage of a nobleman. Hence, Shakespeare's company – who held a patent initially from Henry Carey, the Lord Chamberlain, and later from King James – was called the Lord Chamberlain's Men and, later, the King's Men.

Finally, then, the commercial setting of *The Merchant of Venice* and the commercial setting of the playhouse mirror one another in a multiplicity of ways, even as the Venetian setting of the play and that of early modern London reflected each other during the 1590s. In the most compelling sense, Shylock's 'merchandising' parallels that of the dramatist who wrote the play, and of the actors who marketed it and performed it. Therefore, the marketplace of the Rialto is concurrently the marketplace of the Elizabethan stage. Given this, it hardly surprising that *The Merchant of Venice* is the most thorough exploration and the most forceful demonstration of 'theatrical economics' – in every possible sense of the term – that Shakespeare ever presented.

Chronology

Bullet points are used to denote events in Shakespeare's life, and asterisks to denote historical and literary events.

1564
- • William Shakespeare is born in Stratford-upon-Avon in April
- * Gypsies are expelled from England

1567
- * Red Lion Playhouse built in London; revolt in the Netherlands

1570
- • Shakespeare's father twice accused of lending money at interest

1572
- • Shakespeare's father is accused of illegal wool dealing
- * Statute against vagabonds is passed, which threatens actors without patrons; Thomas Wilson publishes *A Discourse upon Usury*

1576
- * James Burbage builds the Theatre in Shoreditch; laws against Catholics passed

1577
- * Henry Lanham builds the Curtain Playhouse in Shoreditch; Jerome Savage builds a playhouse in Newington Butts, south of London; Francis Drake begins his voyage around the world

1582
- • Shakespeare marries Anne Hathaway

1585
- • Shakespeare's twins, Hamnet and Judith, are born

1587

* Philip Henslowe builds the Rose Theatre in Southwark; Mary, Queen of Scots executed

1588

• Shakespeare probably enters the London theatre around this time
* Spanish Armada defeated

1589

* Christopher Marlowe's *The Jew of Malta* performed in London around this time

1592

• Shakespeare's father fails to go to church for fear of process for debt; *King Richard III, The Comedy of Errors*
* James Burbage's son Richard performs with Shakespeare's company as the lead actor; plague breaks out in London

1593

* Christopher Marlowe murdered; church attendance made compulsory; plague rages in London and the playhouses are closed temporarily

1594

• Lord Chamberlain's Men founded, with Shakespeare as one of the company's players; *The Taming of the Shrew, Titus Andronicus*
* Marlowe's *The Jew of Malta* continues in the repertory of the Lord Admiral's Men; Francis Langley builds the Swan Theatre; rebellion in Ireland

1595

• *Romeo and Juliet, A Midsummer Night's Dream, King Richard II*
* Treasurer of the Queen's Chamber records payments to Shakespeare and other actors in his company for performing plays before the Queen during the Christmas season, 1594

1596

• Shakespeare's son Hamnet dies; *The Merchant of Venice* probably written around this time; *King Henry IV Part 1*
* *The Jew of Malta*, temporarily dropped from the repertory of the Lord Admiral's Men, again performed; Earl of Essex attacks Cadiz harbour and destroys Spanish galleons, one of which is called the *San Andrés* ('The Andrew'); food shortages create a crisis throughout England; James Burbage, owner of the Theatre, purchases leases to build a private theatre in the Blackfriars; neighbourhood residents prevent him from opening a playhouse there

1597

- Shakespeare purchases New Place, a fine house, in Stratford-upon-Avon, but defaults on paying taxes in London
* James Burbage's sons, Cuthbert and Richard, purchase additional property in the Blackfriars

1598

- Shakespeare again defaults on paying taxes; Richard Quiney, an acquaintance from Stratford-upon-Avon, approaches Shakespeare for a loan; *The Merchant of Venice* is entered in the London Stationers Register and probably in performance by this time; *Much Ado About Nothing, King Henry IV Part 2*; a lease is granted for property in Southwark to the Burbages, together with actors William Shakespeare, Augustine Phillips, Thomas Pope, John Heminges and William Kempe

1599

- The Burbages, with members of the Lord Chamberlain's Men (including Shakespeare) build the first Globe Theatre in Southwark; *King Henry V, Julius Caesar, As You Like It*
* The Archbishop of Canterbury publicly burns satires and pamphlets

1600

- Shakespeare again fails to pay taxes due earlier; *Hamlet* performed; *The Merchant of Venice* first published in quarto
* Philip Henslowe and Edward Alleyn build the Fortune Theatre in Middlesex; a private playhouse is built in the vicinity of St Paul's Cathedral; the East India Company is founded

1601

- Death of Shakespeare's father; the Lord Chamberlain's Men are paid by Essex and other conspirators to perform *Richard II* on the eve of their rebellion; *Twelfth Night, Troilus and Cressida*
* The Earl of Essex and his followers attempt rebellion and fail; the Earl and other traitors are executed

1602

- Shakespeare extends his property holdings in Stratford-upon-Avon, purchasing another house and an additional tract of land

1603

- The Lord Chamberlain's Men, Lord Admiral's Men and Worcester's Men are granted royal patronage. Shakespeare's company becomes the King's Men; First Quarto of *Hamlet* published
* Queen Elizabeth dies; James VI and I accedes; plague again rages in London and the theatres are temporarily closed

1604

- The King's Men participate in the coronation for the new king; they are paid to attend upon the Spanish ambassador at Somerset House; *Othello, Measure for Measure*
* Aaron Holland builds the Red Bull Playhouse in Middlesex

1605

- Shakespeare purchases lands in Stratford-upon-Avon; the Master of the Revels pays Shakespeare's company to perform seven plays at Court, including *The Merchant of Venice*, played twice, as 'commanded by the King's Majesty'; *King Lear*

1606

- *Macbeth, Antony and Cleopatra*
* Expedition to colonise Virginia

1607

- Shakespeare's daughter Susanna marries John Hall, a prominent doctor in Stratford-upon-Avon; *Coriolanus*
* Defeated Irish earls flee to the Continent

1608

- The Burbages, together with Henry Evans and some members of the King's Men, form a syndicate to operate a theatre in the Blackfriars
* A private playhouse is built in the Whitefriars; conflict erupts between King James and Parliament

1609

- The King's Men begin to occupy the Blackfriars theatre, thereafter using it alternately with the Globe as their winter playhouse

1610

- *The Winter's Tale*
* Parliament petitions the King with 'grievances'; Richard and Cuthbert Burbage purchase more properties in the Blackfriars

1611

- Shakespeare returns to Stratford-upon-Avon around this time; *The Tempest*
- Actor John Underwood acquires a share in the Blackfriars theatre some time after 1611; William Sly dies and his share is transferred to actor William Ostler
* Parliament is dismissed by King James; a translation of the Bible is authorised by the King

1612

- The Burbages acquire additional property in the Blackfriars
* Prince Henry, son to James VI and I, dies; his brother Charles becomes next

in line to the throne; the Prince's Men find patronage with Frederick, Elector Palatine, and become known as the Palsgrave's Men

1613
- Shakespeare purchases the deed for an expensive property in the Blackfriars; the first Globe playhouse burns down and is rebuilt by Richard Burbage, William Shakespeare and fellow players from the King's Men; *The Two Noble Kinsmen* is written by Shakespeare and Fletcher around this time
* Henslowe and Alleyn build the Hope Playhouse in Southwark, on the site of the former Bear Garden, near to the Globe

1614
- Richard and Cuthbert Burbage purchase additional properties in the Blackfriars
- William Ostler's share in the Blackfriars is transferred to his father-in-law John Heminges following Ostler's death

1616
- Shakespeare's second daughter Judith marries Thomas Quiney; Shakespeare dies in April
* Philip Henslowe, owner of the Rose and Hope playhouses, dies; the First Folio of Ben Jonson's plays is printed in London; a playhouse called the Cockpit (Phoenix) is built in Drury Lane

1619
- The Second Quarto of *The Merchant of Venice* is printed, an unauthorised reprint with the false date of 1600
* Queen Anne dies; Richard Burbage dies

1621
* The Fortune Playhouse burns down and is rebuilt by Edward Alleyn

1623
- The First Folio of Shakespeare's plays, including *The Merchant of Venice*, is printed in London

1626
* Edward Alleyn, owner of the Fortune Playhouse, dies

1629
- The original leases owned by the shareholders of the Blackfriars theatre are terminated, leaving Cuthbert Burbage, together with the widows of Richard Burbage and Henry Condell, to represent the original shareholders
* A new playhouse called Salisbury Court is built near the old site of the Whitefriars

Historical Contexts

The Commercial Playhouse

From **Philip Henslowe, _Henslowe's Diary_** (1591), ed. R. A. Foakes and R. T. Rickert (Cambridge: Cambridge University Press, 1961), pp. 16–17

From 1593 to 1607 Philip Henslowe kept a memorandum book containing – amongst other things – accounts relating to the Rose Theatre. These include loans to the various Rose-playing companies for playbooks, costumes and other production expenses. There is also a section of receipts from the Rose play-house covering the period from mid-February 1591 to early November 1597, with some gaps. _Henslowe's Diary_ is a unique document: no other account book exists for other playhouses or playing companies during Shakespeare's era. Consequently, it reveals much about the ways in which the Rose repertory functioned, and the kinds of expenses and income that could be expected of a theatrical business. From Henslowe's receipts it appears that the plays in the repertory changed frequently, and that even the most popular plays were not performed day after day, but were rotated along with the other, less popular plays. The receipts section of the _Diary_ also suggests that Henslowe's income would have been substantial. The income recorded in the list below, which is a short section from Henslowe's accounts, totals just under £70. Of course, as a theatrical investor Henslowe also loaned money to the acting company that performed at the Rose, so, ultimately, not all of the money recorded was pure profit. Nonetheless, the income recorded here is impressive and it must have been substantial enough for Henslowe to continue in his role as a theatre entrepreneur until his death in 1616.

The plays in the following list include a variety of comedies, English histories and foreign histories. They are: _Friar Bacon and Friar Bungay, Muly Mollocco, The Spanish Comedy_ (also called _Don Horatio_), _Orlando Furioso, Henry VI_ and _Henry of Cornwall, Machiavel, Pope Joan, Clorys and Orgasto, Jeronimo, The Looking-Glass, Zenobia, Four Plays in One_ and _Bendo and Richardo_. Also included is Christopher

Marlowe's play, *The Jew of Malta*, which, some critics argue, had an influence on Shakespeare's *The Merchant of Venice* (although other critics argue that 'influence' is too strong a term).[1]

In the key passages below, taken from the Foakes and Rickert edition, the italicised letters, included by the editors, indicate expansions of Henslowe's manuscript abbreviations.

Rd at fryer bacvne th*e* 19 of febreary . . . satterdaye	xvij s iij d
Rd at m*v*lomvrc*o* the 20 of febreary	xxix s
Rd at orlando th*e* 21 of febreary	xvj s vj d
Rd at spanes comodye donne oraci*o*e the 23 of febreary	xiij s vj d
Rd at sy*r* John mandevell th*e* 24 of febreary	xij*s*vj d
Rd at harey of cornwell th*e* 25 of febreary 1591	xxxij*s*
Rd at the Jewe of malltuse th*e* 26 of febrearye 1591	l s
Rd at clorys & orgasto th*e* 28 of febreary 1591	xviij s
Rd at mvlamvlluco the 29 of febrearye 1591	xxxiiij s
Rd at poope Jone the 1 of marche 1591	xv*s*
Rd the matchevell the 2 of marche 1591	xiiij*s*
Rd at harey the vj the 3 of marche 1591	iij*li* xvj*s*8 d
Rd at bendo & Richardo th*e* 4 of march*e* 1591	xvj s
Rd at iiij playes in one th*e* 6 of marche 1591	xxxj s vj d
Rd at harey the vj the 7 of marche 1591	iij li
Rd at lockinglasse th*e* 8 of marche 1591	vij*s*
Rd at senobia the 9 of marche 1591	xxij s vj d
Rd at the Jewe of malta th*e* 10 of march*e* 1591	lvj s
Rd at harey the vj the 11 of marche 1591	xxxxvij*s* vj*d*
Rd at the comodey of doneoracio th*e* 13 of march 1591	xxviiij*s*
Rd at Jeronymo th*e* 14 of march 1591	iij li xj s
Rd at harey the 16 of march*e* 1591	xxxj s vjd
Rd at mvlo mvllocco th*e* 17 of marche 1591	xxviij s vj*d*
Rd at the Jewe of malta th*e* 18 of march*e* 1591	xxxix s
Rd at Joronymo th*e* 20 of march*e* 1591	xxxviij s
Rd at constantine th*e* 21 of march*e* 1591	xij s
Rd at Q Jerusallem the 22 of march*e* 1591	xviij s
Rd at harey of corwell th*e* 23 of march*e* 1591	xiij s vj d
Rd at fryer bacon the 25 of marche 1591	xv*s* vj*d*
Rd at the lockinglasse the 27 of march*e* 1591	lv*s*
Rd at harey the vj the 28 of march*e* 1591	iij*li* viij s
Rd at mvlimvlucko the 29 of march*e* 1591	iij*li*ij s

---

1   M. M. Mahood argues that *The Jew of Malta* is 'not in the conventional sense a source [. . .] It is a persistent presence which Shakespeare manipulates with confidence and skill' (Cambridge: Cambridge University Press, 1987), p. 8.

Rd at doneoracio the 30 of marche 1591   xxxix s
Rd at Joronymo the 31 of marche 1591   iij li
Rd at mandefell the 1 of ap^{r}ell 1591   xxx s
Rd at matchevell the 3 of ap^{r}ell 1591   xxij s
Rd at the Jewe of malta the 4 of ap^{r}ell 1591 xxxxiij s
Rd at harey the vj the 5 of ap^{r}ell 1591   xxxxj s
Rd at brandymer the of ap^{r}ell 1591   xxij s
Rd at Jeronymo the 7 of ap^{r}ell 1591   xxvj s
Rd at mvle mvloco the 8 of ap^{r}ell 1591   xxiij s

From **Philip Henslowe, *Henslowe's Diary*** (1598), ed. R. A. Foakes and R. T. Rickert (Cambridge: Cambridge University Press, 1961), p. 240

In 1597–8, Philip Henslowe, owner of the Rose Theatre, signed bonds with six actors who, by these agreements, became bound to perform at the Rose. Two of these are reproduced below. In the first document William Borne bound himself to play with the Lord Admiral's Men at the Rose Theatre for three years. Borne had been a player with the Pembroke's Men earlier on, but an ill-fated production of a play entitled *The Isle of Dogs* (the subject and circumstances of which remain a mystery) forced the closure of the Swan Theatre. (The closure of other playhouses soon followed.) After this, Borne and several other players (including Thomas Downton, see Document 2 below) joined (or rejoined) the Admiral's Men who performed at Henslowe's Rose. The demands of the bond include the fact that Borne shall not perform at any other public playhouse, and that he will forfeit a hundred marks should he fail to keep his promise. Nevertheless, it is difficult to know precisely how serious a breach of contract would have been. (Borne never seems to have tested the water in order to find out.) The fact that Henslowe used an informal method of contract, rather than having a more formal contract drawn up and enrolled in one of the London courts, combined with the fact that he himself signed all of the witnesses' names, raises the question of whether the bonds would have had much, if any, force under law.

In the second document Thomas Downton bound himself to Henslowe for two years under much the same terms as Borne, mainly to perform exclusively at the Rose.

It is unclear as to whether actors in other playing companies signed similar agreements. If so, none of these documents has survived. After 1599, many of Shakespeare's fellow actors at the Globe playhouse invested in the theatre; and many before this time had invested in the company as shareholders. These investments might well have been of sufficient magnitude to 'bind them' to the company that performed there, without necessitating that the players sign formal bonds. In the case of the Rose Theatre, the players never owned shares in the theatre, and the players who signed bonds with Henslowe weren't apparently shareholders at the time that the bonds were drawn up, although Downton might well have owned a share earlier, in 1595.

In presenting the following documents I have first printed the transcription of the original manuscript versions of the bonds as they appear in Henslowe's *Diary*, ed. Foakes and Rickert (1961). I have followed these versions with modernised versions in order to assist readers who are unfamiliar with early modern manuscripts. Readers will notice that in the original, manuscript version certain letters ('u' and 'v', or 'i' and 'y') were interchangeable, and that spelling and punctuation were not yet standardised. Also, Henslowe simply abbreviated some words in his own idiosyncratic manner (such as 'M^{r}dom' for 'Memorandum'). Because the manuscripts weren't drawn up by a professional clerk it is likely that Henslowe would probably have been either making up the language of the bonds from other bonds that he had signed, or he might well have been using language from a legal formulary, many of which were printed and available for purchase during this period.

1.

Original Manuscript Version

M^{r}dom that the 10 of aguste 1597 w^m borne came & ofered
hime sealfe to come and playe wth my lord admeralles mean
at my howsse called by the name of the Rosse setewate one the back
after this order folowinge he hathe Receued of me iij d vpon & A
sumsette to forfette vnto me a hundrethe marckes of lafull
money of Ingland yf he do not performe thes thinges folowinge
that is presentley after libertie beinge granted for playinge to
come & to playe wth my lordes admeralles men at my howsse
aforsayd & not in any other howsse publicke a bowt london
for the space of iij yeares beginynge Imediatly after this Re
straynt is Recaled by the lordes of the cownsell wch Restraynt
is by the menes of playinge the Ieylle of dooges yf he do not
then he forfettes this asumset afore or ells not wittnes to this

EAlleyn & Robsone

Modernised Version

Memorandum: that the 10th of August 1597 William Borne[1] came &
offered

---

1 William Bird alias Borne was an actor in the Lord Admiral's Men (later, the Prince's Men, then Palsgrave's Men) from 1597 on, and he remained with that company until 1622.

himself to come and play with my Lord Admiral's Men[2]
at my [play]house called by the name of the Rose,[3] situated on the
   Bank[side].[4]
After this order following he hath received of me 3d.[5] upon &[6]
   assumpsit[7]
to forfeit unto me a hundred marks[8] of lawful
money of England if he do not perform these things following:
that is, presently after liberty being granted for playing to
come & to play with my Lord Admiral's Men at my [play]house
aforesaid & not in any other house public[9] about London
for the space of three years beginning immediately after this Restraint is recalled by the Lord of the Council,[10] which restraint
is by the means of playing the Isle of Dogs.[11] If he do not
then he forfeits this assumpsit afore[said] or else not, witness to this
                                        E[dward] Alleyn & [———] Robson[12]

2.

Original Manuscript Version

M[r]dom that the 6 of october 1597 Thomas dowten came & bownd
hime seallfe vnto me in xxxx[li] in [covenante] & a somesett by the
   Receuing
of iij d of me before wittnes the covenant is this that he
shold frome the daye a bove written vntell sra*f*tid next

---

2   One of the two acting companies that were pre-eminent between the early 1590s and 1603 when
    they were taken over by Prince Henry and changed their name to Prince Henry's Men. Upon the
    Prince's death in 1613 they were taken over by Frederick, Count Palatine of the Rhine, who
    married King James's daughter Elizabeth in February 1613.
3   The Rose playhouse, built in 1587, was used by the Lord Admiral's Men until the autumn of 1600.
4   Bankside was the area south of the River Thames, near to St Saviour's, Southwark, in which the
    Rose, Globe and Hope playhouses were all eventually located.
5   Three pence was a small amount of money, more a token of exchange than a formidable gift.
6   Henslowe probably means 'an' here, i.e. 'an assumpsit', rather than 'and'.
7   An assumpsit refers simply to an actionable contract or promise.
8   In England, the mark was money of account, rather than an actual coin. One mark was worth 13s.
    6d., so 100 marks was worth £67 10s. Thus, the default that William Borne agreed to pay was
    markedly higher than the £40 Thomas Downton agreed to pay if he defaulted on his bond. (See
    Document 2, below.)
9   By 'house public' Henslowe is referring to 'public playhouses'.
10 Henslowe is referring to the fact that only a few months earlier, on 28 July 1597, the Privy Council
    declared that all of the playhouses in and around the city of London should be closed and pulled
    down. However, Henslowe clearly had some sense that the demolition part of the order would
    never come to pass. By October, the playhouses were still closed, but doubtless they were expected
    to open shortly. By 11 October Henslowe was again collecting receipts on performances at the
    Rose.
11 The production of a play entitled *The Isle of Dogs* (subject unknown) at the Swan playhouse
    brought the closure of the playhouses. It was at this point that Bird joined the Admiral's Men.
12 Edward Alleyn was a leading actor in the Admiral's Men; he married Henslowe's stepdaughter in
    1592. 'Robson' has not been identified. Henslowe signed both names to the bond.

come ij yeares to playe [wthme] in my howsse [. . .] & in no
other a bowte London pvblickeley yf he do wth owt my
consent to forfet vnto me this some of money a bove writte*n*
wittnes to this   EAlleyn   Robarte shawe
                         w^{m}borne   John synger
                         dick*e* Jonnes

Modernised Version

Memorandum: that the 6th of October Thomas Downton[13] came &
   bound
himself unto me in £40 in covenant[14] & assumpsit[15] by the receiving
of 3d. of me before witness. The covenant is this that he
should from the day above written until Shrovetide[16] next,
come two years to play with me in my [play]house & in no
other about London publicly. If he do without my
consent to forfeit me this sum of money above written.
Witness to this   E[dward] Alleyn   Robert Shaw
                         William Borne   John Singer
                         Dick Jones[17]

Venice and Venetian Life

From **Jan Morris, 'Islanders' in** *The World of Venice* (rev. edn, New
York: Harcourt, Brace, & Co., 1993), pp. 21–6; pp. 21–4

Jan Morris, one of the best-known modern travel writers and a Fellow of the
Royal Society of Literature, describes some of the many distinctive features that
merge to create both the myths and the realities that surround the historical
and mythological 'world' of Venice. In this brief description Morris evokes the
complex socio-political and cultural dimensions that made the city so unique in
early modern times, and that also made the setting so intriguing for writers and
travellers of Shakespeare's day. Although Shakespeare, and most of his contemporaries, had never travelled to Venice, they had, through their contact
with merchants and travellers in the bustling port city of London, heard tell
of Venice's infamous riches, its exotic treasures and its equally seductive

---

13 Thomas Downton performed with the Admiral's/Prince-s'/Palsgrave's Men until *c.* 1618.
14 Agreement.
15 An 'assumpsit' is an actionable contract or promise.
16 'Shrovetide' consists of the three days before Ash Wednesday.
17 The witnesses were all actors with the Admiral's Men at the time that the bond was signed,
    although Henslowe signed the names himself.

decadence. Consequently, some of the elements in Morris's description below – the opulence, money-worship and utter enslavement of the Venetian society to trade – reappear in Shakespeare's play. It is this complex image that influenced Gregory Doran's production of *The Merchant of Venice*, performed in 1997 by the Royal Shakespeare Company (**pp. 126–7**).

So the Venetians became islanders, and islanders they remain [. . .] The squelchy islands of their lagoon, welded over the centuries into a glittering Republic, became the greatest of trading States, mistress of the eastern commerce and the supreme naval power of the day. For more than a thousand years Venice was something unique amongst the nations, half eastern, half Western, half land, half sea, poised between Rome and Byzantium, between Christianity and Islam, one foot in Europe, the other paddling in the pearls of Asia. She called herself the Serenissima,[1] she decked herself in cloth of gold, and she even had her own calendar, in which the years began on 1st March, and the days began in the evening. This lonely hauteur, exerted from the fastnesses of the lagoon, gave to the old Venetians a queer sense of isolation. As their Republic grew in grandeur and prosperity, and their political arteries hardened, and a flow of dazzling booty enriched their palaces and churches, so Venice became entrammelled[2] in mystery and wonder. She stood, in the imagination of the world, somewhere between a freak and a fairy tale.

She remained, first of all, uncompromisingly, a city of the waters. In the early days the Venetians made rough roads in their islands [. . .] but presently they evolved the system of canals, based on existing water-channels and rivulets, that is to this day one of the piquant wonders of the world. Their capital, the city of Venice proper, was built upon an archipelago[3] in the heart of the lagoon. Their esplanade[4] was the Grand Canal, the central highway of this city, which swung in a regal curve through a parade of palaces. Their Cheapside[5] or Wall Street was the Rialto, first an island, then a district, then the most famous bridge in Europe. Their Doges[6] rode in fantastic golden barges, and outside each patrician's house the gondolas lay gracefully at their moorings. Venice evolved an amphibious society peculiar to herself, and the ornate front doors of her mansions opened directly upon the water.

Against this extraordinary physical background, the Venetians erected a no less remarkable kind of State. At first a kind of patriarchal democracy, it became an aristocratic oligarchy of the tightest kind, in which (after 1297) power was strictly reserved to a group of patrician families. Executive authority passed first to this aristocracy; then to the inner Council of Ten; and later, more and more, to the still

1 'Her Most Serene Highness'.
2 Netted, caught up.
3 Group of islands.
4 Level space used as a public promenade.
5 A prominent London business district.
6 The doge was the chief magistrate of Venice.

more reclusive and reticent Council of Three, which was elected in rotation, a month at a time. To maintain this supremacy, and to prevent both popular risings and personal dictatorships, the structure of the State was buttressed with tyranny, ruthless, impersonal, bland, and carefully mysterious. Sometimes the stranger, passing by the Doge's Palace, would find a pair of anonymous conspirators hanging mangled from a gibbet, or hear a whisper of appalling torture in the dungeons of the Ten. Once the Venetians awoke to discover three convicted traitors buried alive, head downwards, among the flagstones of the Piazzetta,[7] their feet protruding between the pillars [. . .] by these means, at once fair and ferocious, she outlived all her rivals, and preserved her republican independence until the very end of the eighteenth century.

All this was wonderful, but no less marvellous was the wealth and strength of Venice—which was, so the Venetians assiduously let it be known, divinely granted [. . .]

In Venice the Orient began [. . .] She was a place of silks, emeralds, marbles, brocades, velvets, cloth of gold, porphyry,[8] ivory, spices, scents, apes, ebony, indigo,[9] slaves, great galleons, Jews, mosaics, shining domes, rubies, and all the gorgeous commodities of Arabia, China and the Indies. She was a treasure-box [. . .]

She was never loved. She was always the outsider, always envied, always suspected, always feared. She fitted into no convenient category of nations. She was the lion who walked by herself. She traded indiscriminately with Christian and Muslim, in defiance of ghastly Papal penalties [. . .]

And as the centuries passed, and she lost her supremacies, and the strain of the merchant princes was weakened, and she sapped her energies in endless Italian squabbles and embroilments, and became a mainland Power—as she sank into her eighteenth-century degeneracy, she became another kind of prodigy. During her last century of independence she was the gayest and worldliest of all cities, a perpetual masque[10] and revelry, where nothing was too daring, too shameful or too licentious. Her carnivals were protracted and uninhibited. Her courtesans were honoured. The domino and the Ace of Spades were her reigning symbols. The dissolute of the western world, the salacious and the mere fun-loving flocked to her theatres and gaming-tables, and respectable people all over Europe looked towards her as they might, from a safe distance, deplore the goings-on of a Sodom or a Gomorrah.[11] No other nation ever died in such feverish hedonism.

---

7 The area in front of the ducal palace on which stand two famous columns bearing sculptures of the famous Venetian lion and an odd crocodile-fish-dragon, symbols of the city's patron saints (St Mark and St Theodore).
8 Hard rock with large crystals in fine-grained mass, thought a rarity in earlier times.
9 An unusual blue-violet dye, used to colour cloth.
10 Literally, an extravagant court drama; used here metaphorically to denote 'riotous festivity'.
11 Sodom and Gomorrah were ancient cities, destroyed because of their sinfulness and corruption (Genesis: 18–19).

From **W. D. Howells, 'The Ghetto and the Jews of Venice' (1866)** in *Venetian Life* (Marlboro, Vt.: The Marlboro Press, 1989), pp. 151–9; pp. 153–4

William Dean Howells, an American writer whose work included countless novels, autobiographical volumes, travel narratives and plays, was rewarded with the post of consul of Venice after he wrote an important campaign biography for Abraham Lincoln in 1860. Howells arrived in Venice in 1862 and remained there until 1865. Because the job required very little of Howells he turned his hand to writing a detailed description of Venice. His fascination for the place lasted for years beyond his departure and his narrative is still read for its attention to detail and shrewd journalistic insight. However, it is altogether different from the Venice that was 'so dream-like and unreal'. Howells's description of the Jewish ghetto, ringed about by walls and gates – its guards paid for by the Jewish inhabitants themselves – remains one of the best verbal illustrations of the geographical, political and psychological separation of Jews and Christians in the district that Howells found marked by 'the discomfort and rank savor of the dark ages'.

In the fifteenth century all the riches of the Orient had been poured into the lap of Venice, and a spirit of reckless profusion took possession of her citizens. The money, hastily and easily amassed, went as rapidly as it came. It went chiefly for dress, in which the Venetian still indulges very often to the stint[1] of his stomach; and the ladies of that bright-colored, showy day bore fortunes on their delicate persons in the shape of costly vestments of scarlet, black, green, white, maroon, or violet, covered with gems, glittering with silver buttons, and ringing with silver bells. The fine gentlemen of the period were not behind them in extravagance; and the priests were peculiarly luxurious in dress, wearing gay silken robes, with cowls of fur and girdles of gold and silver. Sumptuary laws[2] were vainly passed to repress the general license, and fortunes were wasted and wealthy families reduced to beggary. At this time, when so many worthy gentlemen and ladies had need of the Uncle to whom hard-pressed nephews fly to pledge the wrecks of prosperity[3] [. . .] and the demand for pawnbrokers becoming imperative, the Republic was obliged to recall the Hebrews from the exile into which they had been driven some time before, that they might set up pawnshops and succor necessity. They came back, however, only for a limited time, and were obliged to wear a badge of yellow color upon the breast, to distinguish them from the Christians, and later a yellow cap, then a red hat, and then a hat of oil-cloth. They could not acquire houses or lands in Venice, nor practise any trades, nor exercise any noble art but medicine. They were assigned a dwelling place in the vilest and

1 Limited supply (of food).
2 Laws governing requirements for dress, according to profession and social class.
3 i.e. to beg for money because their financial ventures have gone awry (with an allusion to wrecks, as in shipwrecks).

unhealthiest part of the city, and their quarter was called Ghetto, from the Hebrew *nghedah*, a congregation. They were obliged to pay their landlords a third more rent than Christians paid; the ghetto was walled in, and its gates were kept by Christian guards, who every day opened them at dawn and closed them at dark, and who were paid by the Jews. They were not allowed to issue at all from the Ghetto on holidays, and two barges, with armed men, watched over them night and day, while a special magistracy had charge of their affairs. Their synagogues were built at Mestre, on the mainland, and their dead were buried in the sand upon the sea-shore, whither on the Mondays of September, the baser sort of Venetians went to make merry, and drunken men and women danced above their desecrated tombs. These unhappy people were forced also to pay tribute to the state, at first every third year, then every fifth year, and then every tenth year, the privilege of residence being ingeniously renewed to them at these periods for a round sum; but, in spite of all, they flourished upon the waste and wickedness of their oppressors, waxed[4] rich as these waxed poor, and were not again expelled from the city.

From **Peter Berek, 'The Jew as Renaissance Man'**, *Renaissance Quarterly*, Vol. 51 (1998), pp. 128–62; pp. 130, 134–5, 145, 147–8, 158

In this commentary Peter Berek traces the historical figure of the Marrano Jew (i.e. a person avowing conversion to Christianity who covertly kept his Jewish faith) that served as a model for Jewish characters in English plays of the 1590s. He discusses the various types of anxiety aroused by these figures and demonstrates that the impulse to self-fashioning – so central to the formation of early modern identity – was, in the Marrano model, the object of suspicion and fear. As Berek notes, because the Jews had been banished from England in 1290, they were 'more available to the English as concepts than as persons, more vivid as sites of speculation than as doers of deeds'.

[. . .] Despite being foreign, exotic, or "other," the Jew came to be represented in England as a paradigmatic "Renaissance Man." [. . .] At a moment when a culture was unusually self-aware about the strength of innovation and the rapidity of change, anxiety about both phenomena could be figured paradoxically by an ancient stranger who was also an ancestor [. . .]

[. . .] Marranos [. . .] are plausible representations of the idea that identity is not stable and can be created by individuals themselves. Moreover, emerging ideas about the fluidity of personal identity are closely associated with new entrepreneurship and social mobility. The traditional association of Jews with money-lending and other forms of commercial enterprise makes Jews in Elizabethan England, as they have been since, suitable representations of ambivalent feelings

4   Grew.

about economic innovation and social change. They are attractive in part because the Christian scriptural tradition provides a ready means of condemning that which frightens even as it allures [. . .]

I suggest that this "Marrano" condition was the most important quality of Jewishness in Elizabethan England. This is not so much to characterize the self-perceptions of Jews in England under Elizabeth and James as it is to suggest how they must have appeared to the Christians amongst whom they lived. A "Jew" was likely to be a stranger, a merchant, or a physician, a person who advanced in the world by his own ingenuity and by the accumulation of wealth rather than by any traditional principle of birth or inherited position. A "Jew" was likely not only to deny being a Jew, but in some real sense *not* to be a Jew. He might worship with you in church, partner you in commerce, serve your Queen who was defender of the faith. But throughout all this, you would never know to what extent he "really was" what he gave every appearance of being. Were you seeing a real person or a feigned person? [. . .] the Marrano played a series of roles, all of which were associated with social and economic innovation and change. Associating innovation and change with Jewishness provided Elizabethan Englishmen with a way of acknowledging the mixed feelings they aroused of allure and anxiety [. . .]

All the arguments against usury rest on a common scriptural foundation. Usury is a breach of charity, because the needy should be helped without regard to profit. But the tracts that condemn usury spend little or no time speculating as to the reasons why its prohibition might be desirable, instead simply stressing that Scripture prohibits the practice. References to Jews in these tracts are usually signs of unacknowledged internal conflict [. . . Thomas] Wilson says that the usurer is the most dangerous of villains because the most attractive. Dealing with a usurer is like being bitten by an asp—the victim "dieth in pleasure"[1] [. . .] Because the usurer looks just like an honest man, you can't recognize him when you see him, and you may well think him the best of men rather than the worst. [. . .]

[. . .] intense outrage against usury arises from anxiety about social mobility. Usury is a means by which the low-born can get the land and money of the high-born and thus invert good social order. [. . .]

[. . . For Shakespeare's contemporaries, such as Francis Bacon,[2]] some forms of common and legal business practice are susceptible to being called usurious. It can be hard to tell whether a particular transaction is usurious loaning at interest or a legitimate sale or rental at profit; furthermore, making a profit is a goal all seem to desire, even if the desire could appear, in [the poet] George Herbert's words, "a Jewish choice."[3]

---

1 Thomas Wilson was an eminent cleric and politician of the sixteenth century whose *Discourse upon Usury* (1572) was well known during Shakespeare's time. For excerpts of the *Discourse* see pp. 42–4.
2 See the excerpt from Francis Bacon's, 'Of Usury' (pp. 44–6).
3 Berek is quoting lines from a poem by the English religious poet and cleric George Herbert (1593–1633) entitled 'Self Condemnation' that was originally published in his collection *The Temple* (1633). Lines 7–9 read: 'He that doth love, and love amisse/This worlds delights before true Christian joy/Hath made a Jewish choice.'

The particular circumstances of Marranism in Elizabethan England rendered more plausible the use of Jewishness as a figure for widespread Christian misconduct. Visibly present yet with his real nature concealed, the Marrano or New Christian purported to be like his Christian companions while in truth being crucially different. Even more, the ways in which the Marrano differed paralleled the ways in which Elizabethan English behavior was at variance with official ideology. A culture that officially condemned money-lending watched prominent citizens grow rich on the practice, making a choice which was "Jewish" because it cherished the world and the flesh, and Marrano because it concealed its own variance from dogma. A culture that officially valued inheritance and continuity saw the lowborn rise to power, prominence, and titles, becoming "self-made" as the Marrano was also self-fashioned.

[. . . In] Shakespeare, the Jew becomes a figure who enables [the playwright] to express and at the same time to condemn the impulse in both culture and theater to treat selfhood and social roles as a matter of choice. By becoming theatrical, the anxiety about identity and innovation implicit in the Marrano state gains explicitness and becomes available to the culture at large.

Merchants, Capitalism and the Controversy over Usury

From **Daniel Price, 'The Merchant: A Sermon Preached at Paul's Cross on Sunday the 24th of August Being the Day before Bartholomew Fair. 1607'** (Oxford, 1608), pp. 1–38; pp. 5, 16–17

Daniel Price (1581–1631) was educated at Oxford where he received a bachelor's and master's degree. He was ordained soon thereafter and quickly established himself as a leading preacher. Price was frequently invited to preach at Court, and eventually he became chaplain to Prince Henry and King James I. In the passage below – taken from a sermon dedicated to the London Company of Merchants, and delivered in London in 1607 – Price defends merchants against the common criticism of the time, that they were simply involved in a selfish, materialist enterprise. By contrast, Price argues that merchants exemplified the Christian virtues of charity and holiness. Moreover, as Price suggests, merchants are industrious and are to be praised for their risk-taking. Price's merchant is clearly a kind of model for Antonio in *The Merchant of Venice*, the character who ventures unselfishly for friendship and who is respected by others within the commercial community of the play for his generosity and his outward looking spirit.

As is the case with other sermons of the period, Price ties his sermon to a verse from the Bible. Here, he is interested in Matthew 13:45–6: 'Again, the kingdom of heaven is like unto a merchant man, seeking goodly pearls: Who, when he had found one pearl of great price, went and sold all that he had, and bought it.' For a historical analysis of the social views on merchants and mercantilism that Price was responding to, see Alberto Tenenti's essay below, **pp. 40–2**.

In the following passage, and as was customary during the early seventeenth century, the letters 'u'/'v' and 'ie'/'i'/'y' are interchangeable. Underlined letters represent expanded abbreviations.

The Kingdome of heauen is like to a man, not to everie man but to a marchant man, not to everie marchant but to a marchant that seeketh pearles, nether to one that seeketh al kind of pearles, but to a marchant that seeketh good pearles, nether to one that onlie seeketh but findeth, and hauing found selleth, and hauing sould buieth, and hauing bought exchangeth manie good pearles for one, naie all his good pearles for one goodlie pearle, a pearle of great price, and so you see that the kingdome of heauen is compared to a wise diligent, seeking, finding, buying, selling, exchanging marchant.

The K.[1] of heauen is like to a marchant &c. [. . .] the action of this marchant is not for anie smal, but for great gaine, not for anie carnal, but for spirituall glorie, not for any transitory, but for an eternal treasure [. . .] What trade more honorable then the marchant, what marchandise more honorable than the Kingdome of heauen? Yee are manie of you come hether as buiers, as sellers, as marchants, and therfore at this time what argument more fuasible,[2] more plausible, more forceable, more available than this *the K. of heauen is like to a marchant?* like to a seking, finding, buying, selling, exchanging marchant [. . .]

[. . .] The doctrine I obserue out of the word *Marchant*, is this, that the state of a Christian is not an idle vaine speculation, but must bee a careful, painful, diligent, walking in his vocation. The reason of this doctrine, is proued a *Contrario*[3] by the *Antithesis* between the state of the Godlie, & vngodly, under the name of the foole. The foole[4] fouldeth his hands, and eateth vp his own flesh. Better is on[5] handful, saith he with quietnesse, then two handful with labour and vexation of spirit.[6] But contrariwise, the wise *Marchant*, the true Christian, he seeketh, he taketh paines, he laboureth, hee endeuoureth to follow hard to the marke [. . .] noe peril noe danger, noe cost, noe temptation noe opposition can confront him [. . .]

The second vse of this Doctrine is more particuler, belonging only to those that be Merchants, that seeing the *Merchant* here is so studious, careful, diligent, and earnest in good pearles, that euerie one of them seeke by al meanes to become heavenly *Merchants* to seek, and labour, and endeauour to obtaine this

---

1 King.
2 Feasible.
3 In the contrary.
4 The 'ungodly'.
5 One.
6 An allusion to Ecclesiastes 4:5–6.

Merchandise, to lay vp treasure in heaue<u>n</u>, where neither rust nor moath[7] doth corrupt, & where theeues break not through and steale, that as their trade of life is more honourable then others among men, so God shoulde be more honoured of them then of other men [. . .]

Our marchant seeketh good pearles. I might here stand vpon the colour, splendour, lustre, nature, effect and forme of pearles: The learned knowe their colour to be diuers, their splendor to be gratious, their lustre glorious, their nature and effect miraculous, their orbicular[8] forme most perfit, & surely manie great wonders hath God made known vnto men, in precious pearles [. . .]

From **Alberto Tenenti, 'The Merchant and the Banker'** in *Renaissance Characters*, ed. Eugenio Garin (Chicago, Ill.: University of Chicago Press, 1991), pp. 154–65; pp. 159–60, 164–5

The merchants and their overwhelming financial success prompted a divided response from Christian churchmen and their many publics. In London, as in Venice, the success of the business community and, hence, society as a whole depended upon the strength of its merchants. Nevertheless, merchants were also suspected by the clergy for the ease with which they seemed to earn their substantial livings. Moreover, some church authorities pointed to biblical writings that implied that the 'breeding of money' was sinful. (Shylock takes up this issue in his famous speech on Laban's sheep (1.3).) Nevertheless, the Church concurrently needed and cultivated the financial support of the great merchants who were often pillars of charitable giving. Consequently, the moral identity of the merchant, as well as the state of his soul, was, for some, fraught with controversy. As Alberto Tenenti, an historian of early modern Italy, notes, over time what was once conceived of as a highly conflicted relationship settled into something closer to a symbiotic relationship. Therefore, 'mercantilism and holiness' came to occupy the same social space with a degree of comfort. Merchants eventually made their own inalienable place in society, and the churchmen came to accept this fact of emerging modern life, but not totally without nervousness.

The merchant has a certain stature for his highly indirect and posthumous merits as a predecessor or a first incarnation of the capitalist. [. . .]

[. . . Yet] altogether too much importance has been accorded to what the churchmen wrote on the subject of certain mercantile activities [. . .] some writers are satisfied simply with citing the image the theologians presented of them. When they do so they [. . .] are forced into the position that all merchants were radically and permanently torn between a yearning for riches and an anguished fear of punishment after death for the accumulation of wealth [. . .]

---

7   Moth.
8   Rounded.

[However] the merchant did not stand out [. . .] by virtue of any particular independence from the precepts of the church; even less did he express any misgivings on the subject. He participated in collective piety and was sensitive to the religious tensions of his times. Significantly, merchants played an important role in the diffusion of the Protestant Reformation, although they cannot be said to have rallied in mass to Protestantism, even in northern lands. Many of them differed from the majority of the population in that they were less confined to their own town or area. They traveled often; they had repeated contacts and exchanges of opinion in other lands, particularly in the urban centers in which they congregated. They could read and write, so they had access to an important network of both oral and written information [. . .]

The merchants were first and foremost burghers: men to whom business dealings and family prosperity were of the highest importance. Thus by and large they maintained good relations with an institution as revered and influential as the Church of Rome, as they later did with the various Protestant churches [. . .]

Although we know that the profits to be earned from trade were often high in the era of the Renaissance, it would be naïve to conclude that earnings were anything like regular, let alone automatic. The economic operator's life was a dramatic one, and his faith in his own energy and his daring use of capital far from guaranteed his success. A deeply felt, multifaceted awareness of the value of time was coupled with constant tension as the merchant did his best to cope with distances, to make a profit from the fluctuating availability of goods, and to avoid any number of unforeseeable dangers. Fortune was not a purely allegorical[1] figuration for the merchant: it was a confused mass of perils he knew lay beyond his control and that he could no longer confront simply by calling on God's aid, even if he had no doubts as to God's sovereign power. Andrea Berengo,[2] for example, advised recourse to the Holy Ghost, but he also recommended drawing up an insurance contract [. . .]

The gradual and organized control of time, space, and risk were not the only foundations of the mercantile world of the Renaissance, but they are a first indication of its solidity and its special autonomy. Other, more obviously traditional supports were the structure of the family and the image of themselves that the economic operators proposed to and imposed on society [. . .] The merchant and banker by this time occupied an undisputed and preponderant place in society, but they still encountered resistance to the expression and affirmation of themselves as a type eliciting positive connotations. The long-standing ecclesiastical condemnation of certain of their activities, which had to some extent entered into common opinion, was coupled with traces of the equally ancient, outdated three-part division of society into warriors, priests, and peasants. The merchant was never able to formulate an intellectual challenge to the theologians' prejudices in his regard, nor could he prove how little truth was left in the archaic tripartite division of society. He won his place gradually thanks to the real importance of

---

1　Symbolic, i.e. a concrete character illustrating an abstract idea.
2　A prominent Venetian merchant whose letters (written from 1553 to 1556) offer a detailed picture of commercial life during that period.

his activities and services and to his ability to construct his own range of existential values and operational techniques.

From **Thomas Wilson, *A Discourse upon Usury*** (1572), ed. R. H. Tawney (New York: Harcourt Brace & Co., 1925), pp. 173–384; pp. 231–2, 237–40

Thomas Wilson (?1525–81) was educated at Eton and Cambridge, and he later became a politician. He was twice elected to Parliament. After this he served as Secretary of State (1577–80) and later became Dean of Durham Cathedral. His best-known work is a book on logic and rhetoric entitled *The Arte of Rhetorique* (1553), but he was the author of many works on logic and rhetoric. Wilson's *A Discourse upon Usury* is a classic early Elizabethan statement against usury. Based in scripture, Wilson argues that usury simply runs counter to Christian charity; in other words, a Christian ideally ought simply to lend money to a friend *gratis*, without charging interest. Wilson's discomfort with usury is apparent in the first section where a nameless 'Preacher' states the official Church position with which Shakespeare and his contemporaries would have been familiar. However, Wilson also sees the other side of the argument – that the law allows for usury within certain limits – and so if individuals adhere to these there can be little room for abuse. Moreover, the lending of money can be viewed as a service to one's neighbour in a time of need. Nevertheless, in the end Wilson sides with the preacher's argument.

From the 'Preacher's Oration'

To lende freely is a kynde of liberalitie and bountifulnes, when a man departeth from his owne to help his neighbours want, wythout any hope of lucre or gayne at all; for he is benefited that borroweth and feeleth greate comforte in his great neede. Whereas lending for gayne is a chiefe branch of covetousnes, and makes him, that before might have ben counted bountifull, to be now reconed[1] a greedy gayner for him selfe, seeking his own welfare upon good assurance, without any care at all what becometh of his neighbour, grawing him unmercyfully, to satisfie his own wretched and most greedy hunger, directly turnynge a most bewtifull vertue into a most filthy abhominable vyce. Yea, usurie is a manifest and voluntarye knowen thefte, which men do use knowinglye and wyttingly,[2] for eyther they think they do evil, and forbeare it never a whit, or (that which is worse of all) they thinke they do well, and so, by oft using of this filthines, do lull them selves in sinne without anye sence of feeling of theyr moste wretched wyckednesse and horryble dealynge. Christ for his bitter passion be merciful unto us and geve us his

---

1 Reckoned, determined to be.
2 Intentionally.

feare, that we may live after hys law, and folowe his holye will, for surely, as we lyve now, eyther the byble is not gods word, or else we are not of god, such contrarietie is betwene our lyves and our lessons.

The scripture commaundeth: thou shalt not steale, thou shalt not kyll, thou shalt not commyt aduoutery, thou shalt not beare false witnesse; thou shalt not lende out thy money for gayne, to take anye thinge for the lone of it, and yet we all doe these thinges, as though they were neyther scripture that forbad us, nor heaven for us to desyre, nor hell to eschewe, nor god to honor, nor divell[3] to dread. And this last horrible offence, which I count greater, or as great, as any of the rest, is so common emongst us, that wee have no sense to take it for synne, but count it lawfull bargainynge, and judge them goodlye wyse men that havinge greate masses of money by them will never adventure anye iott thereof in lawfull occupying,[4] either to carrye out our plentye, or to bringe in our want, as good merchants use and ought to doe, but lyvinge idle at home will sett out theire money for profite, and so enrych them selves with the labour and travayle of others, being them selves none other than droanes[5] that sucke the honney which other paynefull[6] bees gather wyth their contynuall travayle[7] of dyvers[8] flowers in everye fielde. And whether these men be profitable or tollerable to a common weale, or no, I reporte me to you. Besydes that, god doth utterlye forbidd them, whose commaundement ought to bee obeyed, yf we be Christians and of god, as we professe to be.

[. . .] What is the matter that Iewes are universallye hated wheresoever they come? For soothe, usurie is one of the chief causes, for they robbe all men that deale with them, and undoe them in the ende. And for thys cause they were hated in England, and so banyshed worthelye, with whome I woulde wyshe all these Englishemen were sent that lende their money of their goods whatsoever for gayne, for I take them to be no better then Iewes [. . .] And howe can these men be of god that are so farr from charitie, that care not howe they get goods so they may have them?

From 'The Lawyer's Oration'

Some therbe that say: all usury is against nature. Whereas I think cleane contrarie. For if usurie weare against nature, it should be universallye evell, but god hath said that to a stranger a man may put out his mony for usury, but if it had bene againste nature, god would not have graunted that libertie [. . .]

The common lawe of England is not against all usury, neither in suche sorte, and so preciselye, as you take usurye. And Statutes there have beene that have

---

3 Devil.
4 Dealing.
5 Male, i.e. non-worker bee.
6 Industrious.
7 Work.
8 Diverse, varied.

permitted usurie, which I woulde they had contynued, to avoide further evell, for (as we say) better it is to suffer a mischiefe then an inconvenience [. . .]

Therefore, I am still of this mind, when none hath harme but both receive benefites, there is none offence committed, but rather great goodnes used. You talke much of charitie, you begin with love. I would you weighted al causes aswell by the rule of charitie [. . .] For surely, wher charity is not hindred, there is no usury committed, such usury onely being forbidden that breaketh charitie and decaiethe the love of my neighboure by extreame cutting and excessive taking.

From **Francis Bacon, 'Of Usury'** (1625) in *Francis Bacon* ed. Brian Vickers (Oxford: Oxford University Press, 1996), pp. 421–4; pp. 421–3.

Francis Bacon (1561–1626) – lawyer, statesman and philosopher – wrote widely on jurisprudence and scientific matters. Some of Bacon's most frequently read pieces, however, are his essays on various subjects, from gardening to the court masque. Bacon's 'Of Usury' is one of his best-known essays. Contrary to many commentators of his day who roundly condemned usurious practices (see Thomas Wilson, **pp. 42–4**), Bacon argued that usury was an activity that was not only acceptable, but necessary in order for the wheels of the commercial market to turn. Without usury, Bacon concluded, English law, which allowed up to 10 per cent interest on loans, was fundamentally hypocritical and economically stifling.

Many have made witty invectives against Usury. They say that it is a pity[1] the devil should have God's part, which is the tithe.[2] That the usurer is the greatest sabbath-breaker, because his plough goeth every Sunday.[3] [. . .] That the usurer breaketh the first law that was made for mankind after the fall,[4] which was, 'in sudore vultus tui comedes panem tuum'; not, 'in sudore vultus alieni'.[5] That usurers should have orange-tawny bonnets,[6] because they do judaize.[7] That it is against nature[8] for money to beget money; and the like. I say this only, that usury is a 'concessum propter duritiem cordis':[9] for since there must be borrowing and lending, and men are so hard of heart as they will not lend freely,[10] usury must be

---

1 Pitiful.
2 One tenth (10 per cent) of one's yearly income was to be paid to the Church. Likewise, the law allowed 10 per cent interest on loans.
3 The Church forbade working on Sunday, but interest accumulated daily.
4 The law made by God for mankind after Adam and Eve sinned in Eden.
5 God commanded 'In the sweat of thy face shalt thou eat bread' (Genesis 3:19), not 'in the sweat of another man's face'.
6 The Jews in the Venetian ghetto were required to wear dark orange and red turbans.
7 Follow Jewish practices.
8 The natural order.
9 'Because of the hardness of heart' (Matthew 19:8).
10 Gratis, i.e. without interest.

permitted. Some others have made suspicious[11] and cunning propositions of[12] banks, discovery of[13] men's estates, and other inventions. But few have spoken of usury usefully [. . .]

The discommodities[14] of usury are, First, that it makes fewer merchants.[15] For were it not for this lazy trade of usury, money would not lie still, but would in great part be employed upon merchandizing; which is the *vena porta*[16] of wealth in a state. The second, that it makes poor merchants. For as a farmer cannot husband[17] his ground so well if he sit at a great rent;[18] so the merchant cannot drive his trade so well, if he sit at great usury.[19] The third is incident[20] to the other two; and that is the decay of customs[21] of kings or states, which ebb or flow with merchandizing. The fourth, that it bringeth the treasure of a realm or state into a few hands. For the usurer being at certainties,[22] and others at uncertainties, at the end of the game most of the money will be in the box;[23] and ever a state flourisheth when wealth is more equally spread. The fifth, that it beats down[24] the price of land; for the employment of money is chiefly either merchandizing or purchasing;[25] and usury waylays[26] both. The sixth, that it doth dull[27] and damp all industries, improvements, and new inventions, wherein money would be stirring if it were not for this slug.[28] The last, that it is the canker[29] and ruin of many men's estates; which in process of time breeds a public poverty.[30]

On the other side,[31] the commodities[32] of usury are, first, that howsoever usury in some respect hindereth merchandizing,[33] yet in some other it advanceth[34] it; for it is certain that the greatest part of trade is driven by young merchants, upon borrowing at interest [. . .]. The second is, that were it not for this easy borrowing upon interest, men's necessities[35] would draw upon them a most sudden undoing; in that they would be forced to sell their means (be it lands or goods) far under

11 Prompting suspicion.
12 Concerning.
13 Investigation into.
14 Disadvantages.
15 Reduces the number of merchants.
16 'Gate-vein', the vein that carries chyle to the liver, i.e. a major vein.
17 Cultivate.
18 Be forced to pay high rent.
19 By paying high interest.
20 Connected naturally.
21 Decline in duties on goods sold or made within the country.
22 Having guaranteed returns.
23 The gambling pot.
24 Reduces, collapses.
25 Acquiring (permanently).
26 Obstructs.
27 Suffocates.
28 Obstacle.
29 Disease.
30 In time it impoverishes everybody (i.e. the public).
31 'On the other hand'.
32 Advantages.
33 Trade, in general.
34 Promotes.
35 Things necessary for daily living.

foot.[36] [. . .] The third and last is, that it is a vanity[37] to conceive that there would be ordinary borrowing without profit; and it is impossible to conceive the number of inconveniences that will ensue, if borrowing be cramped [. . .]

To speak now of the reformation and reiglement[38] of usury; how the discommodities of it may be best avoided, and the commodities retained [. . .]

[. . .] That there be two rates of usury; the one free and general[39] for all; the other under licence only, to certain persons in certain places of merchandizing [. . .] Let the state be answered some small matter[40] for the licence, and the rest left to the lender; for if the abatement[41] be but small, it will no whit[42] discourage the lender [. . .]

If it be objected that this doth in a sort[43] authorize usury, which before was in some places but permissive; the answer is, that it is better to mitigate[44] usury by declaration,[45] than to suffer it to rage by connivance.

Virtuous Women and Learned Ladies

From **Edwin Sandys, 'Sermon Sixteen: A Sermon Preached at a Marriage in Strausborough'** (London, 1585). Reprinted in *The Sermons of Edwin Sandys, D. D.*, ed. John Ayre (Cambridge: Cambridge University Press, 1842), pp. 313–30; pp. 319–21, 324–7

Edwin Sandys (?1516–88) attended Cambridge and adopted its Reformation values, becoming friendly with many leading Protestant theologians of the time. Eventually he became Vice-Chancellor of the university, but in 1553, when Edward VI died and his Catholic sister Mary ascended to the throne, Sandys found himself persecuted for his religious views. He resigned his university position and was imprisoned in the Tower of London. Later, Sandys somehow escaped and went to the Continent where he remained until Mary died and her Protestant sister, Queen Elizabeth I, came to power, at which point Sandys returned to England. Thereafter he was appointed to several prominent positions, serving as Bishop of Worcester (1559) and Bishop of London (1570). By 1576, Sandys was appointed Archbishop of York, the second most significant ecclesiastical office within the Church of England. His collected sermons were published in 1585.

---

36 'Forced [. . .] foot,' i.e. 'forced to sell their assets far below their actual value'.
37 Silly idea.
38 Regulation.
39 Universally applicable.
40 'Let the state be guaranteed some small profit' (known as 'the King's profit').
41 Fee, deduction.
42 In no way.
43 In some manner.
44 Reduce the severity of.
45 Official recognition.

In the following passage Sandys argues, like other Protestant theologians who followed a Catholic view of women, that women must be subservient and dutiful to their husbands, that they should be celibate and chaste (abstinent if unmarried and faithful if married), and that women are 'owned' by their husbands. However, while women are clearly assigned second-class status, Sandys also recognises that husbands and wives should respect each other mutually, and that marriage is a partnership. In particular, Sandys was concerned about the loveless marriages that evolved from convenience or the quest for wealth or social position; and he also warned of the pitfalls of choosing a spouse merely for beauty. Readers of *The Merchant of Venice* will recognise Sandys's stern injunction that children are to accept the advice and assistance of their parents in choosing a spouse. Portia stays within the bounds of the casket lottery, which her dead father has set up in order to choose a husband for her, while Jessica – Shylock's daughter – simply elopes with her love. Standing part-way between these positions is Nerissa who, without parental consent, marries Gratiano, Bassanio's friend. But children who marry without the consent of their parents or tutors were generally condemned by Shakespeare's society for their disregard and disobedience, which is akin to disobeying God. Therefore, Sandys's opinions and attitudes help to explain why Portia adheres to her dead father's wishes and the casket lottery that he has set up to choose a husband for her. As Sandys concludes, a marital union that occurs without the consent of parents is not sanctioned in the eyes of God.

Duties of Honour Required in the Wife

Touching the duties of honour which the wife doth owe to the husband, we find in the beginning of the book of Genesis, that because of her transgression (for Eve seduced Adam, not Adam Eve) God gave her a law of subjection to her husband, that she might ever after be better directed by him, than he had at that time by her [. . .] God hath set the husband over the wife in authority; and therefore she ought willingly and dutifully to obey him: else she disobeyeth that God, who created woman for man's sake and hath appointed man to be woman's governor [. . .] An honest and a modest woman is an honour to her husband; but the dissolute wife and undiscreet is a death. She may not be a gadder abroad,[1] a tattler,[2] or a busybody, but sober, quiet, and demure; not an open teacher but ready to learn of her husband at home; obedient in all lawful things [. . .] Thus the man and wife joining themselves together in true love, endeavouring to live in the fear of God, and dutifully behaving themselves one towards the other, either of them bearing wisely the other's infirmities, doubtless they shall reap joy and comfort by their marriage: they shall find this their estate, which is "honorable in all," happy and profitable unto them.

1 A 'run-around'; one who goes about idly in search of pleasure.
2 A gossip.

The Cause of Irreligious Marriage: The Over-great Respecting of Beauty or Wealth

But the common sort of men [. . .] have chiefly two outward untoward respects, regarding nothing in their choice except it be either beauty or money. The sons of God of old, bewitched with the beauty of the daughters of men, procured the general flood to overflow them all and to wash the defiled world. Sampson took one of the daughters of the Philistines to wife, because she pleased his eye: but what came of it? It cost him a polling,[3] wherein stood his strength; and it lost him both his eyes, which before were ravished in the beauty of that deceitful woman.[4] Others there are yet of a baser note, whose only care is to match themselves wealthily. Their question is with what money, not what honesty, the parties whom they seek are endowed; whether they be rich, not with whether they be godly; what lands they have on earth, not what possessions are laid up in heaven for them. Such as marry for money, as the money wasteth, so their love weareth; neither is there any love or friendship constant, save only that which is grounded in constant causes, as virtue and godliness [. . .] In marriage therefore it behoveth us to be careful, that they whom we choose be of the household of God, professing one true religion with us [. . .]

Marriage without the Consent of Parents

But this is not enough. For although the parties married be such as the law of the Lord alloweth to come together, yet can it not be said that they marry in the Lord, except they also marry in such sort as the law prescribeth [. . .] For orderly entering into the state of matrimony, it is required that they, which be under the tuition and government of others, have the full consent of their parents, tutors, or such as have rule over them, to direct and guide them. Abraham provided a wife for his son Isaac: Isaac sent Jacob into Mesopotamia to his uncle Laban, and there commanded him to take a wife, and he did so.[5] In the law of Moses children are commanded to honour their parents.[6] And what honour is given unto parents, if in this chief case, being the weightiest one of them that can happen in all their life, their advice, wisdom, authority, and commandment be contemned? [. . .] And, as the parents' or tutors' consent is to be had in all good and lawful marriages, so it is against the duty of good parents, either to keep their children longer unmarried than is convenient, or through an over-great desire of enriching them (which is the common disease) to marry them against their liking. Such marriages seldom or never prove well, but are for the most part the cause of great sin and much misery. [. . .] Such then as marry not in the fear of God, making a religious and a godly

---

3   Haircut.
4   Samson, the last and most famous of the judges of Israel, was legendary for his superhuman strength, the source of which resided in his long hair. In an attempt to capture him, the Philistines bribed Delilah to seduce him, after which he was shorn, imprisoned and blinded. (The story of Samson's life is told in Judges 13–16.)
5   Genesis 24:2–4; 28:1–2.
6   Exodus 20:12.

choice, having the full consent of their parents or tutors; doubtless God is no author of their marriage: it is not he that coupleth and joineth them together: their estate is base, and not honourable, in his sight.

From **Juan Luis Vives, *The Instruction of a Christen Woman*** (London, 1529), ed. Virginia Walcott Beauchamp, Elizabeth H. Hageman and Margaret Mikesell (Urbana and Chicago, Ill.: University of Illinois Press, 2002), pp. 45–326; pp. 1–178, pp. 19, 22–4

Juan Luis Vives (1493–1540), the Spanish teacher and humanist philosopher, has long been recognised as the most significant author of sixteenth-century Europe in defining women's roles and educational objectives relating to women. Like other humanist philosophers of the period Vives's concern for education had to do with shaping the ideal person and, in turn, with shaping society as well. *De institutione feminae Christianae* (*The Education of a Christian Woman*), written in 1523, is the first significant study to address exclusively the universal education of women. It was written to influence the education of Princess Mary, the daughter of Catherine of Aragon and Henry VIII, but it appealed to a much wider audience. The text was translated into English by Richard Hyrde, a friend of Sir Thomas More, and published after Hyrde's death around 1529 in London.

Vives covers many topics in his treatise, prescribing both the broad kinds of learning that should be undertaken by young women, as well as the kinds of readings that they should be exposed to. In addition, Vives engages the uses of education to women, in general, and the limitations that should define their education. In the passage below, Vives reminds his reader that education is, in and of itself, a useful thing; however, it must be carefully managed, in order to produce the ideal woman of the period who was supposed to be – in the words of common parlance – 'chaste, silent, and obedient'.

Against this background a character such as Shakespeare's Portia is, at once, highly typical and highly atypical. In outward appearance and behaviour Portia exemplifies the chaste woman who defers (at least partially) to her husband (although whether she defers completely to her father's will or to her husband is open to debate). But in the courtroom scene (Act 4, Scene 1) – and disguised as a male doctor of law – she shows another side of herself where she can be learned, eloquent and confident, in the best sense of that term, while attempting to sidestep the cultural anxieties that accompanied the assertive woman. (See Sandys, **pp. 46–9**.) Thus, Portia – to some degree – maintains the holy virtues of womanhood as Vives defines them, at least in outward appearance, while acting in an autonomous fashion when necessary.

Of the Lernyng of Maydes

Of maydes some be but lytell mete[1] for lernyng: Lykewyse as some men be unapte, agayne[2] some be even borne unto hit, or at lest nat unfete for hit. Therefore they that be dulle are nat to be discoraged, and those that be apte, shuld be harted[3] and encouraged. I perceyve that lerned women be suspected of many: as who sayth, the subtyltie of lernynge shulde be a norishement for the malitiousness of their nature. Verely I do nat alowe in a subtile and a crafty woman suche lernyng, as shulde teche her disceyt, and teche her no good maners and virtues: Natwithstandyng the preceptes of lyvyng, and thexamples of those that have lyved wel, and had knowlege together of holynes, be the kepers of chastite and pureness, and the copies of vertues, and prickes to pricke[4] and to move folkes to contynue in them [. . .]

For the study of lernyng is suche a thyng, that it occupieth ones mynde holly,[5] and lyfteth hit up unto the knowledge of moste goodly matters: and plucketh hit from the remembraunce of suche thynges as be foule. And if any suche thought come in to theyr mynde, eyther the mynde, well fortified with the precepts of good lyvynge, avoydeth them away, orels hit gyveth none hede unto those thynges, that be vyle and foule: whan hit hath other most goodly and pure pleasure, where with hit is delyted. And therefore I suppose that Pallas the goddes of wysedome and counnynge, and all the Muses, were feyned in olde tyme to be virgins. And the mynde, set upon lernynge and wisedome, shall nat only abhorre from foule lust, that is to saye, the moste white thynge from soute, and the most pure from spottes: But also they shall leave all suche lyght and tryflynge pleasures, wherin the light fantasies of maydes have delyte, as songes, daunces, and suche other wanton and pevysshe playes. A woman sayth Plutarche, gyven unto lernyng, wyll never delyte in daunsynge.[6]

But here paraventure a man wolde aske, What lernyng a woman shulde be set unto, and what shall she studye: I have tolde you, The study of wysedome: the whiche dothe enstruct their maners, and enfurme theyr lyvyng, and teacheth them the way of good and holy lyfe. As for eloquence I have no great care, nor a woman nedeth it nat: but she nedeth goodnes and wysedome. Nor it is no shame for a woman to hold her peace: but it is shame for her and abominable to lacke discretion, and to lyve yll. Nor I wyl nat here condempne[7] eloquence, whiche both Quintilian,[8] and saynt Hieronyme[9] folowyng hym say, was preysed in Cornelia

---

1   Suited.
2   Agayne: then again, conversely.
3   Heartened; encouraged.
4   Prickes to pricke: goads to spur, ie. instigators.
5   Wholly.
6   Plutarch (AD c.46–c.120): Greek writer and philospher who was educated in Athens and later opened a school in Rome. Vives draws from his well-known *Lives* as well as from the *Moralia*, a collection of essays covering religion, ethics, politics and society.
7   Condemn.
8   Quintilian (AD c.35–96) was a Roman teacher and rhetorician whose *Institutio Oratoria* discussed, amongst other things, early childhood education for boys.
9   St Jerome (AD c.347–420), an eminent cleric in the Roman Catholic Church, known primarily for his revision of the Bible. Jerome wrote extensively on the concept of chastity which influenced Vives in the writing of *The Education of a Christen Woman*.

the mother of Gracchus,[10] and in Hortentia the doughter of Hortentius[11] [. . .] Whan she shalbe taught to rede, let those bokes be taken in hande, that may teche good maners. And what she shall lerne to write, let nat her example be voyde verses, nor wanton or tryflyng songes: but some sad sentence, prudent and chaste, taken out of holy scripture, or the sayenges of philosophers: whiche by often writing she may fasten better in her memory [. . .]

Finally let her lerne for her selfe alone and her yonge children or her sisters in our lord. For it neither becometh a woman to rule a schole, nor to live among men, or speke a brode and shake off her demurenes and honestie, eyther all together orels[12] a great parte: whiche if she be good, hit were better to be at home within, and unknowen to other folkes. And in company to holde her tonge demurely. And let fewe se her, and none at al here her [. . .] Let a woman lerne in silence with all subjection. But I gyve no licence to a woman to be a teacher, nor to have authorite of the man but to be in silence [. . .] Therfore bicause a woman is a fraile thynge, and of weake discretion, and that maye lightlye be disceyved: whiche thyng our fyrst mother Eve sheweth, whom the devyll caught with a lyght argument. Therfore a woman shulde nat teache, leste when she hath taken a false opinion and beleve of any thyng, she spred hit into the herars, by the autorite of maistershyp, and lightly bringe other into the same errour, for the lerners commenly do after the teacher with good wyll.

---

10 Cornelia (c.190–121 BC) was the daughter of Scipio Africanus the Elder, the Roman hero of the Second Punic War against Carthage. Cornelia was noted for her learning and admired by Cicero for her epistolary style. Her son Gracchus was a noted Roman tribune.
11 Hortensius (114–50 BC) was a Roman orator and politician. His daughter, Hortensia, delivered a speech in 42 BC on behalf of 1400 wealthy women who objected to paying taxes which were imposed by the Roman triumvirs to support their war against Julius Caesar's assassins.
12 Or else.

2

Interpretations

Critical History

Introduction

The title page to the first printing of *The Merchant of Venice* in 1600 presents various elements of the play in very different terms from how we might cast them today. It advertises 'The most excellent Historie of the *Merchant of Venice*. With the extreame crueltie of *Shylocke* the Iewe towards the sayd Merchant, in cutting a iust pound of his flesh: and the obtayning of *Portia* by the choyse of three chests' (see Figure 10 on **p. 138**). From the standpoint of a modern reader it is difficult to know where to begin sorting out the differences between our own critical interests and those of earlier readers who (if the title page is telling) saw the play in dissimilar terms. First, the play is referred to by the printer as a 'history', whereas modern critics and spectators are more inclined to think of it as a 'romantic comedy', even though this label presents certain difficulties. Second, the author of the subtitle (or what was called the running title) emphasises Shylock's 'extreme cruelty', which casts Shylock as a contemptible character. Despite the admission that he takes a 'just' pound of flesh, this is not the Shylock who normally earns at least some sympathy from modern audiences. Third, the running title notes that Portia is 'obtained', which suggests that she has little say in the matter. By contrast, many modern critics like to see Portia as an intelligent, independent woman who, to some degree, controls her own destiny, regardless of the casket test that has been set up by her deceased father. Surprisingly perhaps, there were times in the critical history of the play when commentators would have supported readings that seem unusual in the twenty-first century; and, from time to time, certain fashions in critical thinking seem to return. Nevertheless, despite the fact that *The Merchant* has been discussed by generations of scholars, spectators and theatre practitioners, certain elements of the play – those outlined by the running title, and others – simply seem to defy any neat resolution.

The Early Critical Tradition

It is difficult to pinpoint exactly when a 'critical tradition' concerning *The Merchant of Venice* actually begins. In part this is because the writing of formal literary commentary begins much later than we might imagine. For the first 250 years following the first productions of Shakespeare's play most commentators discussed the play in two ways: first, by writing about specific productions or actors that they had seen perform the play; or, second, by rewriting the play, thereby producing an adaptation that, in a backhanded way, commented upon Shakespeare's original. To confuse matters further, the text that was printed in 1600 was probably not Shakespeare's work alone, but, in reality, a collaborative effort that included the dramatist, his fellow actors who performed the play and the printer who, inadvertently or not, introduced his own changes into the text. Therefore, some critics have spent time trying to sort out questions relating to authorship. As a result, the issues relating to the critical tradition of *The Merchant of Venice* span many broad topical areas. Some of these areas are represented by the readings in the section entitled 'Early Critical Reception' (**pp. 64–78**).

Because much of the early commentary was prompted by specific performances of *The Merchant* it is hardly surprising that the earliest 'critics' were often reviewers who wrote about the elements of the play that interested them, or were offering guides to the play for the prospective playgoer. One example of this type of 'critical history' can be found in Nicholas Rowe's essay (**pp. 64–5**) which responds, in part, to a production of *The Jew of Venice*, a play by George Granville in which Shylock was played as a comic character. Another example is provided by William Hazlitt, who cautions against evaluating Shakespeare's characters through a knowledge of stage productions alone. By 1818, when Hazlitt was writing his piece, such a stage tradition of what he calls the 'malignant Shylock' had been established that it was virtually impossible for spectators, or readers of Shakespeare's play, to see the character any differently (**pp. 73–5**). John Potter (**pp. 69–70**) also uses his many years of experience as a theatrical reviewer in order to produce his commentary on the play. And although Shylock is discussed by Potter in the course of his essay, he is primarily concerned with another issue: whether *The Merchant* observes the 'unities' of time, place and action that were such significant criteria for the late seventeenth-century critics. Nevertheless, readers will find that many early commentators on the play, at some point, mention concerns related to staged productions of the play in shaping their own critical views.

Alongside such commentary a discussion began amongst those writers, such as Nicholas Rowe and Samuel Johnson, who had edited collections of Shakespeare's plays. Rowe's edition appeared in 1709, and Johnson followed with his own edition in 1765. In the passages quoted from Johnson's edition of *The Merchant* (**pp. 65–9**), he bases his text on the first quarto of the play. In various places Johnson comments on the ways in which his text either alters or reconfirms earlier readings of the play. And embedded within Johnson's annotations readers find other kinds of commentary – historical, etymological and critical.

As scholarly commentary developed other issues also emerged. These included questions surrounding how the play should be classified – as a comedy, a tragic-comedy or even as the tragedy of Shylock. But even after considerable debate this proved to be a vexed issue, and George Colman, writing in 1787, concluded that perhaps simply calling Shakespeare's works 'plays' was the best solution. Although he ultimately terms the plays 'dramatick tales', what was most important, in Colman's estimation, was that these pieces were intended 'to delight and instruct', that is, that the plays conveyed moral messages whilst engaging their spectators (**pp. 70–1**).

Whether *The Merchant* was 'realistic' or not had, by this time, become an abiding question for many commentators; and this question ultimately led from a discussion of fantasy and historical reality, in general, to discussions as to whether Shylock was a realistic representation of the Jewish nation. In the eighteenth century (embedded in the then-common consideration of the relationship between 'Art' and 'Nature') Rowe stated that the plot of the play was 'a little too much remov'd from the Rules of Probability' (**p. 65**). Colman found that the plays were founded on fables that were 'unpardonably wild and extravagant in their Circumstances' (**p. 71**). Johnson assessed the two plots of *The Merchant* and decided that 'the probability of one or the other story cannot be maintained'. As the nineteenth century got under way discussions became more focused; and by 1817 Nathan Drake had shifted attention, almost exclusively, to Shylock. Despite his admission that the play is a 'fable' Drake concludes that 'the picture which Shakespeare has drawn [of Shylock] exhibits [. . .] a faithful representation of Jewish sentiments and manners' (**p. 73**). For Hazlitt, Shylock 'seems the depositary of the vengeance of his race' (**p. 74**). Yet by the early twentieth century – as the examples of E. E. Stoll (**pp. 75–6**) and Harley Granville-Barker (**pp. 76–8**) attest – some critics were again viewing the plays as a set of literary and dramatic conventions. For Stoll, Shylock is a stage 'villain', like the devil of the medieval morality tales, and for Granville-Barker the human impulses and characteristics represented by Shylock are 'real, while his story remains fabulous' (**p. 77**).

During the early part of the twentieth century, as literary study was growing into its own professional speciality, other commentators on *The Merchant* begun addressing a related set of questions, some of them based on earlier trends. Chief amongst these was, and continues to be, the many ways in which Shylock and his revenge on Antonio are to be interpreted – both by readers and by spectators observing actual performances. Whether Shylock is simply an intolerant miser, or a man whose anger is justified by the mistreatment he has suffered at the hands of the Venetians is a question that has occupied many critics. Shylock's 'tragic dignity' (as some commentators identified it) was addressed early on, in 1905, by Stopford A. Brooke, and again, in 1913, by William Poel, whose experience as an actor, theatrical manager and producer doubtless shaped his views.[1] Additionally, inherent in their essays and in other early critical work, is the issue of balance.

---

1 Stopford A. Brooke, *On Ten Plays of Shakespeare* (London: Constable, 1905), pp. 127–54, and William Poel, *Shakespeare in the Theatre* (London: Sidgwick & Jackson, 1913).

How much of the play should Shylock be allowed to dominate? Brander Matthews, an early-twentieth-century critic, argued that the modern fascination with Shylock is misdirected since Shylock appears in so few scenes. The play, Matthews states, is a comedy, a tale in which lovers triumph, and they are ultimately at the centre of the play. Therefore the play should not be balanced in the direction of those who would see the play as Shylock's tragedy.[2] Studies such as these exemplify the emphasis, by early critics, on characterisation and dramatic genre. However, not surprisingly, it was only a matter of time before literary conversations began to run full circle, back to their eighteenth-century origins. In 1936 John Middleton Murry called into question the work of the 'realist' commentators by asserting that *The Merchant of Venice* is not a realistic drama, and therefore the characters cannot be expected to act according to realistic motives. For Murry, the play was a 'matter-of-fact fairy tale' that can only operate as a fantasy.[3]

Nevertheless, in an attempt to reconcile the conflict that had developed between 'fairy tale' and 'drama inclining towards realism' many authors attempted to test the 'realism' of the play by addressing specific historical and philosophical issues. For example, in 1935 John W. Draper emphasised that few Elizabethans knew Jews, but many had probably known moneylenders.[4] Two years later Helen Pettigrew discussed Elizabethan courtship customs; and earlier, in 1927, Charles Baskerville had placed Bassanio's love and early modern expectations of gentlemanly behaviour in the context of the famous *Book of the Courtier* (*c.* 1507) written by Baldesar Castiglione, an Italian humanist philosopher.[5] By the 1940s, in an essay addressing the setting of the play Cary F. Jacob decided that Shakespeare's play represented Venice and Venetian life truly; and John W. Draper, supporting this sense of the play, produced a second study examining the historical context of the play, this time using psychological and medical theories involving the humours.[6]

Modern Criticism

Yet despite the many years of critical debate surrounding the play, critics and spectators tend to return to a handful of issues. In particular these concern the nature of Shylock's revenge, the nature of Bassanio's love for both Portia and Antonio, the central theme of justice and mercy, the significance of the two locales in the play (Venice and the mythical Belmont), the nature of the casket test which

2   Brander Matthews, *Shakespeare as a Playwright* (New York: Scribner's, 1913).
3   John Middleton Murry, 'Shakespeare's Method: *The Merchant of Venice*' in *Shakespeare* (London: Cape, 1936), pp. 153–73.
4   'Usury in *The Merchant of Venice*', *Modern Philology*, 33 (1935), 37–47.
5   Helen Purinton Pettigrew, 'Bassanio, the Elizabethan Lover', *Philological Quarterly*, 16 (1937), 296–306; Charles Read Baskerville, 'Bassanio as an Ideal Lover', *The Manly Anniversary Studies in Language and Literature* (Chicago, Ill.: University of Chicago Press, 1923), pp. 90–103.
6   Cary F. Jacob, 'Reality and *The Merchant of Venice*', *Quarterly Journal of Speech*, 28 (1942), 307–15; John W. Draper, *The Humors and Shakespeare's Characters* (Durham, NC: Duke University Press, 1945).

determines which of Portia's suitors will become her husband, the propriety (or impropriety) of the punishments meted out to Shylock in Act 4, Scene 1 (generally referred to as the 'trial scene'), the character of Portia and the ways in which the couples (Portia and Bassanio, Nerissa and Gratiano, and Jessica and Lorenzo) play off against each other. Understandably, since the Second World War critics have also taken up the question of whether Shakespeare's play is anti-Semitic or not. Following upon much critical conversation, most commentators now see *The Merchant* not as a play that supports anti-Semitism, but as one that contains anti-Semitic elements, and which attempts to expose the ugliness of many types of prejudice – religious, racial and ethnic. Still, there is no settled opinion. Some critics continue to think that Shylock is vilified unnecessarily, and many productions are at least somewhat sympathetic to his plight.

Even as Belmont awakens the audience to the possibilities of a softer, more lyrical existence, Venice, after all, remains a place that is driven by a type of hard-bitten commercialism that encourages (perhaps even enables) business-men to put a price on human flesh, to the detriment of everyone involved. In selecting materials for this sourcebook I have chosen to concentrate upon the many modern commentators who have decided that commercialism is one of the most significant defining forces within the play. The first section of the modern interpretations that follow (**pp. 79–88**) outlines the central issues that commodification touches upon, from race and gender to the definition of English identity and the relationship between the dramatist and his audience. The second section (**pp. 88–91**) takes up the specific matters of hazarding, risking and choosing, which are omnipresent in the play. The final section – entitled 'Shylock and Other Strangers' – presents several opinions on Shylock, who both attempts to commodify Antonio by charging 3000 ducats for a pound of his flesh and is, ironically, commodified himself by Antonio at the end of the play (**pp. 91–6**). As the final essays in this collection suggest, however, the traditional readings of Shylock, Portia and Antonio are complicated in interest-ing ways if readers are aware of the ways in which these three characters – often thought of as contrary and discrete – seem to be both complementary and, finally, similar. Like the riddle of Portia's caskets, *The Merchant of Venice* appears to have one correct answer; but, as more than one of the critics below makes clear, riddles are, by their very nature, multi-dimensional. So, it seems is Shakespeare's play.

Commodification and Humanity

The authors represented in the 'Modern Criticism' section of the sourcebook harken back to many of the older critical traditions that inform thinking on the play. However, their work also represents a variety of contemporary critical approaches and fresh views. In keeping with the emphasis of this sourcebook, each essay in the section of 'Modern Criticism' touches upon various types of 'transactions' – actual and metaphorical – that shape the play. The first sub-section, entitled 'The Economic Framework', presents five essays that deal more explicitly than the others with the economic terms and conditions that pervade the play. Of these, Walter Cohen's essay attends to the most broadly based issues (**pp. 79–80**). Cohen suggests that *The Merchant* addresses the anxieties of Shakespeare's society towards the rise of capitalism – with all of the structures that this requires (banking, the need for credit, the eventuality of indebtedness and, of course, moneylending). But simultaneously, for Cohen, the play sets up a 'false dichotomy'. As he points out, in the world of trade there can finally be no 'honest merchant' and 'dishonest usurer'. Both are businessmen whose goal is ultimately the same – the 'breeding of money', as Shylock calls it. To Shakespeare's spectators the Venetian setting represented in *The Merchant* characterised their own commercial world, with all of its liabilities, at a more advanced stage. Cohen sees the discussion of the capitalist enterprise in *The Merchant* as one virtually without ethics. Commerce is capable of great good, but it is also a necessary evil of the modern world. As a result the play becomes a vehicle that exposes many 'merchants', each of whom has his or her own 'interest' in events; and no character is necessarily more ethical than the others.

'Guess Who's Coming to Dinner?' might best be subtitled 'Commodification and National Identity' (**pp. 80–2**). Here, Kim Hall discusses 'commerce and intercourse' to identify the many ways in which the play's economic and social transactions cross over racial and ethnic boundaries. Not only are the relations between Christians and Jews troubled, as is apparent from the interaction between Antonio and Shylock from the beginning of the play, but Portia is dismissive of the Prince of Morocco because, in his racial difference, he 'raises the specter of a monetary and sexual exchange in England' (**p. 82**). Consequently, the calm, golden world of Belmont can 'afford' to be calm and golden because of its economic pre-eminence. However, in reality Belmont rests nervously on the same anxieties that have come to the surface in Venice. According to Hall, the lovers' courtships are akin to 'colonial expansions', and the 'cash flow problem' that plagues Venice is a warning to Christian women 'who are associated with an abundance of wealth' (**p. 82**).

Concentrating on the ways in which the two locales of the play – Venice and Belmont – bear different associations Leonard Tennenhouse outlines the sexual identifications that operate within each locale (**pp. 82–4**). Belmont seems bountiful and maternal whereas Venice is wholly masculine. As a result Jessica (Shylock's daughter) escapes from Venice as quickly as she can, while Portia and Nerissa have to disguise themselves as men in order to enter Venice. In agreement with Kim Hall, Tennenhouse argues that the male lovers from Venice (Bassanio and Gratiano) come as 'adventurers' to Belmont where they not only find worthy wives, but where they can escape the harsh reality of the commercial centre of Venetian society. Still, Tennenhouse, like many other critics, is uncomfortable with the ending of the play. Although the punishments assigned to Shylock can be justified by the need to maintain Venetian law, and to maintain the law within reasonable limits, the 'humour of the ring plot' and the 'isolation of Antonio' are elements that Tennenhouse finds 'disturbing'. But more disturbing, in some sense, are the many fantasies that swirl around the ending of the play, chief amongst which is the fantasy that the lovers can live 'happily ever after'. For Tennenhouse, in a setting in which personal relationships are entwined so closely with financial negotiations, most relationships are, in some way, 'counterfeit'. In this context Portia becomes Bassanio's patron, as much as she is his wife; and marriage in Belmont is about maintaining wealth. The return to order at the end of the play is achieved by returning to the 'status quo', an order in which the Christians are both the authors of the law, its most adroit manipulators, and its chief beneficiaries.

Karen Newman's essay delineates the workings of Elizabethan marriage exchanges in order to expose the '*structure* of exchange itself' (**pp. 84–6**). Portia's ring, an emblem of harmony and the forging of bonds in marriage, 'picks up new meanings' as it, along with the three thousand ducats, pass from hand to hand, and from person to person. While it would appear that commercial relationships within the play are, generally speaking, about 'trafficking in flesh' (together with all of the allusions to hierarchy and slavery that this implies), Portia's ring is a *specific* object through which we can track the ways in which *The Merchant* interrogates Elizabethan attitudes towards sex and gender. In the last scene of the play, when Portia hands her ring to Antonio it is Antonio who hands it back to Bassanio. 'Give him this', she says to Antonio, 'And bid him keep it better than the other.' It is, of course, the same ring that she had given to Bassanio earlier in the play. But the vow that Bassanio makes the second time around will be different, having symbolically given away and regained Portia and her love.

When Lynda E. Boose 'picks up' the thread of critical enquiry, she starts, as does Newman, with Portia's ring (**pp. 86–8**). However, Boose reminds us that this symbol, a circle, leads Bassanio back to Portia; and furthermore, the ring's circularity leads the audience back to the lovers at the end of the play. Yet for Boose, Portia is more complicated than some critics acknowledge, for she, like Shylock and many of the other characters, is also an 'adventurer' and a 'shrewd possessor'. Having made this connection, Boose reminds us of the financial contract shared by the actors and the spectators. The acting company promises to deliver a good performance in exchange for the admission fees paid by the members of the audience. But instead of wielding power over the performance through their approval or disapproval, the audience is drawn into the financial web of the play without knowing it. 'The audience of the play is modeled by the suitors in it', Boose states, by which she implies that Shakespeare's spectators are first drawn into the play by their own interests, which mirror those of Portia's suitors. Then, later in the play the spectators, like Bassanio, learn to risk and venture; or at least they imagine that that is what they are doing. In actuality, however, the suitors and the spectators (who are their mirror images) are ensnared by Portia, who is perhaps the most adept 'merchant' in the play. For Boose, Shylock acts as a 'lightening rod' that draws 'all Christian fears and aggressions', and he is one vehicle through which the audience is forced to confront their own fears and aggressions; but it is Portia who subtly works like a clever spider to ensnare her suitor and the audience.

Hazarding, Risking and Choosing

Joan Ozark Holmer, whose essay (**pp. 88–90**) focuses on risking and hazarding, suggests that former critics have overemphasised the fact that the casket test is constructed specifically to defeat the Prince of Morocco and the Duke of Arragon. In fact, she urges, the unsuccessful suitors are defeated finally by their literal mindedness. Similarly, so is Shylock who is interested more in personal financial gain than in the wiser choice – hazarding for love and friendship. In the trial scene Shylock is easily the most literal-minded character in the courtroom, insisting repeatedly that he will 'have his bond'. No other offer will placate him, and he shows his single-mindedness in the way in which he refuses to back down. As Holmer also points out, Shakespeare shows us, by one clever bit of stage business, that Bassanio will not duplicate the mistakes of Morocco or Arragon. Unlike the other suitors, Bassanio doesn't repeat the mottoes on the individual caskets. Of course, as a matter of mere practicality, Shakespeare spares the audience having to listen to another run-through of what they already know; but, more than this, the dramatist 'presents Bassanio's silent contemplation of the caskets as thinking before speaking'. Bassanio weighs and considers the choices for a much longer time than the previous choosers. This, Holmer states, is a clear indication that he is more considerate and more spiritually aware of the higher values of life than Morocco, Arragon or Shylock.

Catherine Belsey sees love as an ambiguous entity in the play; hence, two entities that don't seem to belong together are joined together in her title – 'Love in Venice' (**pp. 90–1**). Although love is surrounded by the feminine and the musical (or 'lyrical') it leaves traces of other things in the text, including a reading of love as 'anarchic, destructive, and dangerous'. The 'hazarding for love' that is so applauded by audiences invites its participants to wager their own destruction; and once obtained, love in Belmont is almost immediately threatened by the legal actions taken against Antonio in Venice. As Belsey reminds us, there are many riddles in the play, some answered and some never answered. However, riddles remind us that 'meaning is neither single nor transparent'. For Belsey, this is equally true of the characters in *The Merchant*, despite the fact that the audience is drawn to some characters over others. Nevertheless, when we consider 'love' in its broadest sense, Belsey reminds us that it was a man's association with women that was fraught with danger, according to Shakespeare's contemporaries; the free association of men with men, for whatever the level of intimacy that existed in that association, was thought to be less dangerous to men.

Shylock and Other Strangers

In the final sub-section of critical commentaries, three authors take up those issues associated with the many contradictory interpretations of Shylock. John Drakakis posits that Shylock isn't really meant to represent a 'Jew' in any historical or ethnic sense (**pp. 91–3**). Rather, he sees Shylock as a sort of blank screen onto which Shakespeare projects many of the most unpleasant and unethical character- istics of the Christian community in Venice. Furthermore, like Joan Holmer,

Drakakis comments that Portia and Shylock are 'drawn together' in several ways. Both are acquisitive; both 'invest' in human beings; and both are interested in making money 'breed'. However, an unusual symbolic link between Shylock and Antonio is forged at the end of the trial scene. While, in Drakakis's words, the 'transition for Shylock [. . .] is not an easy one', once Shylock is converted he becomes 'Christian' and, therefore, a different kind of threat to the Christian community. For Drakakis, the 'illness' with which Shylock is suddenly afflicted at the end of the trial scene is related to the fact that he has now become part of the Christian community. Not only this, but he has also become a new threat as part of that 'Christianized commercialism' from which Antonio suffers at the beginning of the play.

Following on from Drakakis, James Shapiro analyses the features of ritual murder and evisceration that exist in the trial scene of *The Merchant* (**pp. 93–4**). To Shapiro, the play offers a 'fantasy solution' to economic and social issues that were considered genuinely pressing in Shakespeare's London. The 'threat to the flesh' that lies at the centre of Shylock's flesh bond emanates not only from Antonio's flesh – upon which Shylock has put a price – but from the very flesh of Shylock himself as well. Shapiro details how the threatened emasculation of Antonio is bound up in early modern superstitions regarding the bodily functions of Jewish men and the fables involving the ritualised murder of Christian victims. His analysis helps us to interpret the link between commerce and laceration that seems to take over the play and the audience, almost obsessively, once Shylock's flesh bond is introduced.

The last essay in the collection – Alan Sinfield's – highlights the ways in which contemporary critics analyse the play's homoerotic associations (**pp. 95–6**). However, Sinfield extends the analysis of these ideological structures by relating them not only to Antonio and Bassanio (and their commercial interests) but also to being bound, in general. For Sinfield the play offers 'networks of enticements', some of which have to do with 'trafficking in boys'. For Sinfield the masculine commodification of Venice is directly undercut by the relationship between Antonio and Bassanio because this is the relationship in the play that most threatens the Venetian patriarchy; and coincidentally, it threatens the marriage between Bassanio and Portia. Like Drakakis, and some other critics, Sinfield ultimately thinks that Antonio's racism is related to his sexuality; that by identifying the homosexual impulses within himself, Antonio realises that he is the 'alien other' that he symbolically identifies as the Jew.

Early Critical Reception

From **Nicholas Rowe, *Some Account of the Life, &c. of Mr. William Shakespear*** [1] (London, 1709), pp. i–xl; pp. ix–xx

Nicholas Rowe (1674–1718) was trained as a barrister at the Inner Temple; however, his interests turned to poetry and drama, and eventually he became a dramatist of some repute. His works – which include a Marlovian-styled piece entitled *Tamerlane*, as well as other plays with historical subjects – sparked his interest in other writers of the early eighteenth century, including Alexander Pope. Additionally, Rowe is often remembered as the first editor of Shakespeare's plays. His edition, which appeared in 1709, was his most notable achievement. Amongst other things it contained a preface in which Rowe attempted to write a biography of Shakespeare and a general survey of his works.

It is from Rowe's commentary on Shakespeare's plays that the following passage has been taken. Here, he debates whether Shylock should be viewed as a comic character (as a clown of sorts, similar to the melancholy Jacques in *As You Like It*), or whether he is a tragic character. For readers today it might seem that this is an unusual subject for enquiry; but Rowe's debate was not restricted to circles of literary commentators. One staged version of the play was notable for this interpretation of the character, and Rowe probably saw *The Jew of Venice* (1701), a version of *The Merchant* written and produced by George Granville, Lord Lansdowne, in which Shylock was played as a buffoon. While Rowe rejects this interpretation of the role, Granville's production was popular with audiences for over a generation.

Like other commentators of his time Rowe also judges the quality of the play by its coherence and whether, as art, the play mirrors life (or what he and his contemporaries referred to as 'Nature'). He concludes that indeed the play is 'one of the most finish'd' of Shakespeare's. And while the casket lottery is too

---

1   A common spelling for 'Shakespeare' in the eighteenth and nineteenth centuries.

much removed from the 'Rules of Probability' to be realistic, he concludes that Act 4 (the trial scene) is 'extremely Fine'.

His [Shakespeare's] Clowns, without which Character there was hardly any Play writ in that Time, are all very entertaining; And, I believe, *Thersites* in *Troilus and Cressida*, and *Apemantus* in *Timon [of Athens]*, will be allow'd to be Master-Pieces of ill Nature, and satyrical Snarling. To these I might add, that incomparable Character of *Shylock* the *Jew*, in *The Merchant of* Venice; but tho' we have seen that Play Receiv'd and Acted as a Comedy, and the Part of the *Jew* perform'd by an Excellent Comedian, yet I cannot but think it was design'd Tragically by the Author. There appears in it such a deadly Spirit of Revenge, such a savage Fierceness and Fellness, and such a bloody designation of Cruelty and Mischief, as cannot agree either with the Stile or Characters of Comedy. The Play it self, take it all together, seems to me to be one of the most finish'd of any of *Shakespear*'s. The Tale indeed, in that Part relating to the Caskets, and the extravagant and unusual kind of Bond given by *Antonio*, is a little too much remov'd from the Rules of Probability: But taking the Fact for granted, we must allow it to be very beautifully written. There is something in the Friendship of *Antonio* to *Bassanio* very Great, Generous and Tender. The whole fourth Act, supposing, as I said, the Fact to be probable, is extremely Fine. But there are two Passages that deserve a particular Notice. The first is, what Portia says in praise of Mercy [. . .] the other on the Power of Musick [. . .][2]

From **Samuel Johnson, *The Plays of William Shakespeare, in Eight Volumes, with the Corrections and Illustrations of Various Commentators; to which are added Notes by Sam. Johnson*** (London, 1765), 8 vols; vol. 1, pp. 384–488; pp. 389, 393, 395, 404, 422, 427, 435, 465, 477, 488

Samuel Johnson (1709–84) is best remembered for his dictionary of the English language published in 1755; however, he also wrote literary criticism (*Lives of the Poets*, 1781), as well as a play (*Irene*, 1749), a novel (*Rasselas*, 1769), and many miscellaneous pieces for periodicals such as *The Rambler* and *The Idler*, along with various poems, the best remembered of which is his satiric commentary on human nature entitled 'The Vanity of Human Wishes' (1749). Like Nicholas

2 The first speech to which Rowe is referring is clearly Act 4, Scene 1, lines 180–201 (Portia's 'quality of mercy' speech). The other is less clear. It might be either Act 5, Scene 1, lines 75–88 (Lorenzo's 'If they perchance but hear a trumpet sound', which refers to the 'sweet power of music' at line 79) or Act 5, Scene 1, lines 103–6 (Portia's 'The crow doth sing as sweetly as the lark' speech, which refers to the transforming power of music). Portia also speaks of music just before Bassanio chooses amongst the caskets in Act 3, Scene 2, line 44ff.

Rowe, Johnson prepared an edition of Shakespeare's plays (1765). Its well-known Preface is arguably the best piece of Shakespearean criticism of the eighteenth century. In it Johnson addressed what had become standard topics amongst literary scholars: Shakespeare's talent as a poet of 'nature' (as opposed to being a poet of learning); Shakespeare's ability to create characters that are 'true to life'; and, finally, Shakespeare's ability to represent the full range of human passions and emotions that were felt, by Johnson and his contemporaries, to be significant in creating any successful play. Although Johnson was critical of some aspects of Shakespeare's work he found him unsurpassed in creating what he called 'just representations of general nature' or, in modern terms, in creating art that seems to mirror life. Contrary to some critics of his time, however, Johnson criticised the traditional respect for the classical 'unities of time and place'.[1]

Even though Johnson never wrote a sustained piece of literary criticism on *The Merchant of Venice* his edition of Shakespeare's plays contained footnotes and lengthy endnotes to each of the plays through which a reader can gain some sense of his critical views. Below are ten passages from Johnson's notes to *Merchant* that represent the kinds of issues that concerned him as a critic and an editor. In particular, Johnson was interested in roughly six areas that sometimes overlap. First, he addressed specific textual issues (how his own edition compared with, or altered the First Quarto, and how textual format shaped meaning). These interests are exemplified in Examples 5 and 7 below. Second, Johnson attempted to clarify the text through the provision of etymological or historical glosses, as is seen in Examples 1–3 and 9. Third, Johnson attended to textual issues that would influence the actual performance of the play, as in Examples 5–7. Fourth, Johnson pointed out inconsistencies within the text or illogical elements within the play, as in Example 4. Fifth, Johnson offered his overall impression of the play, as in Example 10. Finally, Johnson was interested in entering into a dialogue with former editors, such as Thomas Warburton or Alexander Pope, as he does in Examples 1 and 8. Additionally, Johnson commented upon particular grammatical and stylistic elements in the play, as well as Shakespeare's stylistic 'habits', i.e. his vocabulary or syntax.

1. On Act 1, Scene 1, line 9, in which Johnson responds to Alexander Pope's note on the word 'Argosies' using his knowledge of historical etymology:

---

1   Rules derived from Aristotle's observations on tragedy that were later refined by French classical dramatists such as Corneille and Racine. The unities of time, place and plot (or action), as defined by the French classicists, required a play to present a single action, represented as occurring in a single location, and within the course of one day. By contrast, English playwrights frequently wrote their plays around two (or more) plots, mingling comedy and tragedy in a single play. Some late seventeenth-century playwrights, such as John Dryden, wrote treatises supporting the unities although they never took hold in England as they had in France. Dryden's *All for Love*, a version of the Antony and Cleopatra story, obeys the unities.

Argosie, a ship from *Argo*.

POPE.

Whether it be derived from *Argo* I am in doubt. It was a name given in our Authour's time to ships of great burthen, probably Galleons, such as the *Spaniards* now use in the *West-India* trade. [p. 385]

> 2. On Act 1, Scene 2, line 38, in which Johnson glosses the historical reference to 'Count Palatine':

I am always inclined to believe, that *Shakespear* has more allusions to particular facts and persons than his readers commonly suppose. The Count here mentioned was, perhaps, *Albertus a Lasio*, a *Polish Palatine*, who visited *England* in our Authour's time, was eagerly caressed, and splendidly entertained, but running in debt, at last stole away, and endeavoured to repair his fortune by enchantment. [p. 393]

> 3. On Act 1, Scene 2, lines 68–9, Johnson raises the possibility that in naming Portia's suitors Shakespeare was alluding to Queen Elizabeth I's suitors:

In *Shakespear*'s time the Duke of *Bavaria* visited *London*, and was made Knight of the Garter.

Perhaps in this enumeration of *Portia*'s suitors, there may be some covert allusion to those of Queen *Elizabeth*. [p. 395]

> 4. On Act 2, Scene 1, line 25, in which Johnson comments on Shakespeare's (mis)use of geography:

Shakespear seldom escapes well when he is entangled with Geography. The Prince of *Morocco* must have travelled far to kill the *Sophy* of *Persia*. [p. 404]

> 5. On Act 2, Scene 7, line 79, in which Johnson discusses the divisions of acts within the First Quarto (1600). He notes that there is no 'act' division here, although he clearly means what a modern reader would call a 'scene division'. Hence, this is the place in the text where Johnson divides Scene 8 from Scene 9, despite the fact that the Quarto doesn't include a division here. Interestingly, Johnson's decision to do so is based on what he regards as the need to provide time between Morocco's exit and Bassanio's eventual entrance into Belmont:

The old quarto Edition of 1600 has no distribution of acts, but proceeds from the beginning to the end in an unbroken tenour. This play therefore having been probably divided without authority by the publishers of the first folio,[2] lies open to a new regulation if any more commodious division can be proposed. The story is itself so wildly incredible, and the changes of the scene so frequent and capricious, that the probability of action does not deserve much care; yet it may be proper to observe, that, by concluding the second act here,[3] time is given for *Bassanio*'s passage to *Belmont*. [p. 422]

6. On Act 2, Scene 9, line 69, in which Johnson points out an inconsistency in the text. Earlier in the play (Act 2, Scene 1, lines 40–2) the Prince of Morocco is told that Portia's suitors must forgo marriage if they fail at the casket test; but the message inside the silver casket tells a different story:

Perhaps the poet had forgotten that he who missed *Portia* was never to marry any woman. [p. 427]

7. On Act 3, Scene 2, line 66, the song sung whilst Bassanio is making his choice in the casket lottery. Johnson questions where the placement of 'Reply, Reply' is, and whether this is a stage direction to singers or part of the song:

These words, *reply*, *reply*, were in all the late editions, except Sir *T. Hammer*'s, put as a verse in the song, but in all the old copies stand as a marginal direction. [p. 435]

8. On Act 4, Scene 1, lines 376–81 of the trial scene, in response to which Johnson writes the following remarks in order to clarify what the terms of the punishment against Shylock are:

The terms proposed have been misunderstood. *Antonio* declares, that as the *Duke* quits one half of the forfeiture, he is likewise content to abate his claim, and desires not the property but the *use* or produce only of the half, and that only for the *Jew*'s life, unless we read, as perhaps is right, *upon* my *death*. [p. 465]

2   The First Folio, the first collection of Shakespeare's plays to be printed, appeared in 1623.
3   At the end of Act 2, Arragon (one of Portia's unsuccessful suitors) has just left the stage. In the next scene (Act 3, Scene 1), Shakespeare returns to a conversation involving Shylock which buys some time before Bassanio has to arrive in Act 3, Scene 2.

Wealth was, at [the] time, the term opposite to *adversary*, or *calamity*. [p. 477]

Of *The Merchant of Venice* the stile is even and easy, with few peculiarities of
diction or anomalies of construction. The comick part raises laughter, and the
serious fixes expectation. The probability of either one or the other story cannot
be maintained. The union of two actions in one event is in this drama eminently
happy. [p. 488]

From **John Potter, *The Theatrical Review; or, New Companion to the Play-House*** (London, 1772), 2 vols; vol. 1, pp. 36–7

The Plot is well contrived, notwithstanding it is irregular; but the Unities of Time
and Place are materially broken. The Characters are well chosen, and in general

supported in a masterly Manner. The Incidents are not only numerous but pleas-
ing and affecting, and many of the Sentiments are truly sublime. In short, tho'
this Piece hath many defects its beauties are infinitely more numerous.—With
what art and perfect knowledge of human Nature in her most degenerated State
has the Poet drawn the Character of *Shylock*! How nobly has he availed himself
of the general Character of the *Jews*, the very Quintessence of which he has
displayed in a delightful manner in order to enrich this Character. And though he
has evidently deviated from a Matter of fact (according to Tradition), in representing the Jew the Hero of Villainy and Barbarity instead of the Christian,
popular Prejudice will sufficiently vindicate him; not that we think he was absolutely bound to adhere to the matter of fact, if it really was so. After all, the
Picture here drawn is so disgraceful to human Nature, that we doubt whether it
ever had an Original.

From **George Colman, *Prose on Several Occasions*** (London, 1787).
Reprinted in *Shakespeare: The Critical Heritage, Vol. 4, 1753–1765*, ed. Brian
Vickers (London: Routledge & Kegan Paul, 1976), pp. 442–3

George Colman the Elder (1732–94) was a leading comic dramatist of the
eighteenth century who sought to revive the works of various playwrights of
Shakespeare's age through adaptations. In 1761 he wrote *The Jealous Wife*, one
of the most stageworthy plays of the period, and in 1766 he collaborated with
the eminent Shakespearean actor and theatre manager David Garrick on *The
Clandestine Marriage*, which proved to be an enormous success. Colman went
on to own and manage theatres as well, purchasing a one-quarter share in the
Covent Garden Theatre, which he managed for seven years, and becoming sole
owner, in 1776, of a summer theatre (The Little Theatre in the Hay,
Haymarket).

In the following passage Colman, like Rowe (**pp. 64–5**) and other eighteenth-century commentators, is concerned with classification, and specifically
whether or not *Merchant* can be classified as a comedy, tragedy or a tragic-
comedy. He concludes, however, that these classification schemes are finally
irrelevant, and that the language of playbills, which simply refer to Shakespeare's works as 'plays', perhaps describes these works most aptly. In the
tradition of earlier commentators writing during Shakespeare's day (such as
the poet and courtier, Sir Philip Sidney), Colman reconfirms the sentiment that
the purpose of plays should be 'to delight and instruct'. (Sidney's well-known
statement, which appeared in his prose treatise, *The Apology for Poetry* (c. 1582),
was that poetry should ideally both 'teach and delight', thereby engaging
readers and educating them simultaneously.) Therefore, for Colman and many
of his contemporaries plays must have a moral purpose if they are to be
respected as art.

These Fables (it may be further objected) founded on romantick Novels[1] are unpardonably wild and extravagant in their Circumstances, and exhibit too little even of the Manners of the Age in which they were written. The Plays too are in themselves a kind of heterogeneous composition; scarce any of them being, strictly speaking, a Tragedy, Comedy, or Tragi-Comedy but rather an ingested jumble of every species thrown together.

This charge must be confessed to be true: but upon examination it will perhaps be found of less consequence than is generally imagined. These Dramatick Tales, for so we may best stile such Plays, have often occasioned much pleasure to the Reader and Spectator, which could not possibly have been conveyed to them by any other vehicle. Many an interesting Story which, from the diversity of its circumstances, cannot be regularly reduced either to Tragedy or Comedy, yet abounds with Character, and contains several affecting situations: and why such a Story should lose its force dramatically related and assisted by representation, when it pleases under the colder form of a Novel, is difficult to conceive. Experience has proved the effect of such fictions on our minds; and convinced us that the Theatre is not that barren ground wherein the Plants of Imagination will not flourish. *The Tempest, The Midsummer Night's Dream, The Merchant of Venice, As you like it, Twelfth Night, The Faithful Shepherdess* of Fletcher, (with a much longer list that might be added from Shakespeare, Beaumont and Fletcher,[2] and their contemporaries, or immediate successors) have most of them within all our memories been ranked among the most popular Entertainments of the Stage. Yet none can be denominated Tragedy, Comedy, or Tragi-Comedy. The Play Bills,[3] I have observed, cautiously stile them Plays: and Plays indeed they are, truly such if it be the end of Plays to delight and instruct, to captivate at once the Ear, the Eye, and the Mind, by Situations forcibly conceived and Characters truly delineated.

From **Nathan Drake, *Shakespeare and His Times*** (London: T. Cadell & W. Davies, 1817), 2 vols; vol. 2, pp. 387–9

Nathan Drake, MD, as he identifies himself on the title page of *Shakespeare and His Times*, was also the author of *Literary Hours* (1800) and numerous essay collections. *Shakespeare and His Times*, from which the following passage is taken, proved to be so popular that it was published in London in 1817 and 1828, as well as in Paris in 1838. Drake's approach is typical of commentary in the nineteenth and early twentieth centuries in which commentators attempted to see the plays of Shakespeare through an historical lens, most often

---

1 Colman is referring to the earlier stories, or romances, which served as the basis for numerous plays of Shakespeare's period.
2 Francis Beaumont and John Fletcher, two dramatists contemporary with Shakespeare.
3 Posters used to advertise theatrical performances.

the lens that they imagined was pre-eminent in the sixteenth century. (John Potter (see **pp. 69–70**) and earlier commentators laid the groundwork for this by asking the question: was Shakespeare's art reflective of Nature (i.e. the world)?)

In the passage below, Drake offers his 'observations' (as they were commonly termed in his time) on the character of Shylock. To the standard 'unities' of time, place and action that were so important to commentators in the later seventeenth and eighteenth centuries,[1] Drake adds his own 'unity of feeling' that, he states, underscores the 'dramatic consistency' in the trial scene (Act 4, Scene 1) of *The Merchant*. This consistency, Drake argues, is based on the fact that Shylock represents the 'generic exemplar' (i.e. a stereotype) of Jews during Shakespeare's time, a point that leads him to the topic of anti-Semitism. Yet despite its professed interest in historical questions, Drake's critical commentary culminates in an off-putting conclusion. Drake suggests that the popularity of Shakespeare's *The Merchant* has resided in the strong anti-Semitism of its audiences who, by implication, delight in seeing Shylock put in his place during the trial scene. Moreover, despite Drake's professed humanitarian bent, his ultimate conclusion is very mixed. Drake's reference to 'conversion' in the final line of the passage echoes Shylock's conversion in the trial scene (Act 4, Scene 1, **pp. 177–88**) of the play.

There is also another unity of equal moment, seldom found wanting, indeed, in any of the genuine plays of our poet, but which is particularly observable in this, that *unity of feeling* which we have once before had occasion to notice, and which, in the present instance, has given an uniform, but an extraordinary, tone to every part of the fable. Thus the unparalleled nature of the trial between the Jew and his debtor, required, in order to produce that species of dramatic consistency so essential to the illusion of the reader or spectator, that the other important incident of the piece should assume an equal cast of singularity; the enigma, therefore, of the caskets is a most suitable counterpart to the savage eccentricity of the bond, and their skilful combination effects the probability arising from similitude of nature and intimacy of connection.

Yet the ingenuity of the fable is surpassed by the truth and originality of the characters that carry it into execution. Avarice and revenge, the prominent vices of Shylock, are painted with a pencil so discriminating, as to appear very distinct from the same passions in the bosom of a Christian. The peculiar circumstances, indeed, under which the Jews have been placed for so many centuries, would of themselves be sufficient, were the national feelings correctly caught, to throw a peculiar colouring over all their actions and emotions; but to these were unhappily added, in the age of Shakespeare, the most rooted prejudices and antipathies; an aversion, indeed, partaking of hatred and horror, was indulged against this

1   See note 1, p. 66.

persecuted people, and consequently the picture which Shakespeare has drawn exhibits not only a faithful representation of Jewish sentiments and manners, the necessary result of a singular dispensation of Providence, but it embodies in colours, of almost preternatural strength, the Jew as he appeared to the eye of the shuddering Christian.

In Shylock, therefore, while we behold the manners and the associations of the Hebrew mingling with every thing he says and does, and touched with a verisimilitude and precision which excite our astonishment, we, at the same time, perceive, that, influenced by the prepossessions above-mentioned, the poet has clothed him with passions which would not derogate from a personification of the evil principle itself. He is, in fact, in all the lighter parts of his character, a generical exemplar of Judaism, but demonized, individualized, and rendered awfully striking and horribly appalling by the attribution of such unrelenting malice, as we will hope, for the honour of our species, was never yet accumulated, with such intensity, in any human breast.

So vigorous, however, so masterly is the delineation of this Satanic character, and so exactly did it, until of late years, chime in with the bigotry of the Christian world, that no one of our author's plays has experienced greater popularity. Fortunately the time has now arrived when the Jew and the Christian can meet with all the feelings of humanity about them; a state of society which, more than any other, is calculated to effect that conversion for which every disciple of our blessed religion will assuredly pray.

From **William Hazlitt, _The Round Table; Characters of Shakespear's_[1] _Plays_** (1817) (London: J. M. Dent & Sons, Ltd., 1936), pp. 320–4

William Hazlitt (1778–1830), best known as an essayist, began his career as a painter, an endeavour which was encouraged by his friends, William Wordsworth and Samuel Taylor Coleridge. However, soon thereafter he turned to philosophy, publishing his first book in 1805, _On the Principles of Human Action_, which launched his career as a professional writer. The best known of his books – _Table Talk_ (1821) and _Plain Speaker_ (1826) – were published late in his life. Additionally, Hazlitt's interest in the drama of Shakespeare's age is evident in his _Lectures on the Dramatic Literature of the Age of Elizabeth_ (1819) and _The Round Table; Characters of Shakespear's Plays_ (1817), the source of the following passage.

In the following passage Hazlitt writes short sketches of the characters in _The Merchant of Venice_, which he finds flawed. However, like other commentators he spends most of his time on Shylock who he judges to be particularly interesting. Hazlitt cautions that stage representations of the play are not necessarily the best place to study Shakespeare's characters, because so often a stage tradition

---

1   The spelling 'Shakespear' was a common variation of 'Shakespeare' in the nineteenth century.

develops that directors and actors simply end up repeating, from one production to the next. For this reason, he thinks that the character of Shylock has
survived, in his own time, as a 'malignant' presence, pushing aside other, more
sympathetic portrayals of the character.

This is a play that in spite of the change of manners and prejudices still holds
undisputed possession of the stage. Shakespear's malignant [Shylock] has outlived
Mr. [Richard] Cumberland's[2] benevolent Jew. In proportion as Shylock has
ceased to be a popular bugbear,[3] 'baited with the rabble's curse,' he becomes a
half-favourite with the philosophical part of the audience, who are disposed to
think that Jewish revenge is at least as good as Christian injuries. Shylock is *a
good hater*; 'a man no less sinned against than sinning.' If he carries his revenge
too far, yet he has strong grounds for 'the lodged hate he bears Anthonio,' which
he explains with equal force of eloquence and reason. He seems the depositary of
the vengeance of his race; and though the long habit of brooding over daily insults
and injuries has crusted over his temper with inveterate misanthropy, and hardened him against the contempt of mankind, this adds but little to the triumphant
pretensions of his enemies. There is a strong, quick, and deep sense of justice
mixed up with the gall and bitterness of his resentment [. . .] but even at last, when
disappointed of the sanguinary revenge with which he had glutted his hopes, and
exposed to beggary and contempt by the letter of the law on which he had insisted
with so little remorse, we pity him, and think him hardly dealt with by his judges.
In all his answers and retorts upon his adversaries, he has the best not only of the
argument but of the question, reasoning on their own principles and practice.
[. . .]

After this [Antonio's insult[4]], the appeal to the Jew's mercy, as if there were any
common principle of right and wrong between them, is the rankest hypocrisy, or
the blindest prejudice [. . .]

Portia is not a very great favourite with us; neither are we in love with her maid,
Nerissa. Portia has a certain degree of affectation and pedantry about her, which
is very unusual in Shakespear's women, but which perhaps was a proper qualification for the office of a 'civil doctor,' which she undertakes and executes so
successfully. The speech about Mercy is very well; but there are a thousand finer
ones in Shakespear. We do not admire the scene of the caskets: and object entirely
to the Black Prince, Morocchius. We should like Jessica [Shylock's daughter, who
elopes with Lorenzo, a Christian] better if she had not deceived and robbed her
father, and Lorenzo, if he had not married a Jewess, though he thinks he has a
right to wrong a Jew [. . .]

---

2   Richard Cumberland (1732–1811) wrote plays infused with a sentimental spirit. One of these, a
     play entitled *The Jew* (1794), was an adaptation of *The Merchant of Venice*. It enjoyed great
     success on the London stage.
3   Object of baseless fear; cause of annoyance.
4   Act 1, Scene 3, lines 122–3: 'I am as like to call thee so again,/To spit on thee again, to spurn thee
     too.'

Gratiano is a very admirable subordinate character. He is the jester of the piece
[. . .]

When we first went to see Mr. [Edmund] Kean[5] in Shylock, we expected to see, what we had been used to see, a decrepid old man, bent with age and ugly with mental deformity, grinning with deadly malice, and the venom of his heart congealed in the expression of his countenance, sullen, morose, gloomy, inflexible, brooding over one idea, that of his hatred, and fixed on one unalterable purpose, that of his revenge. We were disappointed, because we had taken our idea from other actors, not from the play. [. . .] That he has but one idea, is not true; he has more ideas than any other person in the piece; and if he is intense and inveterate in the pursuit of his purpose, he shews the utmost elasticity, vigour, and presence of mind, in the means of attaining it. But so rooted was our habitual impression of the part from seeing it caricatured in the representation, that it was only from a careful perusal of the play itself that we saw our error. The stage is not in general the best place to study our author's characters in. It is too often filled with traditional common-place conceptions of the part, handed down from sire to son, and suited to the taste of *the great vulgar and the small*.

From **Elmer Edgar Stoll, 'Shylock'**, *Shakespeare Studies* (New York: The Macmillan Co., 1927), pp. 255–336; pp. 262–3, 268, 317–18

Edgar Stoll was an academic who wrote many books and essays on Shakespeare and other writers of his time. In the following passage, taken from one of Stoll's best-known essays, he focuses on two moments in the play – the well-known 'Hath not a Jew eyes?' speech and the trial scene – in order to argue that Shylock, a 'comical villain', is given a 'villain's due'. In Stoll's view Shylock's 'justification of his race' (Act 3, Scene 1, lines 46–57) paves the way for the final judgment he suffers at the hands of the Christians in Venice during the trial. For Stoll, any sympathy for Shylock and the Jewish race is undercut by the fact that Shylock allows himself to be blinded by revenge.

[. . .] The time is past for speaking of Shakespeare as utterly impartial or inscrutable: the study of his work and that of his fellows as an expression of Elizabethan ideas and technique is teaching us better. The puzzle whether the *Merchant of Venice* is not meant for tragedy, for instance, is cleared up [. . .]

Hero or not, Shylock is given a villain's due [. . .]

Only twice does Shakespeare seem to follow Shylock's pleadings and reasonings with any sympathy—'Hath a dog money?' in the first scene in which he appears, and 'Hath not a Jew eyes?' in the third act[1]—but a bit too much has been made of this. Either plea ends in such fashion as to alienate the audience. [. . .]

5   A well-known actor of the nineteenth century (see **p. 100**).

1   Act 1, Scene 3, lines 107–14 and Act 3, Scene 1, lines 45ff.

Shylock's celebrated justification of his race runs headlong into a justification of his villainy: 'The villainy which you teach me I will execute, and it shall go hard but I will better the instruction'[2] [. . .]

[. . .] Shylock's disappointment [in the trial scene] is tragic to him, but good care is taken that it shall not be to us. Shakespeare is less intent on values than on the conduct and direction of our sympathies through the scene. This he manages both by the action and the comment. The scene is a rise and a fall, a triumph turned into a defeat, an apparent tragedy into a comedy; and the defeat is made to repeat the stages of the triumph so as to bring home to us the fact—the comic fact—of retribution. When fortune turns, almost all the steps of the ladder whereby Shylock with scales and knife had climbed to clutch the fruit of revenge he must now descend empty-handed and in bitterness; and what had been offered to him and refused by him, he is now, when he demands it again, refused. With the course of the action the comment is in perfect accord and unison, marking and signalizing the stages of Shylock's fall. The outcries against the Jew and his stony heart, of the Duke, Bassanio, and Gratiano—protested against by Antonio as futile—give place to the jeers of Gratiano and the irony of the fair judge. Gratiano is not the only one to crow [. . .] But for more than the meagre mercy which Shylock is shown there is neither time nor place, the crowing fits the latter part of the action as perfectly as the indignant comment had fitted the earlier, and we must equally accept it or divest the scene of meaning and sense. The Jew's very words are echoed by Portia and Gratiano as they jeer, and at every turn that the course of justice takes (welcomed by Shylock, while it was in his favour, with hoarse cries of gloating and triumph) there are now peals and shouts of laughter [. . .] How can we here for a moment sympathize with Shylock unless at the same time we indignantly turn, not only against Gratiano, but against Portia, the Duke, and all Venice as well?

From **Harley Granville-Barker, *Prefaces to Shakespeare. Second Series*** (London: Sidgwick & Jackson, 1948), pp. 67–110; pp. 67, 84–5, 87

Harley Granville-Barker made his mark as a playwright, producer and theatrical critic. He is remembered for his productions of the early plays of George Bernard Shaw, and also for his naturalistic stagings of plays, which contrasted with the taste for artificiality in the late nineteenth- and early twentieth-century theatre. He also introduced the plays of Henrik Ibsen and Gilbert Murray's translations of Greek tragedies to the London stage. The latter part of Granville-Barker's career was given over to writing five series of *Prefaces to Shakespeare* (1927–48), which have become touchstones of criticism for those interested in the kind of critical commentary that is informed by production experience. The second series of Granville-Barker's 'prefaces' – from which the

---

2   Act 1, Scene 3, lines 56–7.

following passage was taken – was first published in 1930 following the success of his first series, published three years earlier.

In the following passage (much of which is an analysis of the character of Portia), Granville-Barker suggests that Shakespeare's plays are complete fairy tales. Yet within this context (and in contrast to critics such as William Hazlitt (**pp. 73–5**) or Mervyn Rothstein (**pp. 119–20**), and actresses who have performed the part, such as Sinead Cusack (**pp. 120–2**)) he finds Portia to be the model heroine. For Granville-Barker she is simultaneously a strong, independent woman who controls the Venetian court and a 'laughing school-girl' who jests with her husband after he has given away his wedding ring. Yet while Granville-Barker finds the plot unbelievable, he suggests that the characterisation of Portia seems to possess a kind of reality to which the audience can relate. In this way the many sides of Portia become, for Granville-Barker, 'all one Portia'. However, finally he finds Portia a dynamic character that grows, throughout the play, into a heroine who seems 'real' on some level, even though the plot of the play never rises above the artificiality of a fairy tale.

The Merchant of Venice is a fairy tale. There is no more reality in Shylock's bond and The Lord of Belmont's will than in Jack and the Beanstalk.

Shakespeare, it is true, did not leave the fables as he found them. This would not have done; things that pass muster on the printed page may become quite incredible when acted by human beings, and the unlikelier the story, the likelier must the mechanism of its acting be made. Besides, when his own creative impulse was quickened, he could not help giving life to a character; he could no more help it than the sun can help shining. So Shylock is real, while his story remains fabulous; and Portia and Bassanio become human, though, truly, they never quite emerge from the enchanted thicket of fancy into the common light of day [. . .]

[. . .] Shakespeare can do little enough with Portia while she is still the slave of the caskets; incidentally, the actress must resist the temptation to try and do more. She has this picture of an enchanted princess to present, verse and prose to speak perfectly, and she had better be content with that. But we feel, nevertheless [. . .] that here, pent up and primed for escape, is one of that eminent succession of souls: Rosaline, Helena, Beatrice, Rosalind[1]—they embodied an ideal lodged for long in Shakespeare's imagination; he gave it expression whenever he could. Once he can set his Portia free to be herself, he quickly makes up for lost time [. . .] He does not very deliberately develop her character; he seems by now to know too much about her to need to do that. He reveals it to us mainly in little things, and lets us feel its whole happy virtue in the melody of her speech. This it is that casts its spell upon the strict court of Venice. [. . .] To the very end she expands in her fine freedom, growing in authority and dignity, fresh touches of humour enlightening her, new traits of graciousness showing. She is a great lady in her

1 Strong female characters in Shakespearean comedies (*Love's Labour's Lost*, *All's Well That Ends Well*, *Much Ado About Nothing* and *As You Like It*).

perfect simplicity, in her ready tact (see how she keeps her guest Antonio free from the mock quarrel about the rings), and in her quite unconscious self-sufficiency (she jokes without embarrassment about taking the mythical Balthasar to her bed, but she snubs Gratiano the next minute for talking of cuckoldry, even as she snubbed Nerissa for a very mild indelicacy—she is fond of Nerissa, but no forward waiting-women for her!) Yet she is no more than a girl [. . .]

Set beside this the Portia of resource and command, who sends Bassanio post haste to his friend, and beside that the schoolgirl laughing with Nerissa over the trick they are to play their news lords and masters. Know them all for one Portia, a wise and gallant spirit so virginally enshrined; and we see to what profit Shakespeare turned his disabilities. There is, in this play, a twofold artistry in the achievement. Unlikelihood of plot is redeemed by veracity of character; while the artifice of the medium, the verse and all its convention, and the stylised acting of boy as woman, re-reconciles us to the fantasy of the plot.

Modern Criticism

The Economic Framework

From **Walter Cohen, 'The Merchant of Venice and the Possibilities of Historical Criticism'**, English Literary History, vol. 49 (1982), pp. 765–89; pp. 766–9, 771

In the following commentary Walter Cohen employs the approach of Marxist criticism to discuss the ways in which economic structures shape the meaning of Shakespeare's play.[1] He argues that the play's representations of class, state and religion are interrelated, and that these elements complicate our reading by criticising emerging aspects of capitalism, even though the play seems simultaneously to be pro-capitalist. In the end Cohen asks whether Shakespeare wasn't pointing up the hypocrisy of a society that judges merchants and usurers so differently when, in fact, they appear to have so much in common. Both are ultimately interested in what Shylock refers to as the breeding of money.[2]

The Merchant of Venice (1596) offers an embarrassment of socio-economic riches. It treats merchants and usurers, the nature of the law, and the interaction between country and city. But since it is also about the relationship between love and friendship, the meaning of Christianity, and a good deal more, a thematically minded critic, regardless of his of her persuasion, may be in for a bit of difficulty [. . .]

Critics who have studied The Merchant of Venice against the background of

---

1 Marxist critics ground their theory on the economic and cultural theory of Karl Marx and Friedrich Engels, and their followers. In accordance with this, a Marxist critic typically analyses literature by 'revealing the economic, class, and ideological determinants of the way an author writes', and examining 'the relation of the resulting literary product to the social reality of that time and place' (M. H. Abrams, A Glossary of Literary Terms, 5th edn (New York: Holt, Reinhart & Winston, Inc., 1988), pp. 218–22; p. 219.

2 Act 1, Scene 3, line 88 (p. 154).

English history have justifiably seen Shylock, and especially his lending habits, as the embodiment of capitalism [. . .] Behind this fear [of usury] lay the transition to capitalism: the rise of banking; the increasing need for credit in industrial enterprises; and the growing threat of indebtedness facing both aristocratic landlords and, above all, small, independent producers, who could easily decline to working-class status [. . .]

[. . .] But not only do Shakespeare's other plays of the 1590's show few signs of hostility to capitalism, *The Merchant of Venice* itself is quite obviously pro-capitalist, at least as far as commerce is concerned. It would be more accurate to say that Shakespeare is criticizing merely the worst aspects of an emerging, ongoing system, rather than the system itself [. . .]

In addition, the penalty for default on the bond is closer to folklore than to capitalism [. . .] To be sure, Shakespeare is literalizing the traditional metaphorical view of usurers [. . .]

To the English, and particularly to Londoners, Venice represented a more advanced stage of the commercial development they themselves were experiencing [. . .]

Obviously, however, the use of Italian materials in *The Merchant of Venice*, for all its historicity, remains deeply ideological in the bad sense, primarily because of the anti-Semitic distinction between vindictive Jewish usurer and charitable Christian merchant. Shylock's defense of usury is not so strong as it could have been, nor was Shakespeare's preference for an Italian merchant over a Jewish usurer universally shared at the time. Indeed, the very contrast between the two occupations may be seen as a false dichotomy, faithful to the Renaissance Italian merchant's understanding of himself but not to the reality that self-conception was designed to justify.

From **Kim Hall, 'Guess Who's Coming to Dinner? Colonisation and Miscegenation in *The Merchant of Venice*'**, *Renaissance Drama*, vol. 23 (1992), pp. 87–111; pp. 88, 93–100

In this passage Kim Hall employs the methods of New Historicism[1] in order to explore the ways in which *The Merchant* reflects the interconnectedness of economic and social concerns during Shakespeare's time. In so doing she identifies aspects of the exchanges created by mercantile culture and the kinds of anxieties that these raised. As Hall suggests, the merchant's transactions (buying and selling across geographical, racial and cultural boundaries) ultimately blur the boundaries between cultures and peoples, which, in turn, raises anxieties

---

1   The New Historicism treats literature as part of history, and as 'an expression of forces on history [. . .] The *New Historicism* tends to be social, economic, and political, and it views literary works (particularly Renaissance dramas and Victorian novels) as instruments for the displaying and enforcing of doctrines about conduct, etiquette, and law' (William Harmon and Hugh Holman, *A Handbook to Literature*, 9th edn (Upper Saddle River, NJ: Prentice Hall, 2003), p. 338).

related to 'miscegenation' (intermarriage and interbreeding amongst different races) in the early modern period. Therefore, Portia's interactions with Morocco and Arragon, as well as Antonio's business dealings with Shylock, are all shaped by similar forces.

[. . .T]he exchange of goods (or even the circulation of money) across cultural borders always contains the possibility of other forms of exchange between different cultures [. . .]

It is this problem of "commerce and intercourse," of commercial interaction inevitably fostering social and sexual contact, that underlies representations of miscegenation in the early modern period. In addition to addressing domestic anxieties about the proper organization of male and female (particularly the uncontrolled desires of women), the appearance of miscegenation in plays responds to growing concerns over English national identity and culture as England develops political and economic ties with foreign (and "racially" different) nations [. . .]

The acute sense of privation amid plenty is signaled through *Merchant*'s ubiquitous images of starvation that are interwoven with the incessant eating in the play [. . .]

The associations with eating and starvation link outsiders, particularly Shylock, with one of the most compelling tropes of colonialist discourse: the cannibal [. . .]

The language of eating in *The Merchant of Venice* situates Shylock within this framework by merging images of cannibalism with older accusations of blood libel [. . .]

Shylock's reluctance to eat with the Christians displays the fear of "be[ing] subsumed . . . by a hostile host," [. . .] Economic exchanges with an outsider like Shylock open up Venice to sexual and commercial intercourse with strangers; this breach brings with it the threat of economic upheaval and foreign invasion [. . .]

[. . .] Shylock exposes the fears of a chauvinist culture by revealing the Venetians' problematic economic position, suggesting that, in such an open system, the slaves among them may just as well become sons-in-law [. . .]

The potential dangers of Antonio's mercantile involvement with foreign Others, read as seductive sexual union, are offset by the rejection of difference in the golden world of Belmont. Bassanio's discussion of his intent to woo Portia suggests an interesting inversion of Antonio's economic adventures. The narrative of his romantic quest is filled with economic metaphors, and his description of Portia makes it obvious that there is an unfavorable balance of trade on the marriage market.[2] Rather than bringing wealth into the country, suitors are coming to Belmont to win away Portia's wealth [. . .] While Antonio participates in the expansion of Venice's economic influence, Bassanio insulates the sexual

---

2   See Act 1, Scene 1, lines 160–75.

economy of Venice from foreign "invasion." [. . . Morocco] frames his own court-ship as colonial enterprise and religious pilgrimage when he chooses [a casket . . .] At the very moment in which he loses the game by making the wrong choice, Morocco raises the specter of a monetary and sexual exchange in England with the image of Portia as an angel in a golden bed [. . .]

[. . .] The sexual and the monetary anxieties of a Venetian state that is open to alien trade are displayed and dispelled in the casket plot, which allows Portia to avoid the threat of contact with others [. . .]

The economic issues which underlie the romantic world of Belmont rise to the surface in Venice, where there appears to be a real cash-flow problem. Most of the Christian men, it seems, are on the verge of bankruptcy [. . .]

In contrast to the males, the women are associated with an abundance of wealth [. . .]

Economic alliances in the play are made with expectations of one-way exchange, which is often troped through conversion. Thus, Bassanio and Antonio stress Shylock's "kindness" when making the deal in order to give Shylock the illusion of a communal interest and identity rooted in Christian values. Antonio takes his leave, claiming, "The Hebrew will turn Christian, he grows kind" (1.3.174), a phrase which only serves to remind Shylock and the audience that his "kindness" is still contingent. The pun on "kind" used throughout this scene reminds us that the courtesy and "kindness" shown in the play's world is only extended to those who are alike and judged of human "kin" by Christians [. . .]

The imagery associated with Shylock in the play reveals an ongoing link between perceptions of the racial difference of the black, the religious difference of the Jew, and the possible ramifications of sexual and economic contact with both.

From **Leonard Tennenhouse, 'The Counterfeit Order of The Merchant of Venice'** in The Merchant of Venice: Critical Essays, ed. Thomas Wheeler (New York: Garland, 1991), pp. 195–215; pp. 198–202, 210–11

In this essay, Leonard Tennenhouse employs the methods of psychoanalytical criticism,[1] tracing the ways in which Venice and Belmont, each with specific associations, are played off against each other throughout The Merchant of Venice. Towards the end of his commentary he explores some reasons as to why the play has to end in Belmont although, as many modern critics, Tennenhouse sees the end of the play as 'disturbed'.

Shakespeare's use of two locales characterizes the design of many of his plays in which emotionally different areas of action are marked off by means of

1 William Harmon and Hugh Holman, A Handbook to Literature, 9th edn (Saddle River, NJ: Prentice Hall, 2003), p. 409, define psychoanalytical criticism as: 'The emphasis in criticism on the values of symbols and language that, often unconsciously, explains meanings or unconscious intention.'

geographical boundaries. In *The Merchant of Venice*, however, the two locales are associated with sexual identifications and diametrically opposed in a way characteristic of no other play [. . .] Venice seems masculine, competitive, and commercial, operating according to harsh laws that create and perpetuate a scarcity economy and threaten strict punishment for anyone who endangers the economic life of the city. Presented initially as a romance world that promises love and money, Belmont seems contrastingly maternal, bountiful, and generous. To enter and exit Venice, women must disguise themselves as men. Men come to Belmont either as adventurers in search of marriage and wealth, or, in the case of Lorenzo, as a Christian privateer in quest of a safe harbor and a sympathetic monarch.

At the end of the play, Shakespeare does not return [. . .] to the world of social and economic reality. In one sense, of course, he cannot change Venice as he changes other closed worlds [. . .] Venice is associated with Shylock and the emotional reverberations he arouses, but there is another, equally important reason Shakespeare abandons Venice for the resolution of the play. The city, as he represents it, is so firmly rooted in mercantilism that no amount of artistry can wish these economic realities away. Thus, by ending the play in Belmont, Shakespeare distances us from the harsh facts of economic life in Venice. Nonetheless, something seems to have gone wrong with the ending, even after we justify the ending. The translation of the meaning of the bond, the humor of the ring plot resolution, and the isolation of Antonio are disturbing [. . .] that some critics have argued that the fifth act is unified with the rest of the play, that the setting is appropriate, and that the business of the rings is good-natured fun, suggests (to me, at least) that the resolution is in fact an uncomfortable one. Despite its contrast to Venice [. . .] Belmont becomes in the fifth act a less lyrical, less benevolent world—a world of sexual contest, threatened betrayals, and rivalrous competition [. . .]

[. . .] Venice as presented at the opening of the play is an idealized Elizabethan version of a masculine world [. . .] The image of rival suitors, the competition they threaten, the language of venturing and hazarding, and the specific situation of the caskets by which Portia exists as a ward of her dead father—all reflect Shakespeare's condensation into one complex metaphor of the different, culture-specific ways in which young men of the gentry and aristocracy hoped to make their fortunes. By so conceiving the object of the quest, Shakespeare gives voice to a very powerful cultural fantasy.

An equally powerful fantasy revolves around the wealthy merchant who will finance such a venture out of love for the needy courtier [. . .] Significantly, the issues of the venture and the bond arise in a Venice at whose center is a figure of paternal nurturance and whose love is given in the form of wealth [. . .] The network of relationships thus established is based solely on forms of dependence and trust and hence is constantly subject to the threat of betrayal.

The first real betrayal in the play, however, is Jessica's betrayal of Shylock [. . .]

The rules that operate in Venice not only encourage the conversion and flight of Jessica from Shylock but also require the punishment of Antonio for the well-being of the city [. . .] In Venice, the economic life of the city literally starves on inflation; the law invoked by the angry and betrayed father must be observed because it protects the flow of capital into the city [. . .] Given such a law, Portia's bountiful supply of money is useless in Venice, and given such a plaintiff, her call for mercy goes unheeded. It is only when she acts as sternly as her father might have that she is effective [. . .]

[. . .] Portia can come into Venice [. . .] and can free Antonio. But when she leaves Venice, she is, like Shylock, a victim of a betrayal [. . .] her repossession of the ring not only signals that the betrothal vows have been violated, but it also implies, as the joking in the last act makes clear, that she has just cuckolded her husband, even as he has betrayed her. It is in her deeply complicated self-possession that she becomes such a disturbing presence in the play [. . .]

By replacing Shylock with Portia in the triangular relationship with Bassanio and Antonio [. . .] Fidelity to wife [. . .] replaces loyalty to patron-friend. The narcissistic bond between males has been loosened, but Antonio's isolation [. . .] still disturbs the resolution. Moreover, Portia's successful mediation of the crisis in Venice and her triumphant outfacing in Belmont require that she be an andro-gyne [. . .] Portia's sexuality [is] most effective when [it is] counterfeit. For that reason, the play ends in Belmont, where marriage substitutes for patronage and love is wealth.

From **Karen Newman, 'Portia's Ring: Unruly Women and Structures of Exchange in *The Merchant of Venice*'**, *Shakespeare Quarterly*, Vol. 38 (1987), pp. 19–33; pp. 19, 21–2, 28, 32–3

In this commentary Karen Newman employs the methods of feminist criticism[1] to examine the complicated social interactions that underlie Elizabethan marriage exchanges. She argues that the sexual symbolism of transvestism, the transgression of traditional gender roles and the many types of exchange that inform the play – particularly the exchange of Portia's ring – all 'interrogate and reveal contradictions in the Elizabethan sex/gender system in which women were commodities whose exchange both produced and reproduced hier-archical gender relations' (p. 32).

[. . .] any simple binary opposition between Belmont and Venice is misleading, for the aristocratic country life of Belmont shares much with commercial Venice: the matter and mottoes of the caskets suggest commercial values, and Portia's father's will rules her choice of husbands. Though venturing at Belmont is admittedly idealized—Bassanio's quest of Portia is likened to Jason's voyage,[2] thus endowing it with a mythical dimension, and Portia's father's will, through the mottoes, criticizes rather than endorses commercial values—what is important is the

---

1 Feminist criticism analyses 'the works of male authors, especially in the depiction of women and their relation to women readers [. . . Additionally,] *feminist criticism* has become a wide-ranging exploration of the construction of gender and identity, the role of women in culture and society, and the possibilities of women's creative expression' (William Harmon and Hugh Holman, *A Handbook to Literature*, 9th edn (Upper Saddle River, NJ: Prentice Hall, 2003), p. 297).

2 Act 1, Scene 1, lines 170–1.

structure of exchange itself which characterizes both the economic transactions of Venice and the love relationships forged at Belmont. Venice and Belmont are throughout the play compared and contrasted, but the syntax of exchange itself functions in both locales; indeed, it seems universal [. . .]

[. . .] The exchange of Portia from her father via the caskets to Bassanio [. . . motivates] Bassanio's request for money from Antonio and in turn the bond between Antonio and Shylock. Though the disposition of Portia by her father's will, and the financial arrangements between Bassanio and Antonio that permit Bassanio's courtship, lead to heterosexual marriage, the traffic in women paradoxically promotes and secures homosocial relations between men. Read from within such a system, Portia's seeming centrality is a mystification, a pseudo-center, for women in this series of transactions [. . .]

[. . .] Portia's ring, we should remember, does not remain on Bassanio's finger, and *his* gift of the ring to Balthazar does indeed give Portia "vantage to exclaim" [. . .] By following the movements of her ring, we may discover something about how the play both enacts and interrogates Elizabethan structures of figural and sexual exchange. Objects, like words, change their meaning in different contexts; as things pass from hand to hand, they accumulate meanings from the process of exchange itself. Bassanio gives away his ring in payment for services rendered and in doing so transgresses his pledge to Portia. When it begins its metonymic[3] travels from Bassanio to the young doctor, the ring picks up new meanings which contradict its status as a sign of male possession, fidelity, and values; it moves from Bassanio to Balthazar to Portia to Antonio and back to Bassanio again and the very multiplicity of exchanges undermines its prior signification. [. . .] By opening out the metonymic chain to include Balthazar, Bassanio opens his marriage to forces of disorder, to bisexuality, equality between the sexes, and linguistic equivalence in opposition to the decorous world of Renaissance marriage represented by the love pledges in Act III. ii. Bassanio gives his ring to an "unruly woman," that is, to a woman who steps outside her role and functions as subservient, a woman who dresses like a man, who embarks upon behavior ill-suited to her "weaker" intellect, a woman who argues the law.

[. . .] Portia's unruliness of language and behavior exposes the male homosocial bond the exchange of women insures, but it also multiplies the terms of sexual trafficking so as to disrupt those structures of exchange that insure hierarchical gender relations and the figural hegemony of the microcosm/macrocosm analogy in Elizabethan marriage.

[. . .] Behaviors and rhetorics signify within particular discourses, histories, and economies. [. . .] the *Merchant* interrogates the Elizabethan sex/gender system and resists the "traffic in women," because in early modern England a woman

---

3   Metonymy is literally a figure of speech in which one word or phrase is substituted for another. Here, Newman means that when Bassanio's ring changes hands it is given to Balthasar, a male, and by so doing, Bassanio ends up (symbolically speaking) in a relationship to a man as well as to a woman (Portia). For Newman, this opens his marriage up to disorder and other forces that would have been 'indecorous' by comparison with the 'decorous' marriages (between men and women) that were typical of the period and which had already occurred in the play when Bassanio pledged his love to Portia in Act 3, Scene 2.

occupying the position of a Big Man, or a lawyer in a Renaissance Venetian courtroom, or the lord of Belmont, is not the same as a man doing so. For a woman, such behavior is a form of simulation, a confusion that elides the conventional poles of sexual preference by denaturalizing gender-coded behaviors; such simulation perverts authorized systems of gender and power. It is inversion with a difference.

From **Lynda E. Boose, 'The Comic Contract and Portia's Golden Ring'**, Shakespeare Studies, Vol. 20 (1988), pp. 241–54; pp. 241–3, 249–50

In this essay Lynda E. Boose – adopting the approach of feminist criticism[1] – focuses on 'the mediation between play and audience' and how this shapes Shakespeare's sense of comedy. For Boose, the contract, negotiated by audience and playwright, as well as by certain characters within the play, is both financial and physical. Moreover, it is central to defining the role of *The Merchant's* comic heroine, Portia. In addition, the anxiety and unease raised by the play – which are never fully resolved – remind the audience that we are suitors like Morocco who choose 'what many men desire'. The audience of the play is modelled by the suitors in it, Boose argues, and like Bassanio our gratification is 'dearly bought by a wily artist [Portia] who has played the spider' (p. 252).

With its emphasis on social bonds, comedy inherently proposes a structure that is peculiarly dependent upon audience gratification. And all the dramatists in this era, writing as they were for the new commercial enterprise of public theatre, seem acutely aware of a problematic obligation to give their audiences "what you will" or "as you like it." [. . .]

[. . .] For Shakespeare [. . .] the comic contract is *always* fulfilled through a formulaic closure of marriage that at times seems so blatantly imposed on top of a recalcitrant narrative as to approach becoming a device that parodies the demands of the patriarchal formula it so determinedly reproduces. Yet Shakespeare doggedly sticks by this formula, and [. . .] usually even refracts it into multiple images. This "Jack shall have Jill and all shall be well" closure unites the various plot oppositions and emblematically dramatizes a model of social harmony. But more importantly, it re-presents the ultimate wedding between the play and audience and thus fulfills the generic obligations of comic form[2] [. . .] Yet within Shakespeare's complex formulation, fulfilling that indenture provides precisely the context that allows for subverting it. By analogically inscribing the comic contract into the logic of the marriage bond, Shakespeare acquires not only a means through which he can question the terms of both indentures, but a means by which he can effectively reappropriate the debt structure and transform the

1 For a general definition of feminist criticism, see note 1, **p. 84.**
2 It was thought that a comedy should end with a series of happy marriages as a way of restoring order.

playwright's obligation into one that, by closure, the audience clearly owes the artist [. . .] as Shakespeare develops this analogy in his early comedies, what emerges as the most potent strategy for appropriating the debt structure and subverting both its contractual terms is the figure upon whose body both contracts are written—the comic heroine, who first fully emerges in the creation of Portia [. . .]

[. . .] Indeed, by the time this play has been transferred to the hands of its audience, it may well be Portia, its broker, who can best lay claim to being the signified "merchant" of the play's ambiguous title, *The Merchant of Venice* [. . .]

Bassanio opened this play acknowledging an unrequitable debt that bound him to a male friend and mentor: "To you, Antonio,/I owe the most, in money and in love" (I.i.131). Antonio's substantial moral credit in Venice has always depended on driving down Shylock's through rescuing such Christian debtors as Bassanio from their obligations to the Jew. Since the dichotomy between Shylock's reputation as a vicious usurer and Antonio's renown as the generous creditor who "neither lend[s] nor borrow[s]/Upon advantage" (I.iii.66–67) is precisely what has allowed Antonio to accumulate a portfolio of long-term, high-yield ethical obligations in Venice, it is obviously not in Antonio's interest to accept Shylock's offer to "take no doit³/Of usance for my moneys" (I.iii.137–38). To do so would irreparably blur the *real* signifier of difference in commercial Venice that marks Antonio as "Christian" and Shylock as "Jew." In the financial terms that the play invites, it is Portia who has, by the end of the drama, effected a "friendly takeover" of *all* the Venetian lending institutions, moral and financial. The ring game of the final scene, where Antonio steps forward and finally yields his claim on Bassanio, is where Portia acquires control over any remaining male debts owed to the play's initial chief banker. The interest inherent in such reassigned indentures may well be beyond payment. But through the sexual innuendos of the ring game, it likewise becomes clear that Portia's bid implicitly promises Bassanio and Gratiano, the play's central models of male desire, a return interest that neither Antonio nor Shylock can offer as creditors. In terms of the analogue Shylock sets up of Jacob's sagacity in breeding profit,⁴ it is Portia who is this play's shrewd "third possessor," the one who does "not take interest, not, as you would say,/ Directly int'rest" (I.ii.75, 77–78). But by "pilling certain wands" in the "act of generation," Portia, we might say, can offer stock options. [. . .]

[. . .] Like Antonio, Portia builds her own moral credit on Shylock—and not merely by saving the Christians from him, but by enacting their deepest hostilities against him. Portia is regarded by everyone in the play and usually by audiences outside it as the veritable exemplum of generosity. Yet Portia actually never spends or hazards an uninsured ducat of her own; she spends Shylock's money. The "quality of mercy" identity that theater audiences have traditionally ascribed to Portia is, I suggest, possible only because of Shylock, whose threat to Christian privilege and Christian potency, both fiscal and physical, acts in this play like a

---

3 A small Dutch coin of little value. (The reference is to Act 1, Scene 3, line 133.)
4 Act 1, Scene 3, lines 63–82.

lightening rod to draw all Christian fears and aggressions. Thus when audiences recall Shylock, he is imaged with the knife in his hand.

Choosing and Risking

From **Joan Ozark Holmer, *The Merchant of Venice: Choice, Hazard and Consequence*** (New York: St Martin's Press, 1995), pp. 95–110; pp. 95, 102–6, 108–10

> One of the most significant moments in *The Merchant of Venice* consists of the three suitors and their attempt to solve the casket plot. Contrary to some critics who suggest that the test is insulting to Morocco and Arragon and devised in such a way that it will guarantee Bassanio's success, Joan Holmer, using the methods of formalist criticism,[1] underlines other, significant aspects of each of the suitor's choices. Previous to the extract presented below she traces the significance of the casket test in one of Shakespeare's sources, the *Gesta Romanorum*,[2] from which, she notes, Shakespeare has borrowed 'the essential meaning of the marriage test [. . .] at both the literal and allegorical levels of meaning' (p. 96).

In these three chests lies the heart of the play's dramatic meaning, its exploration of the definition and difference between wise love and foolish desire which ideologically unites the seemingly disparate elements of this richly textured play. Indeed, one of Shakespeare's significant verbal changes is to substitute the word 'chest' or 'casket' for his source's 'vessel'. [. . . The] word 'chest' or 'casket' signifies the outer housing for inner contents, either of which may be valueless or valuable. In terms of the animate body the 'chest' houses the 'heart', and Antonio's heart is the flesh Shylock desires and thinks he deserves. Inanimate chests or caskets are containers for earthly treasures (gold, silver, precious stones) as well as for fleshly bodies committed to earth when buried. Shakespeare chooses to develop the truth of noncorrespondence between the outer view and inner worth for the choice of lead and the falsity of correspondence between the outer view and inner worth in the choices of gold and silver [. . .]

Portia incisively sums up why Morocco and Arragon lose: 'O these deliberate fools! When they do choose/They have the wisdom by their wit to lose'

---

1   Formalist critics adopt an approach to analysing texts that emphasises a close reading of their form or structure. As such they pay attention to aspects of the text such as plot, conflict, setting, characterisation and themes, or central ideas that the reader is expected to derive from the text. For a fuller explanation, see William Harmon and Hugh Holman, *A Handbook to Literature*, 9th edn (Saddle River, NJ: Prentice Hall, 2003), p. 217.

2   The *Gesta Romanorum* is a collection of Latin anecdotes and tales, compiled in the fourteenth century, which served as a popular sourcebook for Chaucer and many other writers, including Shakespeare. Modern editions include that edited by Charles Swan, *Gesta Romanorum* (New York: AMS Press, 1970).

(2.9.79–80). The rational deliberations of the worldly wise prove the foolish nature of their seemingly wise wit, their abuse of the letter by their blindness to the spirit. Shakespeare's addition of these two princely suitors refines our perception of worldliness in the play and heightens our appreciation of Bassanio's wisely loving choice. In his first appearance on stage Morocco pleads not to be judged solely on the basis of appearances [. . .] To Portia's credit her objections to Morocco's 'complexion' are not simply skin-deep. The Elizabethan meaning of 'complexion' includes the sense of one's 'temperament' or 'habit of mind' [. . .] Morocco chooses and reveals his inner self [. . .] Morocco's choosing has demonstrated his superficially 'golden mind' [. . .]

[. . .] it is Morocco, not Portia, who cherishes outward show [. . .] his vanity regarding his own physical worthiness is clear from his celebration of his own courageous exploits [. . .]

[Similarly,] Arragon's preoccupation with what 'he deserves' looks inward to self-estimation. Morocco was preoccupied with the outer beauty of Portia, whom many men admire; Arragon is so self-absorbed he barely acknowledges Portia's presence [. . . Arragon] chooses more by the 'show' of the motto than by the show of the metal as Morocco had done. His, like Morocco's, is a literal, not a spiritual, interpretation. Although he sounds clever, his arrogance hoodwinks any true self-knowledge [. . .]

Thus, both Morocco and Arragon fail because they are worldly men who literally interpret the metals and mottos of the caskets they select. Morocco focuses more on the literal significance of the showy metal [. . .] Arragon focuses more on the literal significance of the motto [. . .] Morocco and Arragon earn their death's head and fool's head by their wrongheaded judgements. Morocco is fooled by his false outward gaze, while Arragon is fooled by his false inward gaze [. . .]

The gold and silver choices of Morocco and Arragon serve as dramatic analogues for Shylock's own choices of what he desires and thinks he deserves: his gold and silver gain of usury and his assumption of deserving fleshly revenge according to the rigour of the law. Like Morocco and Arragon, who literally reject the leaden chest, Shylock symbolically rejects it because he considers the true wisdom of giving and hazarding mere foolishness, insisting rather on personal gain, whether of earthly treasure or flesh. Both Morocco and Arragon ironically err exactly where they think they excel, just as Shylock does when he is undone by the letter [of the law] and strict justice. Like Morocco and Arragon, self-preoccupation blinds Shylock to his own presumptive egotism. These mischoosers defeat themselves [. . .] Morocco's, Arragon's, and Shylock's choices are effective foils to Bassanio's choice of lead, the choice of wise love [. . .]

Bassanio, the giver and hazarder, will not make the same mistakes as Morocco and Arragon. By not having him read the mottos aloud, Shakespeare spares the audience unnecessary repetition but, more importantly, presents Bassanio's silent contemplation of the caskets as thinking before speaking [. . .]

Portia's understandable but unwarranted fear is laid to rest with Bassanio's opening couplet: 'So may the outward shows be least themselves:/The world is still deceived with ornament', and later 'Thus ornament is but the guilèd shore/To a most dangerous sea' (3.2.73–4, 97–8) [. . .]

Motivated by true love that seeks to give and risk, not gain and get, that is bred in the heart or head, Bassanio avoids the straits of 'eye' and 'I' that proved such guilèd shores for Morocco and Arragon [. . .] Morocco and Arragon demonstrate reason confounding itself, wit superseding wisdom [. . .] Bassanio's spiritual understanding is properly based on the higher rational faculty, whose function is *sapientia* or wisdom. Given the caskets' various rewards of different 'heads', we should recall Milton's[3] explanation that wisdom will not desert us if we avoid 'attributing overmuch to things/Less excellent' because 'true Love' is 'judicious', has its 'seat/In Reason', not 'carnal pleasure'.

From **Catherine Belsey, 'Love in Venice'**, *Shakespeare Survey*, Vol. 44 (1992), pp. 41–53; pp. 41, 43–6, 48, 52

In this essay Catherine Belsey, writing as a psychoanalytical critic[1], discusses sexual politics in the play by focusing on Act 5, Scene 1 (**pp. 188–95**), in which the lovers come together following the trial scene. The move here is from a new world of men and market forces (Venice) to 'its romantic opposite' (Belmont). Yet the last act of the play is problematical in that it is riddled by equivocation and trickery, thus introducing a second, less idealised understanding of 'love' into the mix of love and friendship that pervades much of the text.

[. . .] Though the nature of their tragedies changes with cultural history, Venice is generally no place for lovers [. . .]

[. . .] Belmont is the conventional critical *other* of Venice, its defining romantic opposite. Belmont, it is widely agreed, is feminine, lyrical, aristocratic – and vanishing – while Venice represents the new world of men, market forces and racial tensions.

[. . . In a former, nostalgic world] love was seen as anarchic, destructive, and dangerous. In the play this world is no longer dominant. Love in *The Merchant of Venice* means marriage, concord, consent, and partnership. It means mutual compatibility and sympathy and support. But the older understanding of love leaves traces in the text, with the effect that desire is only imperfectly domesticated, and in consequence the extent to which Venice is superimposed on Belmont becomes visible to the audience [. . .]

Bassanio is able to solve the riddle of the caskets not only because he sees through outward show, but also because he alone among the suitors recognizes the appropriate emblem of desire [. . .] The Prince of Arragon thinks of his own desert, and the silver casket acts as a mirror for his narcissism, revealing the portrait of a blinking idiot [. . .] Morocco resolves to take his own desert for

---

3   The English poet, John Milton (1608–74), whose epic poem *Paradise Lost* (Book 8, ll. 563–93) is referred to here.

1   For a definition of psychoanalytical criticism see note 1, **p. 82**.

granted [. . .] The golden casket contains death, the destiny of those who serve mammon. Only Bassanio is motivated by desire and knows that lovers give and hazard all they have [. . .]

Riddles too are traditionally dangerous because they exploit the duplicity of the signifier, the secret alterity[2] that subsists in meaning. They prevaricate, explicitly deferring and obscuring the truth. Riddles demonstrate that meaning is neither single nor transparent, that words can be used to conceal it [. . .]

The riddle for Portia's hand is posed, appropriately enough, by a dead father, and solved by the romantic hero. Portia, who has immoderate desires, cannot act on them but waits, a sacrificial virgin, for the happy outcome of the ordeal [. . .] The news from Venice, however, changes everything. Antonio's predicament also poses a riddle: how can he fulfil his contract without losing his life? This time, Bassanio stands helplessly by while Portia and Nerissa turn to men, and Portia-as-Balthasar finds the equivocation which releases her husband's friend: flesh is not blood. An apparently archetypal and yet vanishing order is radically challenged by cross-dressed women who travel from Belmont to Venice and [. . .] intervene [. . .] in the supremely masculine and political world of law, with the effect of challenging the economic arrangements of the commercial capital of the world [. . .]

The full answer to the riddle of the rings is that Portia has more than one identity. There is a sense in which the multiple meanings here recapitulate the action of the play. Portia has always been other than she is [. . .] The equivocations and doubles entendres of Act 5 celebrate a sexual indeterminacy, which is not in-difference but multiplicity [. . .]

And what about the place of homoerotic desire? Perhaps we shall never know [. . .] In practice the whole issue seems to have generated relatively little anxiety [. . .] homosexual acts were perceived as less dangerous to men than heterosexual love, because it was association with women which was effeminating.

Shylock and Other Strangers

From **John Drakakis, 'Historical Difference and Venetian Patriarchy'** in *The Merchant of Venice*, ed. Nigel Wood (Buckingham: Open University Press, 1996), pp. 23–53; pp. 30, 35, 41–4

In this essay John Drakakis employs the methods of Marxist criticism[1] in order to examine the relationship between religion and ideology in *The Merchant of Venice*. Focusing on Shylock, in particular, Drakakis suggests that, in some sense, Shylock is not really a character at all, but a construct and the agency through

---

2   Multi-sidedness.

1   For a general definition of Marxist criticism see note 1, p. 79.

which Venetian institutions are demystified. As such, Shylock becomes the all-important focus through which issues relating to comedy, patriarchy and various discontinuities within the play are tested.

[. . .] Shylock is not primarily a realistic representation, not a 'Jew' in the strictly ethnological sense of the term, but both a subject position *and* a rhetorical means of prising open a dominant Christian ideology no longer able to smooth over its own internal contradictions, and therefore a challenge and a threat [. . .]

[. . .] To this extent the Venetians in the play project onto Shylock a hatred which stems from their recognition of the need of his money to sustain their own society, but they refuse to acknowledge that his means of acquisition, which are in effect a practical necessity, can have either a religious or an ethical validation [. . .] Shylock is the object upon whom Venetian society vents its own hatred of itself, and in this respect his own dramatic characterization is made to incorporate those negative social forces, such as puritanism, which challenge the norms of Venetian/Elizabethan society. It is within this complex web of significations, both as an *effect* of Venetian self-hatred, and as the representative of a historically ostracised ethnic group, that Shylock is forced to eke out a precarious existence, marginal, yet symbolically central to Venice's own perception of itself, tolerated, yet repressed [. . .]

What draws Portia and Shylock together as particular foci of resistance is that they are both possessed of material wealth which Venice needs. What distinguishes them from each other in structural terms is that, while in Portia's case the institution already exists for making that wealth available, and constitutes a legitimate form of acquisition articulated through the discourses of romance and marriage, the stark necessity of Shylock's role in Venetian economic life can only be expressed negatively. Because he is engaged in an 'unnatural' and therefore unchristian practice, the sterile activity of making money breed, Venice can only admit him as a demonization of its own social and economic practices, and as an obstacle, in the sphere of aesthetics, to comic closure. Only when he is coerced fully into the life of Venice by being forced to become a Christian, does he become a reconstituted subject who can then play a full patriarchal role in its affairs, transferring his wealth legitimately to his heirs, and replenishing the coffers of the state. To this extent the play historicizes a key element of the genre, the obstructive father, by effecting what is actually a problematic transformation of its content. The transition for Shylock is, however, not an easy one [. . .] Shylock is himself 'converted' and with that conversion comes an anxiety which he now shares with his adversary Antonio.

[. . . Shylock is] both the focus of Christian history, and that part of it that requires to be repressed and marginalized in order for Venice to continue to function commercially. To this extent he represents that *real* history which Venetian representations overlay with social and cultural forms designed to displace their own anxieties. Indeed, the 'discontent' which Shylock feels as he enters the domain of Christian patriarchy is a registering of that political repression upon which a form of national unity is predicated. Shylock is part of Venice's own unconscious that it can only deal with either by repression, or by transformation into what we might call the Christian imaginary – that set of images and institutions in and through which Venice recognizes its own cultural identity [. . .] That process, however, decentres that human subject, splits him and forces him to live in the world, as it counsels him to disregard worldly practice: forced to accept a normative ethic of wealth accumulation whose operations are attributed to the determining force of a divinely motivated 'Nature', but committed by practical desire to secular intervention. By a subtle manoeuvre, the play first demystifies usury, and then discloses the mechanisms whereby it can be remystified again, transformed into a theatrical practice and dispersed through a series of symbolic representations which aligns the theatre itself with the non-theatrical production of cultural forms. But that mystification, once dismantled, is not easily reinstated. Shylock's 'illness' is the direct consequence of his entry into what is now a deeply decentred Christian patriarchy. His illness becomes, as it were, a form of self-hatred which can only be expressed in terms of a mechanism of displacement.

If Shylock's 'illness' is the condition of his entry into the patriarchal order of Venice, then Antonio's 'sadness' is a condition of his existence within it [. . .] Antonio, we may recall, is committed to accepting a causal link between mercantile success and divine providence, where the operations of God are articulated as the 'risk' which the Christian merchant must always undertake [. . .] in other words, his unease produces in him a failure to recognize himself, and as a consequence, his own identity is unsettled.

From **James Shapiro, 'Shakespeare and the Jews'**, The Parkes Lecture (University of Southampton, 1992), pp. 1–24; pp. 11–12, 15–16, 21–3

In his commentary James Shapiro, writing as an historicist critic,[1] examines Shylock's bond, touching upon the relationship that Shakespeare establishes amongst the flesh (and the flesh-bond), the effeminisation of men and the fear of the 'Other'. In so doing he traces several myths of criminality that connect Jews with ritualised mutilation and witchcraft, and ultimately with racial stereotyping.

[. . .] Act 4 of *The Merchant of Venice* reproduces a number of key features of ritual murder accusations and trials, the most striking of which is its visual representation of the secret and unobserved (except in pictures or plays) bloody rituals of the Jews. We actually watch Shylock sharpen his knife, as Antonio stands with his bosom bared, prepared to meet his fate at the hands of a murderous Jew. The

---

1 'Old' or traditional historicism treats literature 'not as a self-standing transcendent entity capable of analysis on its own terms but rather as a part of history and, furthermore, as an expression or representation of forces on history' (William Harmon and Hugh Holman, *A Handbook to Literature*, 9th edn (Saddle River, NJ: Prentice Hall, 2003), p. 338.

trial in this scene also moves the conflict to a courtroom, the site of legitimate (though contested) legal jurisdiction so crucial to the blood-libel cases. At the same time it reproduces the Jewish strategy of insistently refusing to provide motives for the murderous intent. Finally, it offers the retribution brought upon the Jew for threatening the life of a Christian. In covering this ground Act 4 of *The Merchant of Venice* offers a fantasy solution to some of the pressing social, political, and economic contradictions of early modern European society: a world in which usury was balanced against the need for venture capital; where emerging nationalism was threatened by the internationalism of groups like the Jews who were a "nation" and yet scattered over the world, especially in the economic sphere; where local authority was pitted against central control; where social anxieties about religious faith could be exorcised by the conversion of the Jew [. . .]

For Shylock to take the knife to Antonio's privy members would be to threaten circumcision (and symbolically conversion) since it is a ritual whose complex function is to separate Jew from non-Jew, and Jewish men from Jewish women. Only through the male could the covenant be transmitted, which helps explain why Jewish daughters like Jessica and Abigail can so easily cross the religious lines that divide their fathers from the dominant Christian community; their difference is not physically inscribed in their flesh. Given Antonio's anxious assertion of difference in terms of both gender and faith a potential circumcision is understandably threatening [. . .]

The threat to cut Antonio's "flesh" also suggests that Shylock [. . .] is a Jewish "emasculator," one who somehow threatens to transform Antonio from a man to something other and less than a man. The principle of inversion or substitution that operates throughout the play obtains here as well. The threatened feminization occurs within a larger context in which the dominant early modern Christian culture projected its fear of feminization by investing the Jewish male with female qualities [. . .]

The Jewish male body was, then, a leaky body, and as such a suspect one. Again and again the Jewish man was constructed as a creature of the bodily fluids: spitting, stinking, menstruating, smearing faeces on Christian symbols, constantly falling into privies. In their androgyny, monstrosity, implication in local and unsolvable crimes, apostasy, secret rituals, "Sabbath", and interest in sorcery and magic, the Jews resembled the other great marginal and threatening social group of the early modern period: witches. Indeed, some of the earliest individuals prosecuted for sorcery in England were Jews. There may well be a relation between the banishment of the Jews from England at the close of the thirteenth century and the emergence of witch prosecutions shortly thereafter; certainly, there is a common thread in monstrous allegations, torture, and executions to which both groups were subjected in early modern Europe.

From **Alan Sinfield, 'How to Read *The Merchant of Venice* Without Being Heterosexist'** in *Alternative Shakespeares: Volume 2*, ed. Terence Hawkes (London: Routledge, 1996), pp. 122–39; pp. 128–9, 133–5, 139

In the following passage Alan Sinfield uses queer theory[1] in order to focus his reader's attention on the presumptions of a society committed to a hetero-sexual viewpoint. He argues that this traditional viewpoint is pointless once critics take into account that an historical examination of same-sex relations indicates that these might not have been considered either unusual or outré in Elizabethan England. Sinfield's essay suggests ways in which *The Merchant* – a play in which the love of two men is central – can be resituated in light of its homoerotic situations and overtones. Ultimately, for Sinfield, Antonio's hostility to Shylock is inextricably bound up in his sexual identity, as is his racism.

[. . .] In practice, there are (at least) two routes through the *Merchant* for out-groups. One involves pointing out the mechanisms of exclusion in our cultures – how the circulation of Shakespearean texts may reinforce the privilege of some groups and the subordination of others [. . .] Another involves exploring the ideo-logical structures in the playtexts – of class, race, ethnicity, gender and sexuality – that facilitate these exclusions. These structures will not be the same as the ones we experience today, but they may throw light upon our circumstances and stimulate critical awareness of how our life-possibilities are constructed.

In *The Merchant*, the emphasis on the idea of being bound displays quite openly the way ideological structures work. Through an intricate network of enticements, obligations and interdictions – in terms of wealth, family, gender, patronage and law – this culture sorts out who is to control property and other human relations. Portia, Jessica and Launcelot[2] are bound as daughters and sons; Morocco and Arragon as suitors; Antonio and Bassanio as friends; Gratiano as friend or dependant; Nerissa as dependant or servant [. . .] Antonio, Shylock and even the Duke are bound by the law; and the Venetians, Shylock rather effectively remarks, have no intention of freeing their slaves (IV.i.90–8) [. . .]

My point is not that the dreadful truth of the *Merchant* is here uncovered: it is really about traffic in boys. Rather, that such traffic is casual, ubiquitous and hardly remarkable. It becomes significant in its resonances for the relationship between Antonio and Bassanio because Portia, subject to her father's will, has reason to feel insecure about the affections of her stranger-husband [. . .]

---

1 Quoting Warren Hedges, queer theorists assume that 'sexual identities are a function of representa-tions. Queer theorists [. . .] read texts with a great degree of specificity, attending to what characters take pleasure in, how this is tied to historically specific circumstances, and the represen-tational dynamics and dilemmas in which characters find themselves enmeshed' (William Harmon and Hugh Holman, *A Handbook to Literature*, 9th edn (Saddle River, NJ: Prentice Hall, 2003), p. 417).
2 Shylock's servant who, becoming dissatisfied with his master, leaves his household and joins Bassanio's retinue.

The fact that the text of the *Merchant* gives no plain indication that the love between Antonio and Bassanio is informed by erotic passion does not mean that such passion was inconceivable, then; it may well mean that it didn't require particular presentation as a significant category [. . .] Portia does not express disgust, or even surprise, that her husband might have shared his bed with a young doctor. Her point is that Bassanio has given to another something that he had pledged to her. Nor does she disparage Antonio (as she does Morocco). Shylock, for the social cohesion of Venice, has to be killed, beggared, expelled, converted or any combination of those penalties. Same-sex passion doesn't matter nearly so much; Antonio has only to be relegated to a subordinate position [. . .]

As for using *The Merchant* as a way of addressing problems in gay subculture, the bonds of class, age, gender and race exhibited in the play have distinct resonances for us. The traffic in boys may help us to think about power structures in our class and generational interactions. And while an obvious perspective on the play is resentment at Portia's manipulation of Antonio and Bassanio, we may bear in mind that Portia too is oppressed in hetero-patriarchy, and try to work towards a sex–gender regime in which women and men would not be bound to compete. Above all, plainly, Antonio is the character most hostile to Shylock. It is he who spat on him, spurned him and called him dog, and he means to do it again. (I.iii.121–6). At the trial it is he who imposes the most offensive requirement – that Shylock convert to Christianity [. . . Critic] Seymour Kleinberg connects Antonio's racism to his sexuality [. . . Kleinberg states]: '[Antonio] hates himself in Shylock: the homosexual self that Antonio has come to identify symbolically as the Jew.'[3]

3 [Sinfield's note.] Seymour Kleinberg, '*The Merchant of Venice*: The Homosexual as Anti-Semite in Nascent Capitalism', in Stuart Kellog (ed.), *Literary Visions of Homosexuality* (New York: Haworth Press, 1985), p. 120.

The Work in Performance

Introduction

Shakespeare's Theatre

Although the precise date for the composition of *The Merchant of Venice* is unknown, scholars usually agree that the play was probably in performance by 1598 when it was entered in the Stationers' Register. By this time Shakespeare's career – both as an actor and a dramatist – had moved beyond the apprentice stages, and he enjoyed a relatively stable theatrical environment in which to work. Around 1594, Shakespeare joined an acting company known as the Lord Chamberlain's Men, named for the company's patron, Henry Carey, who then held the office of Lord Chamberlain to Queen Elizabeth I. Within this group Shakespeare worked alongside other players who had experience performing together in the late 1580s and early 1590s (some of them in Shakespeare's early plays). The lead actor in the company was Richard Burbage who is best remembered for his performances in tragic roles such as Hamlet and King Lear. Nevertheless, Burbage was apparently a versatile actor, and it was probably he who performed the role of Shylock in *The Merchant of Venice*.

Throughout the years Shakespeare and the other actors in the Lord Chamberlain's Men – many of whom remained in the company for years – became close professional colleagues. They performed together in London and on tour, and occasionally at Court. What set them apart from many other troupes was that they managed to attract an enormous number of talented actors and dramatists. Moreover, in the 1590s they were fortunate to have a permanent playhouse, called the Theatre, in which to perform. (It was only later, in 1599, that the company moved to a new playhouse, called the Globe, with which Shakespeare is most often associated.) In fact, it was Richard Burbage's father James – a joiner by trade – who built the playhouse in which many of Shakespeare's earliest plays were performed. Thus, a stable acting company, yoked together by their work and their joint ownership of company property, became coupled with an assured venue for performance. This gave Shakespeare's company a competitive edge over many other troupes of actors during the period.

Despite the difficulty of reconstructing the historical aspects of early performance venues, it is often useful to imagine what it might have been like to
see a play performed in its original setting. In order to do so, the physical space
in which the plays were performed becomes significant. From all available evidence it would appear that Burbage's Theatre was a 'typical' Elizabethan playhouse. One early illustration indicates that it was polygonal (i.e. many-sided),
although the precise number of sides, their height and width are all unknown.
For this reason, estimates of the Theatre's size vary; however, many historians
calculate that it held around one thousand people. Like other playhouses of the
period the Theatre would have had a thatched roof and external staircases. It
would also have been open to the sky, with three covered galleries for seating
and a large, open yard around the stage for the many spectators who chose to
stand. Like the Rose playhouse, its contemporary, the Theatre might well have
had a trapezoidal stage which, being longer than it was wide, would have
required much of the onstage action to move from side to side, rather than
from back to front as it does on more modern stages. The Theatre also probably had an area over the stage (called 'the heavens') to hold equipment for
raising and lowering furniture (particularly thrones) onto the stage, a space
below the stage ('the hell') that was accessible from trapdoors on the stage and
a space behind the stage (the 'tiring house') in which costumes, playbooks and
props were stored. The back wall of the stage offered several doors for exits
and entrances, along with a balcony, which was used to house the playhouse
musicians, as well as to perform certain scenes. For instance, the famous balcony scene from *Romeo and Juliet*, or Act 2, Scene 6 of *The Merchant* – the
elopement of Jessica with Lorenzo – in which Jessica throws down, from above,
a casket of her father's money to Lorenzo, would have required the use of the
balcony.

Yet as intriguing as it is to see one of Shakespeare's plays in its original
setting, some features of Shakespeare's theatre would seem unusual to
modern spectators. For instance, the posts that held up the galleries interfered with sightlines, so that members of the audience could not always enjoy
a clear, unobstructed view of the stage. Actors, moving around on the stage
in order to accommodate this, could not always be heard clearly. Spectators
in the pit moved around in order to change position, or they left and re-entered
in order to purchase food or drink; and, in Shakespeare's day, plays were
performed throughout the calendar year, despite the periods of inclement
weather.

Yet regardless of these liabilities the Elizabethan playhouse was a 'poetic playhouse' in which acoustics were central to the theatrical experience, and the physical fabric of the theatre contributed importantly to this. The mortar, which
covered the walls of the playhouse, reflected sound, and the stage, or 'platform' as
it was sometimes called, served as an acoustical backdrop that bounced sound out
into the arena. Because the Elizabethan playhouse was such a unique space some
more recent buildings and productions have tried to re-create these elements.
Recently, buildings such as the new Globe, in London, or the Swan playhouse, in
Stratford-upon-Avon, attempt to approximate the types of physical spaces with

which Shakespeare would have been familiar (even though they do not attempt to produce 'realistic' sets as Prout's or Foster's). Interestingly, both the new Globe and the Swan are products of the twentieth century. Regardless of earlier interest in 'authenticity', the building of playhouses that approximate Shakespeare's own is a fairly recent phenomenon.

Seventeenth- and Eighteenth-century Productions

Although the printing of *The Merchant of Venice* in 1600 would suggest that the play was popular early on, few records of these performances exist. It is known that the play was performed twice at Court before King James in 1605; however, this moment was followed by many years during which there are no recorded performances. Only the printing of a second quarto in 1619 would indicate that *The Merchant* retained its popularity, and was even possibly performed into the 1620s. But for reasons that perhaps have to do with the ambiguous, vexing character of Shylock, the play seems not to have been popular again until 1701; and then it was not Shakespeare's *The Merchant* that attracted audiences, but an adaptation of this play by George Granville, Lord Lansdowne, entitled *The Jew of Venice*. In this version of the play scenes were cut in order to showcase Bassanio as the romantic hero. Additionally, Shylock was played by a well-known comic actor named Thomas Doggett who, from all indications, performed the role in a clownish vein. It was probably some unrecorded version of *The Merchant* influenced by Granville's text that was seen by Nicholas Rowe, the editor of the first critical edition of Shakespeare's plays (1709). In his introductory essay, Rowe remarked oddly that Shakespeare's play was 'Receiv'd and Acted as a Comedy, and the Part of the *Jew* perform'd by an Excellent Comedian'. Still, Rowe apparently disagreed with this interpretation because he subsequently proclaimed: 'I cannot but think it was design'd Tragically by the Author'. (See **pp. 64–5** for Rowe's full commentary.) Without knowing it at the time, Rowe was prophetic in his comments. Historically speaking, virtually every performance from the eighteenth century on is remembered primarily (and sometimes exclusively) for the way in which the role of Shylock has been construed, despite the fact that he appears in only five scenes in the play.

In studying the performance history of *The Merchant of Venice* scholars return to four landmark productions that occurred between Rowe's time and the beginning of the twentieth century. Each of these was distinguished by a different kind of Shylock. The first, a production in 1741 at the Theatre Royal, Drury Lane, starred Charles Macklin, who played the role of Shylock as a terrifying villain. At first, the theatre's managers were wary of such a portrayal, but eventually Macklin prevailed upon them to try it. As a consequence, when the production succeeded Macklin earned a reputation as an eminent actor and, until his death, no other actor could perform the role on the London stage. However, Macklin's Shylock was an extremely unattractive character, 'the moneylender turned monster', a malignant, almost diabolical creature wholly blinded by (and driven by) revenge and justice.[1]

The Merchant in the Nineteenth Century

In 1814 Macklin's characterisation was succeeded by that of Edmund Kean, who performed the role again at Drury Lane. Departing from Macklin's interpretation, Kean decided that Shylock is indeed driven by revenge but that he is a sympathetic character. In contemporary reviews and in the annals of stage history, Kean's Shylock has been described as more human than previous portrayals. In fact, Kean's performance is thought to have been the first in which Shylock was treated with dignity and sensitivity. (By this, modern critics might wonder whether Burbage's original Shylock wasn't therefore an object of fun (like Doggett's portrayal), an extremely foolish man who deserves to be laughed at and mocked.) Like Macklin, Kean made his reputation with this role. When the well-known essayist and critic William Hazlitt reviewed the production for *The Morning Chronicle,* he stated that Kean's Shylock was 'more than half a Christian'. 'Certainly,' he wrote, 'our sympathies are much oftener with him than with his enemies. He is honest in his vices; they are hypocrites in their virtues.'[2] Furthermore, a few years later in his comments in *The Round Table; Characters of Shakespear's Plays,* Hazlitt saw Shylock as representing not only 'a man no less sinned against than sinning', but more broadly as the representative of the Jewish people, 'the depositary of the vengeance of his race' (**p. 74**).

William Charles Macready, who performed Shylock in 1823, was generally harsher than Kean's Shylock; however, he was also more restrained than Kean's portrayal, and he surprised audiences by periodically exhibiting moments of affection. Yet in the 1860s Edwin Booth returned to the softer, sentimentalised Shylock; and in order to focus attention on this role he removed the last act of the play, ending instead after the trial scene. (This kind of Shylock is depicted in Sir John Tenniel's nineteenth-century drawing of an unidentified actor in Figure 7.) When Booth's Shylock was informed that he had to convert to Christianity, he let out a howl, staggered backward and collapsed; and that was, more or less, the end of the play. For Booth, Shylock came close to the tragic figure that Rowe had described over 150 years earlier. Still, to most spectators Booth 'saw the Jew's predicament as primarily an economic one [. . .] This business-like Shylock did not exhibit the religious frenzy of his predecessors'.[3]

Audiences of the later nineteenth century found their most perfect Shylock in an 1879 production starring Henry Irving that ran for 250 nights. Irving's Shylock was both sympathetic and tragic, and the play essentially became Shylock's. The

---

1   Toby Lelyveld, *Shylock on the Stage* (London: Routledge & Kegan Paul, 1961), p. 22ff. See also Denis Donoghue, 'Macklin's Shylock and Macbeth', *Studies,* 43 (1954), 421–30, and William W. Appleton, *Charles Macklin: An Actor's Life* (Cambridge, Mass.: Harvard University Press, 1960).
2   See Hazlitt's reviews on 27 January and 2 February 1814, reprinted in William Hazlitt, *A View of the English Stage* (London: Robert Stodart, 1818), pp. 1–4. More commentary by Hazlitt on *The Merchant of Venice* can be found on **pp. 73–5.**
3   Lelyveld, *Shylock on the Stage*, pp. 63–77 (quotation from p. 68).

THE THIRD ACT.

Figure 5 'The Third Act showing the Rialto Bridge' (n.d.) by Birket Foster.

charming Ellen Terry performed the role of Portia; however, all attention was on Irving who made significant changes in the text and removed all of the bawdry. Nevertheless, Irving's most significant innovation involved the return of Shylock to his home after Jessica had eloped. Dignified and patriarchal, he knocked at the door only to find the house empty and his daughter gone. Apparently Irving's production was full of small touches that garnered the audience's sympathy. By the end of the trial scene Ellen Terry reported that the audience saw Shylock as a heroic saint who, in his last moments, dragged himself from the room, a broken man. So powerful was Irving's depiction that 'the play went on without the benefit of Irving's characterization'; that is, even when Irving did not perform the role audiences demanded that actors imitate his characterisation of Shylock. Actors who substituted for Irving when his production went on tour were virtually forced, by the pressure of audience expectations, to follow Irving's lead.[4]

Twentieth-century Trends

At the end of the nineteenth century William Poel, the actor and director, had tried to return the role to its imagined original, a buffoonish foreigner who was

---

4   *Ibid.* pp. 79–95.

even comical in the trial scene. (During his performance as Shylock, Poel rushed clumsily off the stage at the end of the trial scene instead of exiting the stage with dignity.) By contrast many twentieth-century actors continued to perform the role with some measure of sympathy. Despite this tradition, the issue of Shylock's character is far from settled; and the sense of the play, as a whole, often differs quite radically from one production to the next depending upon the manner in which Shylock is characterised. John Gielgud (1932, 1938) attempted to alter the tradition of allowing Shylock to take over the centre of the play by treating the entire story as a fairy tale. For Morris Carnovsky (1957, 1967) Shylock was a sympathetic character and the Christians were objectionable. In 1970 Jonathan Miller directed *The Merchant of Venice* at the National Theatre, a production in which Sir Laurence Olivier portrayed a terribly businesslike Shylock. There was little comedy in the play as Miller conceived it, and the Christians were, in the manner of Carnovsky's production, arrogant monied types. Increasingly during recent years, and perhaps owing to the commercially conscious time in which we live, this 'business model' has shaped many productions of the play. In 1978 Patrick Stewart's Shylock was a thoroughly professional, more-English-than-the-English immigrant, who sat on stage with scales and balances, counting and weighing his money. Later, in 1981, David Suchet's Shylock presented a more strongly ethnic profile, although his Shylock was also caught up in commercial interests. In 1993, in a modern-dress production, David Calder again depicted the City–Wall Street type, performing against a set that replicated London's banking district.

As might well be anticipated, the performance of Shylock, in particular, and *The Merchant of Venice*, as a whole, has become increasingly complex politically since the Holocaust. Consequently, contemporary productions are often shaped by actors' and directors' interest in, or distance from, issues concerning anti-Semitism. Three recent Shylocks – Ian McDiarmid's (1984), Antony Sher's (1987) and Norbert Kentrup's (1998) – have all provoked an outcry from the press, but for different reasons. In his own statement, Ian McDiarmid (**pp. 122–3**) attempted to create a Shylock who was 'neither hero nor villain'. The 'central problem [. . .] was not so much to divest myself of the paranoias, echoes, concepts, traditions of previous performances, but rather how I might find a way to persuade the audience to do this'. However, regardless of what McDiarmid was attempting to do with the role, reviewer William Frankel (*The Times* 17 April 1984) found McDiarmid's Shylock to be offensive: 'comic, villainous and avaricious, cruel and insolent in success, servile in defeat'.[5]

Similarly, as James C. Bulman notes, (**pp. 125–6**), Antony Sher's Shylock broke with tradition, being 'exotically unassimilated' in flowing robe and turban, smacking his lips as if always looking for his next business deal, and, in large measure, equally as objectionable as the Christians in the play. In fact, Sher's portrayal was judged anti-Semitic by the critics, although he, and the director, had intended the production to focus upon racism more generally.[6] In 1998, a

---

5   Quoted in Miriam Gilbert, *The Merchant of Venice* (London: Thomson Learning, 2002), p. 14.
6   James C. Bulman, *The Merchant of Venice* (Manchester: Manchester University Press, 1991), pp. 119, 120.

production of *The Merchant of Venice* that opened the new Globe (directed by Richard Olivier) cast a German actor, Norbert Kentrup, in the role of Shylock. Large and jolly with a long grey beard, and looking a bit like Falstaff, Kentrup wore a red cap and gown. His thick German accent distinguished Kentrup's Jew from previous characterisations in a manner that ultimately dislocated the audience and appalled some reviewers and spectators who found the production to be anti-Semitic and repellent. The natural sympathy which spectators have come to expect to share with Shylock, was complicated by flashbacks to World War II (provoked by Kentrup's accent, in particular) and the moments in which he projected an off-putting, carefree manner. Although reviewers almost unanimously praised Kentrup for his performance they wondered whether the character of Shylock wasn't being oversimplified. Michael Billington, writing for the *Guardian* (1 June 1998) stated: 'I would argue that *The Merchant* is still morally complex. It is the Globe style that simplifies it. [. . . However] we live, inescapably, in a post-Freudian, post-Holocaust world; you cannot turn the clock back and present *The Merchant* as a play untouched by history.'[7]

The Merchant in Germany

In light of historical circumstances surrounding the Second World War, it is particularly interesting to examine the stage traditions that have emerged within the German theatre. But it is also important to remember that the German stage has enjoyed a long and passionate interaction with Shakespeare's plays and, thus, offers one of the most interesting theatrical traditions within which to discuss *The Merchant of Venice*. For over a century theatre historians have pointed out that touring companies of English actors visited Germany during Shakespeare's time. Performances of various English plays in Germany can be traced back to the 1580s; and although Shakespeare's *The Merchant of Venice* was not adapted for performance until the eighteenth century, another anonymous but seemingly related English play, entitled *Der Jud von Venedig* (*The Jew of Venice*), appears to have been performed at Passau in 1607 and early the next year in Graz. Other performances were recorded in 1611 and 1626.[8] Many critics who study both Shakespeare's *The Merchant* and Christopher Marlowe's *The Jew of Malta* (performed at the Rose playhouse in 1592–3) have ascertained that the German *Jew of Venice* probably owed more to Marlowe than to Shakespeare. Simon Williams writes that 'with the exception of the phrase "a second Daniel" [. . .] nowhere does the text recall Shakespeare's'.[9]

By the mid-eighteenth century Shakespeare's plays were being printed in Germany, but with some alterations, in part because elements of Shakespeare's

---

7   Features Section, p. 13. The responses to the new Globe production (1998) were complex. Some responses can be traced through the 'Archives' section of the website called 'Shaksper', which provides much useful information in a variety of areas. See ⟨http://www.shaksper.net⟩.

8   Ernest Brennecke, *Shakespeare in Germany* (Chicago, Ill.: University of Chicago Press, 1964), pp. 11–12 and 105–6. See also Simon Williams, *Shakespeare on the German Stage, 1586–1914* (Cambridge: Cambridge University Press, 1990), pp. 34–5.

9   Williams, *Shakespeare on the German Stage*, p. 35.

language, which would seem innocuous today, were thought to be vulgar. Therefore, Christopher Martin Wieland published prose translations of Shakespeare's plays, including *The Merchant*, between 1762 and 1766 in a form that would suit the taste of audiences at the time.[10] Friedrich Ludwig Schröder, the actor and director, also produced versions of some of Shakespeare's plays in the 1770s, staging *The Merchant* in 1777 in Hamburg and performing the role of Shylock himself. In 1812 *The Merchant* was the only Shakespearean comedy to be performed at the Weimar Court Theatre, and in 1827 it was staged at the Vienna Burgtheater.[11]

Yet the play's popularity grew slowly and the play continued to present many problems for directors and audiences prior to 1900. When the play was first introduced to the stage in German translation, audiences were 'predisposed towards generic purity in the drama they saw'. Therefore, the play's comic main plot, combined with a more tragic subplot surrounding the character of Shylock, ran contrary to popular taste.[12] Moreover, German audiences preferred to see 'environments and experiences close to their own', a factor that made a character such as Shylock problematical for performers. The first notable Shylock was Friedrich Schröder, mentioned above. Although little evidence of his portrayal has been preserved, it appears that he attempted to use the role to 'extend the audience's understanding of a world that was alien to them.'[13] However, this production was followed by a performance by August Iffland, in 1783, who – being concerned to 'portray the Jew as he appeared through the eyes of prejudice' – ended up making Shylock seem clownish:

> His costume made the character somewhat ridiculous, dressed as he was in a blue coat with fur trimming, a caftan and red stockings [. . .] His performance was an aggregation of small mannerisms, commonly accepted as typical of Jews. He pattered across the stage with mincing footsteps, he walked in circles when worried, he crumpled his cap in distress during the trial scene. The main through-line of his performance was the character's greed, a trait that audiences associated with his race [. . .] Iffland gave no stature to Shylock [. . .] In his interpretation, the character remained [. . .] a subsidiary figure, a dispensable menace, a nuisance rather than a threat. This was apparent particularly in his choice of a knife with which to carve Antonio's flesh. Normally this was a large, forbidding instrument, but Iffland used a small penknife that could hardly be seen from the auditorium. When he collapsed at the end of the trial, he struck a contemporary as being little more than 'a laughable scarecrow'.

As in the performance of other characters, Iffland 'avoided the extremes of experience' preferring instead to 'dignify the average'; however, his Shylock

---

10 *Ibid.*, pp. 3, 57–8.
11 *Ibid.*, pp. 81–2, and 94.
12 *Ibid.*, p. 132.
13 *Ibid.*, p. 133.

seemed to lack all dignity, which, in turn, provided an interpretation that 'in later years might have been described as anti-semitic'.[14]

There followed a succession of Shylocks portrayed by eminent actors of the German theatre, some of whom played the character sympathetically and others who did not. By contrast with Iffland, Ludwig Devrient, in the early nineteenth century, represented Shylock as 'a bowed man, weakened by age, at the end of his life of servitude'. His hatred for the Christian community was 'the dominant concern of his life, making his demand for Antonio's flesh an act of desperate rebellion, a necessary consummation, yet a culmination of years of bitterness, suffering, and martyrdom. Devrient accentuated rather than hid racial differences, playing Shylock either with a distinctly dark skin or speaking in a recognisably Jewish accent, dressed as a Venetian Jew [. . .] or as a Polish or Hungarian Jew'.[15]

In the mid-nineteenth century the Polish-born actor, Bohumil Dawison, became the first Jewish actor to perform the role of Shylock on the German stage. As a precondition of his performance he insisted that the final act of the play – the ring scene – had to be cut altogether from the text so that Shylock's downfall 'was the final impression left with the audience'. One eyewitness who saw Dawison's Shylock wrote that he became 'a hero of hatred, a martyr to the absolute, to noble custom and the gruesomely wounded right of beautiful humanity'.[16] In retrospect, Dawison's portrayal was the most 'idealised' portrait of Shylock in the nineteenth century. Only Friedrich Mitterwurzer – an actor of great experience with Shakespeare's plays – gave a more memorable performance.

In the 1870s Mitterwurzer joined the Vienna Burgtheater where he performed many major roles, including Iago, Richard III and Macbeth. It was during this period that he also performed Shylock. Unlike earlier performances by German actors Mitterwurzer decided that:

> [Shylock's] desire to revenge himself on the Christians was so great that [. . .] he made no attempt to hide it [. . .] But what was most remarkable about his performance was the mixture of burlesque with passages of powerfully naturalistic acting. He attempted no great tragic moments, but oscillated between styles of acting that must have had a most disconcerting effect on audiences who prized stylistic unity above all in their actors. So Mitterwurzer began Shylock with 'a terrible, inextinguishable anger' which became so immense that he showed the character as terrified of himself [. . .] while he was in himself a figure of fury, to the Christians he was an object of ridicule [. . .] an insignificant creature whose downfall was entirely to be desired. Mitterwurzer challenged the idealism of the generation prior to his own by reaching back to the interpretations of the early nineteenth century. He revived the impressively morose and turbulently angry Shylock, but set him in a

---

14 *Ibid.*, pp. 133–4.
15 *Ibid.*, p. 137.
16 *Ibid.*, pp. 142–3.

context that is distinctly reminiscent of the interpretation given the role by Iffland. In this clear disjunction, by which a deeply pathetic, even tragic experience is seen in a framework that ultimately devalues it, Mitterwurzer was no longer looking back to the past, but looking forward to the stylistic incongruity of the twentieth century.[17]

During the twentieth century *The Merchant of Venice* continued to be popular with German audiences. Prior to the Nazi period there were twenty to thirty productions every year, with around 200 performances among them; however, after 1933 the number of productions dropped to around ten per year, and in 1939, to three productions totalling only twenty-three performances.[18] As Wilhelm Hortmann states, although 'the most flattering explanation' would point to a 'sense of shame' that made the play less popular, 'other reasons' probably made directors shy away from performing the play. These reasons included the element of instability within the play: namely, that there was always the chance that the audience would sympathise with Shylock, 'which would have been suicidal'. Or, alternately, as Hortmann suggests, a performance of Shylock as a caricature would have been considered 'tasteless' by many directors: 'Both textual alteration as well as the manner of performance were subject to political interpretation. In this situation, directors either performed the play as a pure comedy suppressing, as far as possible, all tragic and contemporary references, or they openly declared their Nazi convictions by pointedly racist renderings.'[19] Apparently the most notorious of these productions premièred on 15 May 1943 at the Vienna Burgtheater. Hortmann writes: 'The production has been singled out as the most infamous instance of theatre's complicity with the regime during the Nazi period.'[20] Werner Krauss, an established actor who performed the role of Shylock, did so in a manner which one reviewer described as suggesting 'the pathological image of the typical eastern Jew in all his outer and inner uncleanness' [. . .]. Hortmann states that 'even after the war, Krauss failed to see that he had erred [. . .] His plea that the actor's business was to act and that he was basically a neutral and therefore innocent instrument, was frequently used by incriminated actors during the denazification process, where it failed to convince.'[21]

In the post-war decades there have been many multi-dimensional Shylocks on the German stage. Fritz Kortner, an actor and director, prepared a version of *The Merchant of Venice* entitled *Shylock* for Austro-German TV in 1968. 'When it aired,' Hortmann states, 'millions of viewers saw the sufferings of the whole

17 *Ibid.*, pp. 145–6.
18 Charles Edelman states that a persistent myth about *Merchant* is that it was 'the Nazis' favourite play'. However, quoting Hortmann's findings, he states that 'after 1933 the number of productions of the *Merchant* dropped to less than a third of what it had been before Hitler came to power, and Berlin saw only one production during the entire era' (Edelman, *The Merchant of Venice* (Cambridge: Cambridge University Press, 2002), p. 53).
19 Wilhelm Hortmann, *Shakespeare on the German Stage: the Twentieth Century* (Cambridge: Cambridge University Press, 1998), p. 135.
20 *Ibid.*, p. 135, note 43.
21 *Ibid.*, p. 136.

Jewish race engraved in a care-furrowed and time-ravaged face while the many individual nuances of Kortner's acting reminded them that the actual pain was being felt by a human being living in its own and very personal orbit of fears and joys [. . .] In the theatre to come, such nice distinctions were neither possible nor necessary. It painted in bolder strokes and primary colours.'[22]

Other notable twentieth-century productions have followed. Wilhelm Hortmann has written: 'The history of *The Merchant of Venice* on the post-war German stage is a fascinating subject which reflects both guilt and shame – and the compensatory psychological mechanisms – that can also be found in Germany's political treatment of her past. It is a stage history full of oddities and unpredictable reactions.'[23] Hortmann reports that the first attempt, in 1946–7 in Frankfurt, was 'nipped in the bud' and the director was fired. By 1981, sixty productions of the play had been mounted on the German stage. In the 1950s and 1960s 'there was a predominance of noble Shylocks' who were 'driven to extremes by inhuman suffering at the hand of callous Christians'. In 1968, Fritz Kortner (mentioned above) 'presented the first Shylock with definite racial traits, in gesture as well as with a touch of Yiddish in intonation and syntax, whose character as well as his business practice became sharp, monomaniac and deadly, as his sufferings mounted [. . .] his main interest was to present a very human Shylock deserving of compassion as a man deeply attached to his religion and his family, and greatly suffering through both'.[24]

Another landmark production, directed in 1968 by Peter Zadek, a 'taboo breaker by self-appointed vocation', featured a Shylock 'full of malignant treachery'. Zadek's purpose was to expose, 'by grotesque exaggeration [. . .] all the worst anti-Jewish clichés'. Quite understandably, the production created a terrible scandal. 'In fact,' Hortmann explains, 'Zadek was not primarily concerned with teaching a lesson at all. He was concerned with exploiting the play's dramatic and traumatic potential for a full, i.e. sensual and visceral, event.' Because Zadek was a Jewish émigré he was 'above suspicion of anti-Semitism'. Still, critics felt uncomfortable with the production on many levels.

From the 1970s onwards non-Jewish directors favoured an interpretation of the play in which economic concerns came forcefully to the foreground and in which Shylock's usury was treated as outdated by Shakespeare. As Hortmann describes this approach:

> His [Shylock's] hoarding and breeding harks back to agrarian times and stands no chance in the new age of merchant adventurers, i.e. in competition with the new class of the mercantile bourgeoisie whose pooled resources, combined with pluck and enterprise, opened up a fantastic world of commercial wealth. Translated into theatrical terms this interpretation meant that the Shylock–Antonio conflict did not have to be dealt with primarily in psychological, racial or religious terms but could

22 *Ibid.*, p. 216.
23 *Ibid.*, p. 254.
24 *Ibid.*, pp. 256–7.

be presented as having an 'objective' or material basis. In his *Merchant at Düsseldorf* (26 Sept. 1981) Peter Palitzsch [. . .] contrasted Shylock's sobriety with the gamblers' world of Venetian smart operators who, no matter how irresponsible individually, are favoured by the fortune of history. Shylock, under such circumstances was destroyed not by racial hatred but by ideologically subtler means, though just as effectively.[25]

In line with this trend, Zadek produced a version of *The Merchant* (his third production of the play) in Vienna in December 1988, in which Shylock, as a 'Wall Street broker, designer-dressed and equipped with attaché case and pocket computer, momentarily overreached himself in a whimsical deal, losing status, fortune and daughter in the process, but gave every indication of being back on the floor shortly'.[26]

The Merchant in Japan

The stage tradition surrounding *The Merchant of Venice* in Japan, as in the history of the German theatre, begins with adaptations of Shakespeare's text, not necessarily for the stage. The first, a prose adaptation taken from Charles and Mary Lamb's *Tales from Shakespeare* and entitled *The Flesh Pawning Trial* (1883), was written by Udagawa Bunkai for serialised circulation in a newspaper published in Osaka. The story proved so popular that the well-known dramatist, Katsu Genzô, immediately produced a Kabuki adaptation of the story for the stage.[27] This adaptation, entitled *Life is as Fragile as Cherry Blossoms in a World of Money* (1885), was the first Shakespearean production mounted by Japanese theatre professionals. The play ran from 16 May to June 1855 at a theatre in Osaka, and was a sell-out.

The main text was set in Osaka in the feudal Edo period, around 1854 when Japan had opened its doors to foreign influence. Quite predictably, the adaptation altered the story somewhat. Bassanio is a poor scholar, Portia is the sole daughter of Bassanio's mentor and the Nerissa character is an orphan who is under the guardianship of an evil uncle (who is the play's parallel character to Shylock). In the course of the play the Portia character saves Nerissa and then creates a casket test involving caskets of gold, silver and iron, as a way of marrying herself off to the man who chooses the correct casket. In other ways Shakespeare's story is much the same as it is in the original play; however, in the final scene Portia's father miraculously appears. (He was previously thought to be dead.) The evil uncle repents and willingly joins the other characters.

Yoshihara Yukari, a critic who has written on this particular adaptation, explains that, like others of Shakespeare's plays, *The Merchant* was appropriated

---

25 *Ibid.*, p. 259.
26 *Ibid.*, p. 259.
27 Takashi Sasayama, J. R. Mulryne and Margaret Shewring, eds, *Shakespeare and the Japanese Stage* (Cambridge: Cambridge University Press, 1998), p. 258.

by Japan in the age during which a national culture was being constructed. 'What was thereby appropriated was not the Renaissance Shakespeare,' she writes, 'but the National Bard in the age of the British colonization of India.' (The original source for the first adaptation was written by Charles Lamb, and Lamb was a metropolitan officer of the East India Company.)[28] The conflict between native Japanese culture, and the threat of 'invasion' by other, foreign cultures from the West became central to the discussion of those who had seen the play. By the 1880s Japan had adopted many aspects of foreign, particularly English, education that were thought to 'civilise' the Japanese (who were construed as barbarians by some of the foreigners). Hence, many questions relating to Japan's national identity, at a time when this was being challenged, could be raised by adapting some of the elements presented by Shakespeare's *Merchant*. Bassanio is praised in the play for being 'industrious', a trait associated with the industrial superiority of the West. The Portia character in the play is also 'industrious', and 'she believes that industrious scholarship makes women spiritually independent of men'. Portia thus criticises the traditional, feudal relationships between the sexes, while simultaneously valuing educated women for the wisdom that they can bring to a marriage.[29] Finally, the title of the adaptation relates to the ways in which Japan was becoming involved in international economy. The title of this adaptation translates loosely as 'Money isn't everything'. Western civilisation, perceived at the time as a place in which money was worshipped, was seen as a bad example for the Japanese as they considered the future of their culture. Yukari explains: 'By creating a fictional world where money is not everything, [the author] (despite his title) invents a fictional Japanese world where industriousness does not necessarily mean money-worshipping.' Moreover, Bassanio's choice of the iron casket connects with his comparison of iron to the usefulness of paper money. In this way Bassanio's comment becomes 'symbolic of the birth of the Japanese economy' and of the first convertible bank notes which were issued by the Bank of Japan in 1885, the year in which the play was popular.[30]

Genzô's adaptation of *Merchant* was so successful that it was produced again from 31 May to 21 June 1885, by another kabuki company. Yet another company produced the adaptation in February 1886. All productions took place in Osaka. Then, in 1903 Doi Shunsho produced a faithful translation of the trial scene (Act 4, Scene 1) from the play that was performed during that year by two different theatre groups. (In the meantime the Miln Company, based in Chicago, had performed an English version of the play in Yokohama during May 1891, primarily for a student audience at the university there.)[31] During the early part of

28 Yoshihara Yukari, 'Japan as "Half-civilized:" an Early Japanese Adaptation of Shakespeare's *The Merchant of Venice* and Japan's Construction of Its National Image in the Late Nineteenth Century' in *Performing Shakespeare in Japan*, ed. Minami Ryuta, Ian Carruthers and John Gillies (Cambridge: Cambridge University Press, 2001), pp. 21–31. (This quotation from p. 22.)
29 Yukari, 'Japan as "Half-civilized" ', pp. 26–8.
30 Yukari, 'Japan as "Half-civilized" ', pp. 29 and 31.
31 The contribution of the Miln Company to the Japanese theatrical scene has been researched by Kaori Kobayashi, 'Touring in Asia: The Miln Company's Shakespearean Production in Japan' in *Shakespeare and His Contemporaries in Performance*, ed. Edward J. Esche (Aldershot: Ashgate, 2000), pp. 53–72.

the twentieth century various performances of the play, primarily in translation or adaptation, occurred. During the Second World War no productions of the play are recorded; however, these resumed in 1946. Since 1960, *Merchant* (both in the original and in translation) has been produced over twenty-three times on the Japanese stage. Adaptations – such as *I am Portia* (Odashima Yûshi, 1985), *Shylock or Maltreatment* (Abe Ryô, 1986) and *Fake: The Merchant of Venice* (Nakajima Atsuhiko, 1993) – continue to appear.[32] In 2001, *Merchant* was staged as a co-production between Théâtre-du-Sygne & Haiyu-za Company, Tokyo and Bulandra Theatre, Bucharest. Encouraged by the Euro-Japan Theatre Organiza-tion, it was directed by the Romanian actor and director Ion Caramitru and performed at the Other Place in Stratford-upon-Avon as part of the Royal Shakespeare Company's visiting artists programme.

The Yiddish Theatre Production (1901)

There have been many interesting productions of *The Merchant of Venice* in the United States; however, one of the most intriguing was that produced by Jacob Adler. Adler, a refugee from Tsarist Russia, performed the role of Shylock in Yiddish at the People's Theatre on New York's Lower East Side in 1901. Two years later, Adler again performed the role, but this time the supporting cast spoke in English while he spoke the part of Shylock in Yiddish. The production was performed in many major cities in the north-eastern United States, and also on Broadway. Adler commented on the role of Shylock to a reporter from the New York *Evening Telegram*: 'He is a patriarch, a higher being. A certain grandeur, the triumph of long patience, intellect, and character has been imparted to him by the sufferings and traditions that have been his teachers.' According to Adler, Shylock is 'a good man of a persecuted race' who never really intended to carve out Antonio's flesh. Instead he decides to press his case in court 'to show the world that his despised ducats have actually bought and paid for it. His whetting the knife on his sole is a hyperbolical menace: his sardonic smile, accompanying this action, is the only sharp edge that shall cut the self-humiliated Merchant.' Apparently, the reviewers in the Yiddish press were enthusiastic, while the reviewers in the English-language papers 'ranged from respectful to very favourable'.[33]

Elements of Design/Elements of Meaning

As Gregory Doran notes, in describing his own 1987 production, the elements of design within a play (costumes, sets) and the ways in which these define characters

32 Takashi Sasayama, J. R. Mulryne and Margaret Shewring, (eds) *Shakespeare and the Japanese Stage* (Cambridge: Cambridge University Press, 1998) offer a calendar of the performances of Shakespeare's plays in Japan, 1866–1994), pp. 257–331.
33 Charles Edelman, *The Merchant of Venice* (Cambridge: Cambridge University Press, 2002), pp. 29–31; quotations from p. 30.

and locales – in this case Venice and Belmont – are vital, not only in creating the atmosphere of a production but in actually defining what the production is meant to convey to the audience (see **pp. 126–7**). For Doran, the essential contrast in the play is that between the commercial busy-ness and carnival-like quality of Venice, and the garden of Eden that is Portia's Belmont. (By contrast, some designers have depicted Venice by drawing attention to all of its liabilities, with dripping, smelly water and precarious-looking bridges over the canals. See Figures 5 (see **p. 101**) and 6, for example. Figure 5 shows Birket Foster's drawing for the set accompanying Act 3 of the play, which shows the influence of former sets, such as Prout's 'realistic' drawing of the Rialto Bridge.) On the other hand, some productions are very modern, as in those in which the trial scene retains the barren look of a prison camp (see Figure 8), or the polished wood of a richly appointed boardroom. Interestingly, some nineteenth-century productions were less imagistic, being instead more concerned with evoking the exact nature of Venice. This was the guiding influence that shaped the 1841 production at Drury Lane, which featured realistic replicas of the city, including St Mark's Cathedral and the square upon which it sits. In 1875, the Prince of Wales Theatre followed suit, featuring a set that replicated the arches of the Doges' Palace, with merchants, sailors, beggars and Jews passing over the stage to create the look of a heavily trafficked street. Henry Irving's production at the Lyceum Theatre (1879)

Figure 6 'The Rialto, Venice' (1830) by Samuel Prout.

Figure 7 'Shylock' (n.d.) by Sir John Tenniel.

Figure 8 Royal Shakespeare Company performance at the Royal Shakespeare Theatre, 1981, with David Suchet (Shylock), showing the trial scene (Act 4, Scene 1).

included a usable bridge on the stage (presumably with water beneath), a feature that has been imitated frequently in subsequent productions.[34]

In terms of costumes, one highly contested element remains the colour of Shylock's wig. From the earliest times it appears that the red wig was associated with stage Jews. But many actors have either clung to this tradition, or altered it, in order to make their own unique statement about Shylock. Thomas Doggett, William Poel and other actors who were interested in promoting Shylock's comic edge have frequently worn a red wig. Conversely, Edmund Kean (1814) was the first actor on record to have switched to a black wig in order to create a dignified, patriarchal Shylock, a tradition followed later by Henry Irving. By the time that Sir Laurence Olivier performed the role he had dispensed with the wig and beard altogether, playing the role bare-faced. (He was, however, costumed in a rather up-market manner in a frock coat and skullcap, producing his prayer shawl and wrapping himself in it for consolation only when he learned of the loss of his daughter.) David Suchet was clean-shaven, but dressed in plain clothes, with a slightly worn black overcoat and a skullcap. Patrick Stewart's Shylock looked smartly conservative in his suit and vest, not elaborate but to taste, as if he, an immigrant, had adopted the dress of old money rather than the *nouveau riche* (see Figure 9). Antony Sher, garbed as a Levantine Jew, wore a richly coloured kaftan, striped turban and long beard, and went barefoot, sitting cross-legged on pillows. David Calder began his performance wearing a suit just like any other, to show his assimilation into the world of the Christians; but as the play progressed he adopted a different, distinctly 'Jewish style of dress' (with rounded collar and skullcap) in order to signify his growing alienation.

Key Moments

Not only design elements, but the manner in which key moments are performed define a production. In *The Merchant of Venice*, as in other Shakespeare plays, there are many of these; however, two of the most important relate to exits in the play. One of these occurs at the point where Shylock leaves the stage at the end of the trial scene, and the other has to do with the way in which the lovers and Antonio exit the stage at the end of the play. Taking Shylock's exit first, it is useful to note that the 1600 quarto simply states 'Exit', to which many editors add Shylock's name, i.e. 'Exit [Shylock]'. Therefore, it is up to the actor playing Shylock to determine precisely how he is going to exit the stage. Inevitably, this means making up some sort of stage action that is not only plausible within the manner in which the actor has defined the role; it also means finding the right way to shape the final moments in which the audience – which has been so pre-occupied with Shylock – interacts with this character. The solutions to this problem have been extremely notable. Olivier exited the stage letting out a long, barbaric cry, what some reviewers described as a 'terrible cry of despair'. Patrick Stewart left on a forced laugh that became louder and more exaggerated the

---

34 Bulman, *The Merchant of Venice*, pp. 26–7, 29, Illustration 2 (opposite p. 52).

Figure 9 **Royal Shakespeare Company performance at the Other Place, 1978, showing Shylock (Patrick Stewart) and his scales.**

further he moved offstage. Norbert Kentrup left the stage in virtual silence, pursued only by the hissing and booing of the audience. William Poel rushed from the stage, while Henry Irving walked slowly, with pride and dignity. David Suchet exited fawning and scraping, with a polite smile on his face, like a beaten dog hoping that he wouldn't suffer more punishment.

Removing the lovers and Antonio from the stage, at the end of Act 5 of the *The Merchant*, presents a different set of problems. As Robert Smallwood suggests (**pp. 128–30**), there seem to be many possible solutions, all of which are crucial in shaping the audience's final impression of the play. The central issue revolves around the fact that Antonio is the only character who is single at the end of the play, whereas the other characters are coupled and on their way to bed. A secondary issue has to do with the fact that Jessica has married into Christian culture, and one with which she might not be entirely at ease. As Smallwood notes, such 'directorly' choices point up how very much this is now 'the age of the director'. One hears of 'John Barton's *Merchant of Venice*' or 'Bill Alexander's *Richard III*', as if the author had ceased to exist. Nonetheless, as Smallwood points out, it is in the final moments that 'conceptual choices [. . .] bring to a final point interpretative themes pursued throughout the play'. For some directors, the play could only end with the ordered exit of couples, leaving Antonio on stage alone, as he was at the beginning of the play. In other cases, the lovers (particularly Bassanio and Portia) try to incorporate Antonio into their exit as though he is not only a part of their family but, in many ways, the broker of their relationship. At the end of Bill Alexander's 1987 production – not described by Smallwood – the lovers exited leaving Antonio and Jessica on stage. Antonio paused to help Jessica find a crucifix necklace that she had lost. Once he had located it, he held it up, deliberately out of her reach, as the stage lights went down. In Alexander's view, both Jessica and Antonio were to remain outcasts. Regardless of their intimate ties to some of the other characters, they would never fully be part of the 'in crowd'.

Differing Portias and Varied Venetians

As is clear from following the history of *The Merchant* on stage, the play was more easily performed as a romantic comedy in the nineteenth century when audiences seemed more willing to engage in a fairy-tale world than they are now. Audiences in the late twentieth century have embraced Shakespeare's play for different reasons, many of which have to do with the realism that they find in the depiction of a sympathetic Shylock and the cynicism with which they approach the calculating business world of the Venetians. Of course, there are perils in either kind of production; however, it seems that audiences, actors and directors cannot have it both ways. Sympathy for Shylock is inevitably won at the expense of the Christian lovers, who can all too easily seem self-absorbed and uncaring; while the elements of romance and the lovers can only be highlighted at the expense of diminishing the moneylending plot and the Christians' brutality as it is directed toward Shylock. Currently, as Peter Thomson has noted, 'the sheer weight of Shylock displaces the lovers, turns what is dramaturgically a romantic comedy into a tragicomedy'.[35]

But despite the truth of this, it is useful to consider Portia and Antonio as well, both of whom are also complex, albeit ambiguous characters. In her interview about Portia, Geraldine James confessed to having contradictory feelings about the character that were later resolved through the many times in which she performed the role (see **pp. 119–20**). Interestingly, James discovered in Portia a human (and humane) character who has the sophistication and intelligence to move beyond the spoilt rich girl mould. In her personal essay on Portia, Sinead Cusack described a similar uneasiness with the role, and the ways in which many thorny passages were worked out on stage. More than a character that one masters, Cusack implies that Portia is a heroine with whom an actress can only hope to make her peace. Perhaps Portia does not deserve the audience's worship, but ultimately she is worthy of their respect (see **p. 120–2**).

Although the punishments that Antonio metes out to Shylock might seem harsh, it is he and his friends, Bassanio in particular, who end up ruling Venice.

---

35 Peter Thomson, 'The Comic Actor and Shakespeare' in *The Cambridge Companion to Shakespeare on Stage*, ed. Stanley Wells and Sarah Stanton (Cambridge: Cambridge University Press, 2002), pp. 137–54 (quotation from p. 146).

But how are the Venetians to be distinguished from one another? Should Antonio and Bassanio seem a couple of friends who share a Platonic affection; or a 'couple' in all that such a term implies? Moreover, how is the contrast between Antonio and Shylock to be depicted? They are bitter enemies, but necessary business associates. In her essay on the Venetians, Miriam Gilbert outlines the varied ways that costume designers have created what she terms the 'male world' of Venice, and with this, the relationship between Antonio and Bassanio (see **pp. 127–8**). As she explains, in some productions the Venetians almost seem a smug group of white-collar thieves who dress (and, by implication, think) alike, whereas in other productions, Bassanio and Antonio seem poles apart.

The Merchant of Venice on Film

The fact that *The Merchant of Venice* is so frequently performed makes it a rich play for study by production historians. Nevertheless, few film versions of the play have been made. The version that is most accessible was made by BBC Television in association with Time–Life Television and produced by Jonathan Miller in 1990. Jack Gold directed this production that featured Warren Mitchell as Shylock and Gemma Jones as Portia. The director was interested in showing 'the grittier, nastier dealings in Venice' while making Belmont more 'placid'. Also, the courtroom seemed close and confined while the 'dappled moonlight of Belmont' appeared to be a wholly different, more spacious world.[36] Throughout the sets are non-realistic: 'At Belmont, what is most important is not the house or the horticulture but those three caskets.'[37]

Another well-known film version of *The Merchant*, set in nineteenth-century England, featured Laurence Olivier and Joan Plowright as Shylock and Portia. This version was produced in 1973 and directed by Jonathan Miller for BBC TV; however, it is not as successful as the 1990 version. In addition to the fact that the older version now seems somewhat dated, in both its appearance and its attitudes, the film presents other problems and has not been well received in modern times. Many of the scenes that did not include Shylock have been cut out of the text completely; Plowright seems too old to be a persuasive Portia; and Olivier played Shylock as a tragic victim. Although the Venetians appear smug and overly self-confident (a common feature of contemporary productions), most of the characters, other than Shylock, have a curiously one-dimensional feel.

In 2002 a New Zealand company produced the Maori *The Merchant of Venice* derived from a 1945 translation of the play into Maori[38] by the scholar Dr Pei Te Hurinui Jones. It is the first Shakespeare film to be produced in New Zealand, as well as the first to be performed in Maori. The director and executive producer, Don Selwyn, chose *The Merchant of Venice* because its themes of racial and

---

36 Susan Willis, *The BBC Shakespeare Plays* (Chapel Hill, NC: University of North Carolina Press, 1991), pp. 210–11.
37 Willis, *BBC Shakespeare Plays*, p. 212.
38 An eastern Polynesian language that has become one of the two official languages recognised in New Zealand.

religious tension are familiar to the Maori people as a result of the European colonisation of New Zealand. Throughout previous work as an actor and director, in both film and television, Selwyn has developed a distinguished career. Currently, he is a leading proponent of Maori drama, and a noted artistic voice who has dedicated his career to encouraging an understanding of, and respect for, Maori viewpoints, as well as a concern for the preservation of the Maori language. As a result, the director and production designer have integrated Maori art and culture into the film, even though the characters are dressed as seventeenth-century Venetians. Commenting on the production, Selwyn stated: 'The basic story and characterization is unchanged from the original drama. The film adaptation allows us to pursue a more expansive portrayal of the drama overall. The "deal" scene between Antonio (Anatonion) and Shylock (Hairoka) is set within the Venetian Market, surrounded by classic works of art by Selwyn Muru, which portray the historical struggle of Parihaka, New Zealand.' Selwyn also notes that the film provides an adaptation that is 'unprecedented in any Shakespearean film'. The play's main characters are performed by a mixture of professional and first-time actors: Waihoroi Shortland (Shylock), Te Rangihau Gilbert (Bassanio), Scott Morrison (Antonio) and Ngarimu Daniels (Portia).[39] The film, which is not available on video at this time, has English subtitles that translate the Maori text.

Additionally, the American film giant Orson Welles made a colour film of *The Merchant* in 1969, but the theft of two reels prevented its release.[40] (A version of a 1938–9 production, starring Orson Welles, which was performed at the Mercury Theatre in New York, is available only in a sound recording.)

Apart from this, it is interesting to note that seven silent film versions of the play were made between 1908 and 1923, in Germany, Italy and America. And one French version of Shakespeare's play, made early in the twentieth century, deserves special mention for its interesting opening and its other unusual elements. This was Henri Desfontaines's *Shylock* (1913). The film opens with a suave Shylock in white tie and tails who is quickly transformed, through the use of a dissolve, into 'a bearded Shylock, with a large wallet at his waist, clowning to the camera'. As the film continues '[He is] reviled by the Venetian citizenry. [. . .] Seated on cushions on the floor, he has a sensual, almost sexual, relationship with his money bags, caressing them with his cheek. He kisses the hands and robes of the Christians, and grovels to them, and when thwarted he creeps on the floor.'[41]

A list of adaptations, films and sound recordings of *The Merchant of Venice* can be found at the back of this book in the section entitled 'Further Reading' (pp. 199–205).

39 An extensive website, the source of this information and quotations, has been set up at: ⟨http://www.maorimerchantofvenice⟩. It includes comments from the director, a synopsis of the cast and a slideshow of still photographs of the production.
40 Pamela Mason, 'Orson Welles and Filmed Shakespeare' in *Shakespeare on Film*, ed. Russell Jackson (Cambridge: Cambridge University Press, 2000), p. 184.
41 Neil Taylor, 'National and Racial Stereotypes in Shakespeare Films' in *Shakespeare on Film*, ed. Russell Jackson (Cambridge: Cambridge University Press, 2000), pp. 261–73 (quotation from p. 267).

The following extracts are divided into three sections: 'The Debate about Portia', 'Three Shylocks' and 'Staging Issues'. 'The Debate about Portia', below, presents the commentaries of two modern actresses who have performed the role. Whereas Geraldine James describes the contradictory feelings she experienced in coming to terms with the role, Sinead Cusack focuses on the difficulties of playing Portia in three different scenes within the play. The section entitled 'Three Shylocks' (**pp. 122–6**) presents descriptions of three different interpretations of the role of Shylock as performed by modern actors. Ian McDiarmid describes the preparation that he undertook in order to perform the role; Patrick Stewart characterises his concept of Shylock as '*Homo Economicus*' ('The Economic Man'); and James Bulman describes the method of actor Antony Sher in performing Shylock in an openly offensive manner. The final section, entitled 'Staging Issues' (**pp. 126–30**), contains three extracts: first, a commentary by director Gregory Doran, describing the influences that shaped his 1987 production of *The Merchant*; second, an analysis by Miriam Gilbert outlining the kind of influence that some designers' decisions have had upon various productions of the play; finally, a discussion by Robert Smallwood of the complex problems presented in staging the final exit in the play.

The Debate about Portia

From **Mervyn Rothstein, 'For Actress in "The Merchant", Hatred of Portia Turns to Love'**, *New York Times*, 2 January 1990, C. 13 and 17

Geraldine James, an English actress whose depictions of regal figures are well known on the London stage, played Portia in Sir Peter's Hall's production of *The Merchant* in 1989. Dustin Hoffman played Shylock. During the next year the production transferred to New York. In an interview with a reporter from *The Times* she described her love–hate relationship with the role she played.

[. . .] Ms. James's contradictory feelings about Portia mirror those of many critics and scholars, who have described the Shakespeare heroine as noble, simple, humble and pure but who have also called her affected and pedantic and the least lovable of Shakespeare's comedy heroines. Ms. James maintains that the contradictory reactions are natural when discussing a character who has so many contradictions. Here is a rich woman whose father in his will has forbidden her to marry unless her suitor passes a difficult test: choosing which of three boxes, one of gold, one of silver and one of lead, best conveys her qualities. When a Moroccan prince arrives to take the test, Ms. James says, Portia at first seems to be very nice to him. But when he makes the wrong choice, Portia dismisses him contemptuously, saying "Let all of his complexion choose me so."

"And this is a key line for me," Ms. James says [. . .] "She does say something that is a really unacceptable thing to say. But let's look at the sort of person who would say that and yet have those wonderful romantic speeches and have the mental ability and sense of truth she has in the court scene," when Shylock is demanding his pound of flesh from Bassanio.

"Yes, she's a very spoiled rich girl who grows up in a world full of the most appalling prejudices," Ms. James continues. "And it's important that we acknowledge that. The job for us in this production is to show these characters, these Christians, realistically for what they are. This play is about people's intolerance to each other: men to women, whites to blacks, Christians to Jews and parents to children.

"[. . . The director's] key to this whole thing was that the people who talk most easily about mercy are the people who do not hand it out [. . .] But I don't entirely agree with him.

"[. . . In her encounter with Shylock in the trial scene] she's saying, 'For God's sake, don't be stupid. You must be merciful. Mercy is everything.' "

From **Sinead Cusack, 'Portia in *The Merchant of Venice*'** in *Players of Shakespeare*, ed. Philip Brockbank (Cambridge: Cambridge University Press, 1985), pp. 29–40; pp. 36–7, 39–40

At the beginning of her essay on playing Portia, Cusack writes: 'I failed when I played Portia. By which I mean that when I do it again – if I do – I'll do it differently.' After a career in which she performed many Shakespearean roles (e.g. Juliet, Desdemona), in addition to many parts in films and television, Cusack reluctantly played Portia in John Barton's production at the Royal Shakespeare Theatre in Stratford-upon-Avon. Here, in section 1, she addresses the relationship between Portia and Bassanio in the casket scene (Act 3, Scene 2) and beyond. In section 2 she addresses some problems that she and other members of the cast encountered in performing the trial scene (Act 4, Scene 1), particularly in the relationship of Portia to Shylock. In section 3 Cusack explores several aspects of the final scene of the play (Act 5, Scene 1) in which Portia and Bassanio are reunited, noting that the final scene is, in some aspects, another kind of 'trial scene'.

I

[. . .] The staging of the scene's first movement[1] altered from day to day, and was not satisfactorily resolved until we took the play to London. But the staging of Bassanio's choice and of Portia's response was decided early in the rehearsal. John[2] wanted Portia isolated centre-stage, under a spotlight, from the moment when she bids 'Nerissa and the rest stand all aloof.'[3] Bassanio was to circle about

1   Act 3, Scene 2.
2   John Barton, the director of the production.
3   Act 3, Scene 2, line 42.

her in the shadows throughout her speech likening him to Hercules and herself to 'the tribute paid by howling Troy to the sea monster'.[4] At the end of this magnificent speech [. . .] comes the song.

Now, the text does not specify the singer of the song. Traditionally it is given to Nerissa or to a special singer for the occasion but John was determined, stubborn, obdurate and intractable – that Portia should sing it. His reason was valid: Portia is telling Bassanio that appearance is not everything [. . .] John insisted that Portia was dredging up the song from childhood memories and found it apt for that occasion [. . .] it also makes sense that Portia should use every means at her disposal, without dishonouring her oath, to point Bassanio in the right direction [. . .] Portia cries to love to moderate and allay her ecstasy, remembers all she had had to endure in obedience to her father's will [. . .] She breaks out of the terrible prison her father's love has built for her [. . .]

I like to think that both Bassanio and Portia grow wiser and more mature in the course of the play, and particularly in the casket 'trial'. Bassanio begins as a feckless ne'er-do-well and opportunist but it must be love of Portia that moves him to make the right choice [. . .] Bassanio has to rise to the occasion to pass the test, to win both Portia and the gold by making the humble choice of lead. The choice is liberating for them both, for by making it he proves his worth [. . .]

2

[. . .] David [Suchet, i.e. Shylock] and I found a convincing way of playing the courtroom scene.[5] The nature of the rehearsals encouraged the two of us to form a very strong theatrical relationship that excluded the rest of the world and the court. Shylock and Portia are head and shoulders above the rest of the group and are fighting a battle there, just the two of them. I decided that when I entered the courtroom I knew exactly how to save Antonio; my cousin had shown me that loophole in the law which would save him from the bond. A lot of people ask why then does Portia put everyone through all that misery and why does she play cat-and-mouse with Shylock. The reason is that she doesn't go into the courtroom to save Antonio (that's easy) but to save Shylock, to redeem him – she is passionate to do that. She gives him opportunity after opportunity to relent and to exercise his humanity. She proposes mercy and charity but he still craves the law. She offers him thrice his money but he sticks to his oath. It is only when he shows himself totally ruthless and intractable (refusing even to allow a surgeon to stand by) that she offers him more justice than he desires.

3

[. . .] From the start I took the last scene[6] to be another painful trial scene and I

---

4 Act 3, Scene 2, lines 55–60.
5 Act 4, Scene 1, and also see Figure 8.
6 Act 5, Scene 1.

tried to play it that way. Now I see more clearly that it is, after all, Portia herself who wins the ring back from Bassanio. She wins both ways, and is in a wonderful position to know the whole truth about Bassanio in the courtroom, and is therefore in a position to show him something as well as to forgive him.

Three Shylocks

From **Ian McDiarmid, 'Shylock in *The Merchant of Venice*'** in *Players of Shakespeare*, 2, ed. Russell Jackson and Robert Smallwood (Cambridge: Cambridge University Press, 1988), pp. 45–54; pp. 48–50

> In the following extract from McDiarmid's essay, the actor describes the dif-
> ficulties he confronted whilst preparing to perform the role of Shylock in John
> Caird's production at Stratford-upon-Avon (1984). McDiarmid appeared with
> the Royal Shakespeare Company earlier, in 1976, performing various Shake-
> spearean roles as well as modern roles. He has also performed Edward II in
> Marlowe's play of the same name, and in a variety of films, including *The Return
> of the Jedi*. In this extract McDiarmid explains what research he undertook in
> forming his conception of Shylock and how his travels to Venice and Israel
> shaped his performance of certain aspects of Shylock's personality.

Before rehearsals began, I went to Venice [. . .] In the Jewish Quarter, Ghetto Nuovo,[1] I was fascinated to see that all the windows looked inward towards the square. None looked outward to the city and the sea beyond. So, I extrapolated, the Jew was not permitted to look outwards. He had no alternative but to look inwards. Light was shut out. He was left obsessively to contemplate the dark. Less metaphorically, inside were his possessions. His house was itself, and also the sole repository of his property: his wealth ('the means whereby I live') and his daugh-ter Jessica ('the prop/That doth sustain my house').[2] Shylock's wealth and his daughter represented his internal life, 'ducats and my daughter!' and his 'pre-cious, precious jewels!'.[3] When they were stolen by the Christians, I conjectured, it was as if his identity and his heart had been removed at one stroke, his flesh torn away, his inside ripped out. At hand, to assuage the agony, was a sure provider of short term-relief – revenge [. . .]

[McDiarmid then visited Israel.] [. . .] Where was Shakespeare's Jew from? Was he necessarily an Italian Jew? To the Christians he was an 'alien', an immigrant in every sense. 'A diamond gone, cost me two thousand ducats in Frankfurt!'[4] Did he hail from Germany, I speculated; funnelled, as so many had been, from free cities

---

1 'The New Ghetto', a walled-in part of Venice that was home to the early modern Jews who were required to live there. For a more detailed description, see W. D. Howells, **pp. 35–6**.
2 The reference is to Act 4, Scene 1, lines 370–3.
3 The reference is to Act 2, Scene 8, lines 15–22.
4 The reference is to Act 3, Scene 1, lines 66–7.

into imprisoning ghettos where they were to remain, fossilised, for years? The question of whether or not to use an accent had vexed me. It was clear that Shylock's language was unlike that of anyone else in the play [. . .] If an accent were to be employed, German seemed quite appropriate, but a bastardised German. All around me there was the evocative sing-song sound of Yiddish, the language frowned on by some but spoken by many who regard Hebrew as a holy language to be used only in prayer. Yiddish: the language of the ghetto, but, no doubt because of its origin, a language of great energy. It has the potency and self-deprecating humour, born of years of oppression. This, I was now convinced, should be the accent of Shakespeare's bastard Venetian.

From **Patrick Stewart, 'Shylock in The Merchant of Venice'** in *Players of Shakespeare*, ed. Philip Brockbank (Cambridge: Cambridge University Press, 1985), pp. 11–28; pp. 15–19

Patrick Stewart, best known to modern television audiences as the commander of the *Enterprise* on *Star Trek: the Next Generation*, has many stage performances to his credit. He has appeared both in modern and classic roles, including the King in both parts of Shakespeare's *Henry IV*, Titus in *Titus Andronicus* and Enobarbus in the 1978 production of *Antony and Cleopatra*, for which he won the Society of West End Theatre Award for Best Supporting Actor. His performance of Shylock in 1978 was directed by John Barton at the Other Place in Stratford-upon-Avon (see Figure 9, **p. 115**). In formulating his own unique depiction of Shylock – and counter to the trend amongst actors that leads many to emphasise Shylock's Jewishness over other aspects of his character – Stewart decided to underscore the many commercial elements within Shylock.

During my early work on the play I was strongly influenced by a theme that runs throughout but is particularly marked in the early scenes. Images of money, commerce and possessions abound, and even people seem to have a price. The value of assets and possessions always seems to dominate and colour relationships. This theme, where it touches Shylock, appears as a series of alternatives for comparison. People, feeling, religion and race versus commerce and material security. Shylock's choices are surprising but – with one exception – consistent. This evidence, and what it seemed to indicate about his personality, became the foundation for my characterization of Shylock [. . .]

A picture emerges of a man in whose life there is an imbalance, an obsession with the retention and acquisition of wealth which is so fixated that it displaces the love and paternal feelings of father for daughter. It transcends race and religion and is felt to be as important as life itself. It inhibits warm, affectionate responses and isolates him from his fellow man. There is a bleak and terrible loneliness in Shylock which is I suspect the cause of much of his anger and bitterness. This sense of loneliness and how he copes with it became increasingly important to me throughout the life of this production. Indeed, there were occasions when its presence became almost dangerously overwhelming. Of course, it is not loneliness that the actor *shows,* but its compensating aspects: false gregariousness, ingratiating humour, violence and arrogance [. . .] A man does not spring into the world unhappy, cruel and mean. It is his experience of the world, its treatment of him and his attempts to cope, that shape and form or bend and warp him. Shylock and his kind are outsiders, strangers, feared and hated for being different. They belong to the world's minorities. They are, as the laws of Venice state, alien, stamped by that world to be always vulnerable and at risk; therefore survival is paramount. Shylock is a survivor. He has clung to life in Venice and he has prospered [. . .] Only Antonio, his competitor in business whose senses are sharpened by commerce, smells the contempt that hides behind Shylock's jokes [. . .]

In the early scenes, however, I was anxious to minimize the impression of Shylock's Jewishness. Whenever I had seen either a very ethnic or detailedly Jewish Shylock I felt that something was lost. Jewishness could become a smokescreen which might conceal both the particular and the universal in the role. See him as a Jew first and foremost and he is in danger of becoming only a symbol, although a symbol that has changed over the centuries as society's attitudes have changed [. . .]

Because of the Nazis' Final Solution and six million deaths, those passages of anti-semitic expression in *The Merchant* will reverberate powerfully for any audience in this second half of the twentieth century. Actor and director will not need to emphasize them, nor must they be avoided. An audience must witness the intolerance of Antonio, the shallowness of Bassanio, the boorishness of Gratiano and the cynicism of Lorenzo. The unease we feel at these characterizations is important. It complicates these men who are at the heart of the romantic story of *The Merchant,* makes us less happy to accept them or not question their motives. Indeed there is an ambivalence in every corner of the play, so that no matter how well a director may bathe Act 5 in the lyrical wash of romance and fairy tale, the memories of cruelty, dishonesty and selfishness will cast troubling shadows across the Belmont dawn. But however important Jewishness and anti-semitism are in the play they are secondary to the consideration of Shylock, the man: unhappy, unloved, lonely, frightened and angry. And no matter how monstrous his cold-blooded attempt on Antonio's life, it is the brave, insane solitary act of a man who will defer no more, compromise no more. Taking Antonio's life is his line of no retreat and, although justified on commercial grounds, this murder is also, therefore, symbolic. Perhaps this makes of Shylock a revolutionary in modern terms.

From **James C. Bulman, 'Cultural Stereotyping and Audience Response: Bill Alexander and Antony Sher'** in *The Merchant of Venice* (Manchester: Manchester University Press, 1991), pp. 117–42; pp. 119–21

In 1987 Bill Alexander directed *The Merchant of Venice* for the Royal Shakespeare Company. Antony Sher performed the role of Shylock in what was judged, by most critics at the time, to be a fresh and a unique portrayal. A few years earlier Sher had dominated the London stage as Richard III, playing the dysfunctional king as a far more physical character than had been seen previously by audiences. Throughout the play he bounded around the stage on a set of black elbow crutches, alternately currying sympathy from others or menacing them with these unusual 'weapons'. He appeared as a hybrid creature, part beetle and part spider. From that point on, Sher has become known, amongst other things, for the unique physicality that he has been able to bring to the characters he plays. This showed in his depiction of Shylock as well.

Sher deliberately made Shylock offensive – so offensive, in fact, that the production itself was attacked for promoting an anti-Semitic stereotype. Although such attacks unduly simplified the moral complexity of the production, Alexander[1] nevertheless encouraged audiences on a visceral level to loathe Shylock and, consequently, to suspect that they were being coaxed into the very racial intolerance which, according to Sher, the production took pains to expose. In outward appearance, Sher's Shylock was exotically unassimilated – 'a lip-smacking, liquid-eyed Levantine[2] bargain hunter' [. . .] Squat, bear-like and barefoot, dressed in bulky gaberdine[3] with unkempt hair and a straggly beard, Shylock was played with the coarse physicality for which Sher is noted: he gestured 'with not just his hands but his entire body' [. . .] and his gait was 'a sort of seafaring waddle interrupted with sudden ferocious descents to a crouching position' [. . .] Grimly determined, he moved through Venice with 'the thrusting quality of someone used to pushing his way . . . through stone-throwing, catcalling mobs [. . .] This portrayal, then, in its dangerous unpredictability, recalled unassimilated Shylocks of earlier times [. . .]

[. . .] In defiant rejection of the patrician, westernised Shylock who had held the stage for so long, Sher – a South African and a Jew by birth – portrayed an Eastern Jew closer to his own Semitic roots. [. . .] Sher sought to overturn the tradition of 'English' characterisation and to play Shylock afresh. He conceived of characters [. . .] from an alien perspective, in light of cultural models different from those traditionally offered to British actors. Thus, where Olivier's Shylock was elderly, dignified, and patriarchal [. . .] Sher's was younger, earthier, and crass – a rug dealer at a bazaar [. . .]

1 Bill Alexander, the director of the production.
2 Eastern Mediterranean; hence, thought to be exotic.
3 Strong, twilled cloth.

[. . .] Sher, therefore, drew his image of Shylock not from Jews who today, in Israel as elsewhere, are largely westernised, but from other Semitic peoples far more threatening to the middle-class audiences who flock to Shakespeare in London and Stratford: Arabs, Palestinians, Iranians, peoples who are associated in the western mind with frightening and unpredictable extremes of behaviour, with Islamic fundamentalism, death threats, and acts of political terrorism. Sher's Shylock invoked the image of such alien and often misunderstood peoples, ignorance of whose traditions and values all too readily has led to racial prejudice. His behaviour at the trial played on audiences' fears of religious fanaticism, the blood ritual recalling not Judaism, but the vengeful outburst of an ayatollah bent on destroying the Great Satan [. . .]

Staging Issues

Gregory Doran, 'Directing *The Merchant of Venice*', interview printed in RSC Interactive Education Pack, 1987, p. 11

Gregory Doran played the part of Solanio in Bill Alexander's 1987 production of *The Merchant*, performed by the Royal Shakespeare Company, starring Antony Sher as Shylock (see Bulman, **pp. 125–6**). A decade later, he directed *The Merchant* for the same company. Doran's production is one of the most thoroughly commodified productions in the history of Shakespearean production. In all aspects – set design, costume and interpretation – it emphasised the commercial hubbub of Venice. The city was simultaneously an impressive centre of trade and the brothel of the commercial world. In Doran's production, both the merchants and the courtesans, for which Venice was famous, were 'prostituting themselves' for gold.

Let's start with the title: *The Merchant of Venice*. It's a play about a merchant, who lives in Venice. Obvious enough. But what is a merchant? [. . .] A man who deals in the market place, a place where value is negotiable, where rates are set, where gambles are taken, where risk is strategically evaluated as part of the game.

Our merchant, Antonio, is a Venetian merchant. Not just any old merchant. In Shakespeare's day the republic of Venice was an oligarchy[1] of merchants [. . .] So Antonio is an aristocrat among merchants, a tycoon [. . .]

Venice was the very epicentre of trade in the Renaissance; she was a treasure box, a place of silks and spices, jewels, slaves, ivory and velvets, all the gorgeous commodities of Arabia, India and China. Antonio has ships, argosies – the equivalent of today's tankers – trafficking all over the world. Portia, on the other hand, in Belmont has suitors pouring in from every corner of the globe to 'view' her. She is in some sense a commodity, and a rich one. It seemed to us that this

---

1   A state ruled by one particular group.

theme of trade linked the two plots of Belmont and Venice very directly, and we wanted to heighten that.

Viewed in this light the play revealed itself as a story about value, the true value we place upon things and the value at which we set human life [. . .]

I also wanted to clarify the plot about the Masquing,[2] under which device Lorenzo steals Jessica from her father's house [. . .] They [Lorenzo and his friends] intend to take Jessica along as a torchbearer, disguised as a boy. This suggested to us that we might extend the idea of Masquing and incorporate it into a wider carnival atmosphere [. . .]

The sense of Venice as a place both of trade and of decadent carnival allowed us to heighten the difference between the city scenes and Portia's home in Belmont, which, as the name implies, is somehow a place of beauty and privilege above the dark, dangerous sink of Venice.

From **Miriam Gilbert, 'The Venetians'** in *The Merchant of Venice* (London: Thomson Learning, 2002), pp. 44–66; pp. 46–9

> Miriam Gilbert, a production historian who studies the ways in which Shake-speare's plays are performed on stage, here concentrates on *The Merchant of Venice*. In order to do so she has targeted representations of various aspects of modern productions, including representations of Shylock, the world of Belmont and the trial scene. In this extract she concentrates on the many ways in which Antonio, as the central character who knits together many of the other characters, has been represented by costume and make-up designers. As she points out, these differences in physical presentation can alter greatly the audience's image of what sort of a character he is, as well as define his relationship to Bassanio and the other Venetians.

Whatever the designer's choices, the Venice of the named characters (as con-trasted with any extras) seems an exclusively male society. No one is married, although Bassanio is thinking about it – and to a woman who lives somewhere else, in Belmont. No one mentions a mother, daughter, sister – except of course for Shylock, who remembers his wife Leah, and who loses his daughter Jessica [. . .] Within this male-dominated and male-focused world, we discern several overlap-ping groups, connected through their association with Antonio [. . .] In perform-ance, Antonio himself is almost always separated from the others, by looks, age or costume. In 1956, Anthony Nicholls was dark and bearded in contrast to Basil Hoskins's blond Bassanio, who resembled 'a Greek god in disguise' [. . .] Fre-quently, Antonio has been cast as older than Bassanio, perhaps as a hold-over from the source for the bond story [. . .] Depending on the age difference, he can

---

2 Doran is referring to Act 2, Scene 6, lines 1–60, the scene in which Shylock's daughter Jessica elopes with Lorenzo who, with his friends, is disguised as a masquer attending carnival.

seem an older brother; [. . .] he can be an avuncular figure; [. . .] he can be a surrogate father [. . .]

One choice [. . .] is to distinguish Antonio by class rather than by age or temperament. Antonio normally appears in dark colours, the outward reflection of that mysterious sadness [. . .] Sometimes the dark colours are particularly evident, as in the 1984 production where the rest of the Venetians wore bright, even garish costumes decorated with sequins resembling (for several reviewers) matadors' outfits [. . .] In the trial scene[1] Tony Church's black-clad Antonio contrasted sharply with the white worn by Bassanio, fresh from his Belmont wooing. Sometimes the difference is less marked, as in 1981 when both Antonio (Tom Wilkinson) and Bassanio (Jonathan Hyde) wore dark colours, but Bassanio sported a flowing cape while Antonio wore a less flamboyant overcoat. But although Antonio looks more restrained, sombre, grave, mature [. . .] he seems to be of the same social class as Bassanio, even though the latter is referred to as 'my Lord Bassanio', as if he's a nobleman, with all the money problems traditionally associated with that rank. In part, the lack of social distinction may be related to period costume, since modern audiences are unlikely to spot subtle differences. The 1993 modern-dress production at Stratford was able to distinguish Antonio and Bassanio, not only by age, but by financial status; Clifford Rose's Antonio seemed the type to have his own office while Owen Teale's Bassanio, more casually dressed, appeared to work in the general office, on the upper level of the unit set [. . .] And in 1999, at the Royal National Theatre, Trevor Nunn's production, set in the 1930s, presented a clear distinction between David Bamber's Antonio, who wore an ill-fitting blue suit and wire-rimmed glasses, and carried a briefcase, and everyone else, from Salerio and Solanio in their three-piece suits to a dapper young Bassanio; not only was this Antonio someone who worked (he actually looked like a clerk rather than a successful merchant), he was treated by the others as the man who would pay for their drinks.

From **Robert Smallwood, 'Directors' Shakespeare'** in *Shakespeare: An Illustrated Stage History*, ed. Jonathan Bate and Russell Jackson (New York: Oxford University Press, 1996), pp. 176–96; pp. 193–4

Robert Smallwood, whose critical essays and accounts of production history offer evidence of many years of close contact with the Royal Shakespeare Company and its productions, reminds us that, while every production is a collaboration between many parties, the actors are only some of those who ultimately create a theatrical experience for the audience. And although it is the actors who dominate the stage there is no production that does not have the director's hand clearly evident in it. In this essay Smallwood explores the ways in which the director becomes, by implication, a part of the live onstage

---

1   Referring to the 1971 production.

performance through the decisions that he or she makes about key moments in the play. In *The Merchant of Venice* the manner in which the actors make their final exit has a more significant determining effect than might be expected.

'Exeunt' says the Folio (and the Quarto) text at the end of *The Merchant of Venice*: please, director, just get these seven principal players [. . .] off the stage. The method of removing them is up to the director, for the text offers absolutely nothing beyond the one word 'Exeunt'. And this single example is explanation enough of why a 'director', in one guise or another, will always be necessary, for someone has to make the decision. In making it, of course, it has to be borne in mind that six of the seven are three pairs of lovers [. . .] at least one of whom, but by implication the others, are leaving to go to bed to consummate a marriage which took place in Act III but which was then left unconsummated because of urgent business in a Venetian court of law. The seventh person is Antonio [. . .] Earlier generations [. . .] would have lowered a curtain on a final 'tableau'; and a modern director might, perhaps, similarly 'freeze' the scene before a final black-out. But a tableau or a freeze requires the placing of the actors in some series of relationships, so hardly avoids decision-making. The usual method nowadays is to obey the direction and get the actors off the stage [. . .] Every recent production in my experience has made firm conceptual choices here that bring to a final point interpretative themes pursued through the play. Let us consider a selection of them.

[Referring to Terry Hands' production at Stratford-upon-Avon, 1971:] As the play ended the three pairs of lovers left the stage in turn, hand in hand, in their vivid and beautiful costumes [. . .] Portia and Bassanio moved off last and Antonio was left alone, pale and serious, in his black suit, his unanswered, undeclared love for Bassanio thwarted. Our last image was of him caught in a narrow spotlight in a solitariness that somehow recalled the loneliness of Shylock's exit at the end of the preceding scene [. . .] The production throughout had concerned itself with the isolation of Shylock and Antonio, and it pressed its point home at the close.

[Referring to John Barton's production at Stratford-upon-Avon, 1978:] There was no such barrier to the gracious, easy friendship of Antonio and Bassanio [. . .] When the time came to get three pairs of lovers and Antonio off the stage, therefore, Gratiano and Nerissa and Lorenzo and Jessica made their exits first, leaving Portia, Bassanio, and Antonio on stage. To celebrate the legal victory (and the weddings) champagne had been served [. . .] and at the end Antonio refilled three glasses, drank a final toast to Portia and Bassanio, and walked briskly from the stage, leaving them to make their departure slowly, hand in hand, as the sound of the dawn chorus of birds began.

Neither of these productions may be accused of distorting the play, of not allowing it to 'speak for itself', for both had most meticulously observed all the information provided by the text—and in the process had found quite opposite meanings in the play's closing moments, and thence in the piece as a whole. [. . .]

[Referring to John Caird's production at Stratford-upon-Avon, 1984:] The two minor pairs of lovers [exited] first, then Portia taking Bassanio's arm [. . . seemed] about to turn upstage past an Antonio who had throughout been a dark, gloomy, unknowable presence. But as she passed him, in a moment of remorse, or compassion, something possessed her to take his arm, and the three of them left together. As they did, and the lights went down, the thought popped alarmingly into one's head 'he'll be there for breakfast . . . And I bet he'll stay a month', the idea of 'love me, love my friend' that had pervaded the play thus brooding over its final moments. [. . .]

3

Key Passages

Introduction

Although *The Merchant of Venice* is purportedly about love, loyalty and friendship, the play crescendoes to one of the most contentious trial scenes in Western drama. One man, Antonio – the so-called 'merchant' and 'borrower' of the play – kneels before his 'lender', chest bared, ready to receive his penalty. While he waits nervously, the Jewish moneylender named Shylock sharpens his knife as he prepares to cut just a pound of flesh – no more, or less – from the area near to Antonio's heart. 'I will have my bond!' Shylock insists repeatedly. Determined in his task, he is undeterred by pleas for mercy or extravagant offers of money from Antonio's friends. Although extreme in his demands, Shylock covets the long-awaited justice that has eluded him throughout his career as a businessman in Venice. At this point in the play he has become embittered by years of injustice and humiliation from Antonio and other members of the Christian community. But, for obvious reasons, the magistrates cannot grant Shylock's request. To do so would unleash an insidious kind of 'justice' on society, one that would sanction revenge and its ruinous consequences.

The Merchant of Venice opens on 'a street in Venice', perhaps even one near to the Rialto, the chief 'business district' of the play. Antonio, a wealthy merchant who is generous but melancholy, promises to lend Bassanio, his younger friend, money to finance his love suit to try to win the hand of Portia, a beautiful, wealthy heiress in Belmont. However, because all of Antonio's money is tied up in commercial ventures, he encourages Bassanio to borrow the money upon his well-established credit. Bassanio approaches Shylock for a loan of three thousand ducats – a considerable sum – for three months, with Antonio consenting to serve as co-signer for the bond. Shylock agrees to the arrangement, even though he hates Antonio because Antonio has previously interfered with his profits and treated him with contempt. Nevertheless, there is a catch in the agreement: if the loan is not repaid on the assigned day then Antonio must forfeit a pound of his flesh, to be cut from whatever part of his body Shylock chooses. As the play progresses the due date for the bond approaches, and it appears that Antonio is financially ruined. When, a short time hence, Antonio defaults on the bond, Shylock takes him to court. In his loyalty to Bassanio, Antonio agrees that he must simply accept the consequences of defaulting on the bond by paying with his life for money he owes.

In a parallel plot Portia and her waiting-maid, Nerissa, watch as numerous suitors present themselves to venture their futures on a casket test that Portia's father arranged before he died. Each suitor is presented with three caskets – in gold, silver and lead – on which are inscribed different mottoes. He who chooses successfully wins Portia's hand in marriage and her accompanying wealth. Two suitors attempt the test and fail; but then, quite predictably, Bassanio manages to choose the correct casket. While he is engaged in making his choice, his friend Gratiano falls in love with Nerissa. For a moment the tension dissipates, and the couples seem relieved to have found true love; however, their celebrations are interrupted when they learn that Antonio is financially ruined and expects to be arrested by Shylock. Immediately, Bassanio and Gratiano rush off to court in an attempt to buy off Shylock, while Portia and Nerissa disguise themselves as a lawyer and a lawyer's clerk in order to defend Antonio in court. As the trial progresses numerous twists and turns keep the audience on tenterhooks. Yet just when it appears that Shylock will get his wish Portia notes that he can only take his pound of flesh if, concurrently, he fails to take a drop of blood. This places Shylock in a disadvantaged position. He cannot take the requisite flesh without extracting blood. Seeing that he is beaten, Shylock states that he will instead accept the money (actually Portia's money) offered previously by Bassanio; but, owing to his reprehensible behaviour, Shylock is denied this by the court. As punishment for attempting the life of a fellow citizen several penalties are dealt out to Shylock by Antonio and Portia, including the demand that Shylock must convert to Christianity.

Two notable subplots run through the play as well. In the first, Shylock's daughter Jessica elopes with Lorenzo, a Christian friend of Bassanio, taking much of her father's money and other valuables with her. In the second subplot Shylock's servant, Lancelot Gobbo, leaves in order to enter service with Bassanio. Consequently, at the end of the play Shylock is a beaten man in every possible way, abandoned by both his only daughter and his servant, and bereft of the fortune that he worked a lifetime to accumulate. The last scene of the play is given over to the reunion of the couples who, by contrast with Shylock, look optimistically to a bright future. Yet, ironically perhaps, although his ships return home safely and he becomes wealthier than ever before, Antonio stands alone, as he did at the opening of the play.

In writing *The Merchant of Venice* Shakespeare drew upon a combination of several sources, rather than one particular source. For the most part he was influenced by the tale of 'Giannetto of Venice and the Lady of Belmont' written in the late fourteenth century by Ser Giovanni of Florence for his collection entitled *Il Pecorone* (*The Simpleton*). Although there was no English translation of this story in Shakespeare's time he might well have read the original in Italian. Giovanni's narrative supplied the central portions of Shakespeare's play, including the love story between Bassanio and Portia, the flesh-bond plot and the ring test that occurs in the last scene of the play. Clearly it was also from Giovanni that Shakespeare's *The Merchant* takes on its fairy-tale-like cast. Another source – the *Gesta Romanorum*, an anonymous collection of medieval tales – contributed the story of the gold, silver and lead caskets. Additionally, there is reason to believe that Antony Munday's romance entitled *Zelauto, or the Fountain of Fame* (published in 1580), which features a story of young lovers caught up in a bond plot, might have served as a third source for the play. Furthermore, many modern critics see a relationship between Barabas, the Jew in Christopher Marlowe's play *The Jew of Malta* (performed in the early 1590s at the Rose playhouse), and Shylock in Shakespeare's play.[1]

There was only one printing of *The Merchant of Venice* during Shakespeare's lifetime. This was a small volume called a 'quarto', which was the equivalent of today's mass-market paperback. It appeared in 1600 and is commonly referred to by scholars as 'Q1' (see Figure 10, **p. 138**). The current text is based on this particular printing of the play, which is generally regarded by editors to be the best text to use in the preparation of modern editions. How it came to be printed remains a mystery. There is no evidence that Shakespeare agreed to its publication or collected any profits from the printer who created it. Nor is there any sense that Shakespeare 'authorised' this text.

In presenting the text here, spellings and punctuation have been modernised, and a few stage directions have been added to provide clarification. Although the quarto texts of Shakespeare's day are not divided into acts and scenes I have added these in accordance with former editors. Speech prefixes have been standardised, including those spoken by Shylock. (His lines, in the 1600 printing, are sometimes attributed to 'Iew[e]', i.e. 'Jew'.) Latin stage directions appear in their original form (e.g. 'Exeunt', 'They exit'). Because there are no line numbers in Q1 I have keyed my lineation to that in the full-text edition prepared by M. M. Mahood (Cambridge: Cambridge University Press, 1987). In the prose passages these are approximate. The most significant textual variations are noted in footnotes; complete lists of textual variations are offered by Mahood, as well as by many other editors of full-text editions. (For a list of these, see 'Further Reading', **pp. 199–205**.) In accordance with what has become standard practice, square brackets ([ ]) indicate where I have added material.

Some information relevant to production history is included in the notes. Readers should be reminded that Jonathan Miller directed *Merchant* in 1970 and, again in 1973. On both occasions, Joan Plowright played the role of Portia, and Laurence Olivier played the role of Shylock. Similarly, John Barton directed two productions – in 1978 and 1981 – but he used different casts.

List of Key Passages

The passages presented here have been chosen with the major goals of the sourcebook in mind as these are outlined in the Introduction to this volume (**pp. 1–4**). They are taken from the following portions of the play:

---

1 (For a comprehensive reproduction of sources see Geoffrey Bullough, *Narrative and Dramatic Sources of Shakespeare* (London: Routledge & Kegan Paul, 1957), I, 445–514.)

1. (**pp. 140–5**) Act 1, Scene 1, lines 1–57 and 118–84: The opening scene in which Bassanio approaches his friend Antonio for a loan and Antonio agrees to allow Bassanio to raise the necessary funds on the promise of his credit.
2. (**pp. 146–50**) Act 1, Scene 2, lines 19–110: The scene in which Portia and Nerissa speculate on the prospects of the many suitors who woo Portia for her wealth. Although Portia is flooded with suitors it is clear that she favours Bassanio.
3. (**pp. 150–7**) Act 1, Scene 3, lines 32–174: Bassanio approaches Shylock for a loan for three thousand ducats. Antonio agrees to the terms of the bond, which require that he surrender a pound of his flesh if he defaults on the bond.
4. (**pp. 157–9**) Act 2, Scene 1, lines 1–31: The Prince of Morocco, Portia's first suitor, declares his intention to attempt the casket test. Portia grows nervous.
5. (**pp. 159–64**) Act 2, Scene 7, lines 1–79: The Prince of Morocco takes the casket test and fails.
6. (**pp. 164–7**) Act 2, Scene 9, lines 30–83: The Prince of Arragon, Portia's second suitor, takes the casket test and fails.
7. (**pp. 167–70**) Act 3, Scene 1, lines 40–103: Gossip on the streets in Venice indicates that Antonio's ships have been lost and that he is financially ruined. Shylock plans immediate legal action, in order to ensure that the terms of the bond are met.
8. (**pp. 170–7**) Act 3, Scene 2, lines 40–214: Bassanio makes the casket choice successfully and wins the hand of Portia, much to her relief. His friend Gratiano announces that he will wed Portia's waiting-maid Nerissa; however, their mutual joy is interrupted by the news that Antonio expects that he will be forced to default on the bond with Shylock.
9. (**pp. 177–88**) Act 4, Scene 1, lines 169–396: Shylock takes Antonio to court and tries to claim the terms of his bond. He is defeated and punished by the magistrates of the court. Portia and Nerissa, still in disguise, demand the rings of Bassanio and Gratiano as payment for their legal services.
10. (**pp. 188–95**) Act 5, Scene 1, lines 161–307: The final scene of the play in which the lovers are reunited in their happiness, but not before Portia and Nerissa have had fun with Bassanio and Gratiano by asking them where their rings – symbols of their union with Portia and Nerissa – have gone.

Although the following passages doubtless speak for themselves, I would offer one final word of advice: in studying the key passages readers will find that reading the play out loud is a useful way to begin to engage with the text. More specifically, it will assist readers in three ways: first, it will help to clarify the language of the play by bringing out its natural metre; second, it will direct attention to the many poetic devices through which meaning is created; and third, it will give readers some sense of how Shakespeare's verse actually works on the stage. Additionally, reading aloud will point the reader in another productive direction – towards an understanding of the text as Shakespeare would have viewed it, as a blueprint for a production that only takes on life when it is spoken and performed. Most Elizabethans who saw a play performed on stage referred to 'hearing a play', not 'seeing a play'. Therefore, 'hearing the play' will allow the modern reader to imagine a staged performance, in all of its marvellous intricacy, rather than simply treating the text as a museum object, to be handled carefully and gazed at from afar.

Abbreviations

I have used the following abbreviations in the headnotes and footnotes:

Bulman   James C. Bulman, *The Merchant of Venice* (Manchester: Manchester University Press, 1991)
Edelman   *The Merchant of Venice*, ed. Charles Edelman (Cambridge: Cambridge University Press, 2002)
Gilbert   Miriam Gilbert, *The Merchant of Venice* (London: Thomson Learning, 2002)
Mahood   *The Merchant of Venice*, ed. M. M. Mahood (Cambridge: Cambridge University Press, 1987)

The most excellent

Historie of the *Merchant* of *Venice*.

VVith the extreame crueltie of *Shylocke* the Iewe
towards the sayd Merchant, in cutting a iust pound
of his flesh: and the obtayning of *Portia*
by the choyse of three
chests.

As it hath beene diuers times acted by the Lord
Chamberlaine his Seruants.

Written by William Shakespeare.

AT LONDON,

Printed by *I. R.* for Thomas Heyes,
and are to be sold in Paules Church-yard, at the
signe of the Greene Dragon.
1600.

Figure 10 Title page from the First Quarto of *The Merchant of Venice*
(1600).

Key Passages

Dramatis Personae[1]

The Duke of Venice
The Prince of Morocco, suitor to Portia
The Prince of Arragon, suitor to Portia
Antonio, a wealthy merchant
Bassanio, Antonio's friend and Portia's suitor
Gratiano, friend to Antonio and Bassanio, and Nerissa's suitor
Salarino and Solanio,[2] friends to Antonio and Bassanio
Lorenzo, friend of Bassanio, in love with Jessica
Shylock, a Jewish moneylender
Tubal, a Jewish moneylender and Shylock's friend
Lancelot Gobbo, a clown, initially Shylock's servant (though later Bassanio's servant)
Portia, the wealthy heiress of Belmont
Nerissa, Portia's waiting-woman and confidante
Jessica, Shylock's daughter, in love with Lorenzo
Magnificoes[3] of Venice, Officers of the Court of Justice, Servants, Attendants, Musicians

---

1 The 'Dramatis Personae', or handlist of characters – a device familiar to modern readers – would not have appeared in any of the early printings of the play. However, it is included here to assist readers in identifying characters. The characters in this handlist are restricted to those that appear in the Key Passages that follow.

2 The speech prefixes in early printings of *The Merchant* suggest that Shakespeare created three characters with similar sounding names (Salerio, Salarino and Solanio). However, some early editors, questioning this evidence, conflated Salerio with one of the other characters (most often Salarino). Modern editors, following the extensive analysis by M. M. Mahood in her Cambridge edition (1987, pp. 179–83), tend to retain the distinction among the three characters, identifying 'Salarino' and 'Solanio' as Venetian gentlemen and friends to Antonio while 'Salerio' is identified as 'a messenger'. This text follows these conventions. Only Salarino and Solanio appear in the Key Passages that follow.

3 The customary term for Venetian dignitaries.

Act I, Scene I, lines 1–57 and 118–84

A street in Venice: as the play opens Antonio – one of the play's many 'mer-chants' – is troubled by melancholy, the root of which is unidentifiable. Two friends, Venetian gentlemen, speculate upon the cause. Bassanio enters and relates his desire to borrow money from Antonio so that he can woo Portia, the wealthy heiress of Belmont who is currently being pursued by many suitors. Because all of Antonio's capital is tied up in commercial ventures Bassanio decides to borrow money on Antonio's credit.

The opening scene of the play – which divides informally into two parts, with the arrival of Bassanio at line 57 – introduces the audience to the masculine, commercial world of Venice, suggesting the many ways in which issues related to trade, friendship and loyalty will shape the action of the play. Although the First Quarto, from which this text (and virtually all others) is taken, is devoid of information that locates the scenes of the play, it has become customary to associate Antonio and commercial aspects of the play with Venice, while the romantic aspects of the play are associated with Belmont, a mythical place, where Portia resides. Therefore, the opening of the play might simply be on a street or a café in Venice, or in some more obvious place in which business is transacted, as on, or near, the Rialto Bridge, which marked the central business district of the city. Throughout the play the physical setting of Venice is sug-gested primarily by numerous allusions to ships. In some ways such scant detail allows directors enormous freedom in determining where they will set indi-vidual scenes. In some productions – for instance, that directed by David Thacker in 1993 at the RSC – the stage sets have included dripping water and rickety bridges, as though Venice was the cesspool of the Mediterranean, phys-ically and morally.

As Leonard Tennenhouse notes, Venice is the masculine world of the play, a place which operates 'according to harsh laws that create and perpetuate a scarcity economy and threaten strict punishment for anyone who endangers the economic life of the city' (p. 83). The economic dimension of the play has been emphasised in many productions. As director Greg Doran comments: 'In Shakespeare's day the republic of Venice was an oligarchy of merchants [. . .] So Antonio is an aristocrat among merchants, a tycoon [. . .] Venice was the very epicentre of trade in the Renaissance; she was the treasure box, a place of silks and spices, jewels, slaves, ivory and velvets, all the gorgeous commodities of Arabia, India and China' (p. 126). As historians comment, the risk-taking nature of the Venetians was also legendary, as was the over-confidence of the merchants, which was characterised by William Dean Howells as 'a spirit of reckless profusion' (p. 35). Thus, a general sense of 'trade' – whether it involves goods or people – and the potential dangers that commercial endeavour raises pervade the play from its very opening to its conclusion. It is embedded in the friendship shared by Antonio and Bassanio, in all of the mar-riages that eventually take place and in the final meting out of justice to Shylock in Act 4, Scene 1. Moreover, when Bassanio describes Portia to Antonio for the first time (line 160ff.), she is 'rich' first, and 'fair' second. Thus, virtually every human arrangement within the play seems to have an economic edge.

According to John Drakakis (**p. 93**), Antonio's melancholy, which is evident in the opening line, is a condition of his existence within the overwhelming commercialism of Venice. However, other critics point out that it is also a product of his intimate relationship with his young friend, Bassanio, and of the fear that he will lose Bassanio to a woman. Alan Sinfield discusses the homoerotic overtones of their relationship, noting that the 'traffic in boys' was unremarkable both in the play and in Shakespeare's time (**pp. 95–6**). Additionally, Miriam Gilbert (**pp. 127–8**) explores the relationship by reporting on various aspects of past productions that have shaped their audience's understanding of the relationship between Antonio and Bassanio within the male society of the play.

For Shakespeare and his fellow actors the manner in which a trading company mirrored an acting company would also have been obvious. As the merchant who risks all by sending out ships, the playing company takes risks by 'sending out' plays on the stage, hoping to make a return, as 'merchants of entertainment and culture'. Their investment in theatre, from a business angle, was substantial. Every player who became a shareholder in a playing company, or a playhouse, was continually immersed in commercial transactions, without which the public playhouses could not have functioned (see **pp. 17–19**).

Enter ANTONIO, SALARINO, *and* SOLANIO.

ANTONIO In sooth[1] I know not why I am so sad.
It wearies me, you say it wearies you;
But how I caught it, found it, or came by it,
What stuff 'tis made of, whereof it is born,
I am to learn;[2]   5
And such a want-wit[3] sadness makes of me
That I have much ado to know myself.
SALARINO Your mind is tossing on the ocean,
There where your argosies[4] with portly[5] sail,
Like signors[6] and rich burghers[7] on the flood,   10

---

1 Truth.
2 Have yet to learn. The blank space following suggests six syllables of silence.
3 Fool, dullard.
4 Large merchant ships. Samuel Johnson doubted the link between the word 'argosies' and 'Argos' (**p. 67**).
5 Majestic.
6 Gentlemen.
7 Wealthy citizens.

Or as it were the pageants[8] of the sea,
Do overpeer[9] the petty traffickers[10]
That curtsy[11] to them, do them reverence,
As they fly by them with their woven wings.

SOLANIO   Believe me, sir,[12] had I such venture forth,   15
The better part of my affections[13] would
Be with my hopes abroad. I should be still[14]
Plucking the grass to know where sits the wind,[15]
Peering[16] in maps for ports and piers and roads,[17]
And every object that might make me fear   20
Misfortune to my ventures, out of doubt[18]
Would make me sad.

SALARINO   My wind[19] cooling my broth
Would blow me to an ague[20] when I thought
What harm a wind too great might do at sea.
I should not see the sandy hour-glass run   25
But I should think of shallows[21] and of flats,[22]
And see my wealthy Andrew[23] docked in sand,
Vailing her high-top lower than her ribs[24]
To kiss her burial.[25] Should I go to church
And see the holy edifice of stone   30
And not bethink me straight[26] of dangerous rocks
Which, touching but my gentle vessel's side,
Would scatter all her spices on the stream,
Enrobe the roaring waters with my silks,
And, in a word, but even now worth this,   35
And now worth nothing? Shall I have the thought
To think on this, and shall I lack the thought

---

8 'Floats' in a procession.
9 Tower over, look down upon.
10 Smaller ships.
11 Bow, i.e. bob up and down upon the waves.
12 The use of 'sir' suggests that the men are friends but not intimates.
13 Concerns.
14 Always.
15 Holding up a blade of grass (or throwing it into the air) to see in which direction the wind is blowing.
16 Q1 prints 'Piring', i.e. 'looking closely', which has a different sense than 'peering' ('look searchingly'), (Mahood, p. 58). However, many modern editors continue to use 'peering'.
17 Harbours.
18 Without doubt.
19 Breath.
20 Fit of shivering.
21 Shallow waters.
22 Sandbanks.
23 The name of a ship. All English ships were referred to as feminine objects, despite their masculine names.
24 Lowering her topmast below her wooden sides.
25 The sand in which the ship is being buried.
26 Immediately.

That such a thing bechanced would make me sad?
But tell not me; I know Antonio
Is sad to think upon his merchandise.   40
ANTONIO   Believe me, no. I thank my fortune[27] for it,
My ventures are not in one bottom[28] trusted,
Nor to one place; nor is my whole estate
Upon the fortune of this present year.
Therefore my merchandise makes me not sad.[29]   45
SOLANIO   Why, then you are in love.
ANTONIO   Fie, fie![30]
SOLANIO   Not in love neither? Then let us say you are sad
Because you are not merry; and 'twere as easy
For you to laugh, and leap, and say you are merry
Because you are not sad. Now, by two headed Janus,[31]   50
Nature hath framed strange fellows in her time:
Some that will evermore peep through their eyes[32]
And laugh like parrots at a bagpiper,[33]
And other of such vinegar[34] aspèct
That they'll not show their teeth in way of smile   55
Though Nestor[35] swear the jest be laughable.
Here comes Bassanio, your most noble kinsman [. . .]

Enter Bassanio with Gratiano and Lorenzo. Exeunt Salarino and Solanio.
Following a comic interchange, Gratiano and Lorenzo exit leaving Antonio and
Bassanio to converse.

ANTONIO   Well, tell me now what lady is the same[36]
To whom you swore a secret pilgrimage,
That you today promised to tell me of.   120
BASSANIO   'Tis not unknown to you, Antonio,
How much I have disabled mine estate
By something showing a more swelling port

---

27 Both 'luck' and 'wealth'.
28 Ship.
29 Antonio claims that all of his fortunes are not tied up in his recent ventures though later on it is
    clear that this is not the case. His current ventures are critical.
30 Nonsense!
31 A Roman god with two faces, one sad and one happy.
32 i.e. because the eyes are half-closed when one laughs.
33 The parrot, noted for its foolishness, laughs even at the drone of a melancholy bagpipe.
34 Sour.
35 The oldest and most dignified Greek general involved in the Trojan wars.
36 The one.

Than my faint means would grant continuance,[37]
Nor do I now make moan[38] to be abridged[39]   125
From such a noble rate; but my chief care
Is to come fairly off from the great debts
Wherein my time, something too prodigal,
Hath left me gaged.[40] To you, Antonio,
I owe the most in money and in love,   130
And from your love I have a warranty
To unburden all my plots and purposes
How to get clear of all the debts I owe.

ANTONIO   I pray you, good Bassanio, let me know it,[41]
And if it stand, as you yourself still do,   135
Within the eye of honour, be assured
My purse, my person, my extremest means,
Lie all unlocked to your occasions.

BASSANIO   In my schooldays, when I had lost one shaft,[42]
I shot his fellow of the selfsame flight   140
The selfsame way with more advisèd watch
To find the other forth; and by adventuring[43] both
I oft found both. I urge this childhood proof
Because what follows is pure innocence.
I owe you much, and, like a wilful youth,   145
That which I owe is lost; but if you please
To shoot another arrow that self[44] way
Which you did shoot the first, I do not doubt,
As I will watch the aim, or to find both
Or bring your latter hazard back again   150
And thankfully rest debtor for the first.

ANTONIO   You know me well, and herein spend but time
To wind about my love with circumstance;[45]
And out of doubt[46] you do me now more wrong
In making question of my uttermost   155
Than if you had made waste of all I have.
Then do but say to me what I should do
That in your knowledge may by me be done,

---

37 'By exhibiting a more lavish lifestyle than my modest means would allow me to continue'. In Peter
    Hall's production (1989) Bassanio's hose were tattered, an outward sign of his penury (Edelman, p.
    97, n. 57).
38 Complain.
39 'Because I have been forced to reduce my expenses'.
40 Engaged, i.e. bound in debt.
41 Bassanio's scheme.
42 Arrow.
43 Risking.
44 Same.
45 'To approach my love in an indirect way'. Antonio loses patience with Bassanio who, he thinks,
    doubts his friendship and integrity.
46 Certainly.

And I am pressed unto it:[47] therefore speak.

BASSANIO   In Belmont is a lady richly left,[48]   160
And she is fair and, fairer than that word,
Of wondrous virtues. Sometimes from her eyes
I did receive fair speechless[49] messages.
Her name is Portia, nothing undervalued[50]
To Cato's daughter, Brutus' Portia;[51]   165
Nor is the wide world ignorant of her worth,
For the four winds blow in from every coast
Renownèd suitors, and her sunny locks
Hang on her temples like a golden fleece,
Which makes her seat[52] of Belmont Colchis' strand,[53]   170
And many Jasons come in quest of her.
O my Antonio, had I but the means
To hold a rival place with one of them,
I have a mind presages me[54] such thrift[55]
That I should questionless be fortunate.   175

ANTONIO   Thou know'st that all my fortunes are at sea,
Neither have I money nor commodity[56]
To raise a present sum. Therefore go forth –
Try what my credit can in Venice do;
That shall be racked,[57] even to the uttermost,   180
To furnish thee to Belmont, to fair Portia.[58]
Go presently inquire, and so will I,
Where money is, and I not question make
To have it of my trust or for my sake.[59]

Exeunt.[60]

---

48 i.e. who has inherited substantial riches. The mercantile rhetoric and the language of love are here
    intertwined as they frequently are elsewhere in the play. Edelman notes two interesting directorial
    decisions pertaining to this section of the play. First, in one production Bassanio rubbed his fingers
    together at the words 'richly left'. Second, in some productions directors have revealed Portia in the
    background at this moment (p. 100, n. 160–75), though others have left Portia's appearance to the
    audience's imagination.
47 Ready to do it.
49 Unspoken.
50 No less worthy than.
51 The historical Portia was daughter of Cato, the honest Roman general, and wife to Brutus who led
    the conspiracy against Julius Caesar.
52 House.
53 Shore. In Greek mythology, Jason and the Argonauts journeyed to Colchis (on the Black Sea) in
    search of a ram with golden fleece.
54 Prophesies to me.
55 Success (also, profit).
56 Goods, i.e. collateral.
57 Strained.
58 Some Antonios make their sexual jealousy of Portia clear in this line (Edelman, p. 101, n. 181).
59 'I have no doubt that I will be able to borrow the money either on my credit or as a personal favour'.
60 In John Barton's production (1981), Bassanio left Antonio to pick up the tab. A similar strategy
    was employed by Trevor Nunn (1999), who directed Bassanio to leave ahead of Antonio, so that
    Antonio was left to pay everyone's bill. Jonathan Miller (1970) had Antonio leave ahead of Bas-
    sanio. When the waiter who brought Bassanio his gloves extended his hand for a tip Bassanio 'slaps
    the waiter's hand with his gloves and laughs nastily' (Edelman, p. 101, n. 183b–4).

Act 1, Scene 2, lines 19–110

Belmont, Portia's house:[1] Portia and her gentlewoman, Nerissa, consider a variety of potential suitors; however, Portia is bound by her deceased father's dictate that all suitors must choose amongst three caskets – made of gold, silver and lead – one of which contains Portia's picture. He who ventures correctly wins Portia's hand in marriage. At the end of the scene the Prince of Morocco, one of Portia's suitors, arrives.

As noted by Leonard Tennenhouse (pp. 82–4), this scene presents the feminine world of Belmont (a vivid contrast to Venice) in which terms such as 'trade' and 'profit' are applied to romantic love despite its 'maternal, bountiful, and generous' nature. Reading Portia's character is more complex, however. It appears that early critics, modern critics and even actresses who have played the part seem to be divided over whether she is an effective character and even as to what sort of character she is. William Hazlitt (1817) found her 'not a very great favorite' with those of his time who saw the play; nor did they seem to like Nerissa any better (p. 74). Harley Granville-Barker, the theatrical producer and critic, remarked that 'Shakespeare can do little enough with Portia while she is still the slave of the caskets' and 'the actress must resist the temptation to [. . .] do more'. Early on in the play, Granville-Barker characterises Portia as 'an enchanted princess' (who later is awakened by her true love in fairy-tale style). Yet he also believes that Portia gains stature as the play unfolds. At the beginning she is 'the schoolgirl laughing with Nerissa' whereas by the end she is 'the Portia of resource and command'. Therefore, for Granville-Barker, it is Portia's marriage to Bassanio in Act 3, Scene 2 that liberates her from the casket lottery (and her father's constraints), allowing her finally to develop into a mature substantial woman (pp. 76–8). Karen Newman interprets Portia's eventual marriage as an 'exchange [. . .] from her father via the caskets' so that Portia becomes 'a pseudo-center' and, in some ways, merely another in the series of transactions through which the play evolves (pp. 84–6).

Modern actresses express different, though complementary, opinions about Portia. In reviewing the 1989–90 performance of Portia by Geraldine James, Mervyn Rothstein suggested that the actress had contradictory feelings about Portia, feelings that, in turn, created a character that was 'affected and pedantic and the least lovable of Shakespeare's comedy heroines' (p. 119). However, contradictory responses are only natural when – as both James and Rothstein believe – a character seems to possess so many contradictions inherently. (For actress Sinead Cusack, who performed Portia in 1981, the role also created a palpable sense of discomfort (pp. 120–2).) Geraldine James is quoted by Rothstein as summing up Portia in this way: 'She's a very spoiled rich girl who

---

1   Again, the setting is vague. The presence of Portia and Nerissa signals that the setting has changed to Belmont; but whether the characters are speaking from inside Portia's house, from an opulent garden outside or from another country location is unclear.

grows up in a world full of the most appalling prejudices' (p. 120). Nevertheless, as Edwin Sandys makes clear in a sermon delivered in 1585, couples were not free to choose their future spouses without the consent of parents (pp. 46–9). Therefore Portia's 'choice' – as she makes clear in the opening of this scene – is very much prescribed by the casket lottery that her dead father has set up.

Enter PORTIA *with her waiting-woman,* NERISSA.

[. . .]

PORTIA[2]   [. . .]   O me, the word 'choose'! I may neither choose who   20
  I would, nor refuse who I dislike; so is the will[3] of a living daughter
  curbed by the will of a dead father. Is it not hard, Nerissa, that I
  cannot choose one nor refuse none?

NERISSA   Your father was ever virtuous, and holy men at their death
  have good inspirations; therefore the lott'ry that he hath devised in   25
  these three chests of gold, silver, and lead, whereof who chooses his
  meaning[4] chooses you, will no doubt never be chosen by any rightly[5]
  but one who you shall rightly love. But what warmth is there in your
  affection towards any of these princely suitors that are already come?

PORTIA   I pray thee overname[6] them; and as thou namest them, I   30
  will describe them and, according to my description, level[7] at my
  affection.

NERISSA   First there is the Neapolitan prince.[8]

PORTIA   Ay, that's a colt[9] indeed, for he doth nothing but talk of his
  horse, and he makes it a great appropriation to his own good parts[10]   35
  that he can shoe him himself. I am much afeard[11] my lady his mother
  played false with a smith.[12]

NERISSA   Then is there the County Palatine.[13]

2 Some critics have hypothesised that Portia and Nerissa speak in prose, instead of verse, because the
   scene is comic.
3 Portia plays with two meanings: 'desire' and 'testament'.
4 The one that Portia's father meant him to choose.
5 Correctly (also, truly).
6 Name from first to last.
7 Guess.
8 The following catalogue of suitors is sometimes seen as tedious, and so some directors have added
   stage business – miming, life-sized chessboards with pieces that represented suitors, viewing pictures of the suitors, etc. – in order to create additional interest (Edelman, p. 104, n. 30ff.).
9 Awkward young man.
10 A great addition to his abilities.
11 Afraid.
12 Blacksmith.
13 Count Palatine ruled territories having royal privilege. Samuel Johnson comments that this reference alluded to a Polish Palatine (p. 67).

PORTIA   He doth nothing but frown, as who should say 'An[14] you
will not have me, choose.' He hears merry tales and smiles not; I fear   40
he will prove the weeping philosopher[15] when he grows old, being so
full of unmannerly sadness in his youth. I had rather be married to a
death's-head[16] with a bone in his mouth than to either of these. God
defend me from these two!

NERISSA   How say you by the French lord, Monsieur le Bon?   45

PORTIA   God made him, and therefore let him pass for a man. In
truth, I know it is a sin to be a mocker, but he! – why, he hath a horse
better than the Neapolitan's, a better bad habit of frowning than the
Count Palatine. He is every man in no man.[17] If a throstle[18] sing, he
falls straight a-cap'ring.[19] He will fence with his own shadow. If I   50
should marry him, I should marry twenty husbands. If he would des-
pise me, I would forgive him; for if he love me to madness, I shall
never requite him.

NERISSA   What say you then to Falconbridge, the young baron of
England?   55

PORTIA   You know I say nothing to him, for he understands not me,
nor I him: he hath neither Latin, French, nor Italian, and you will
come into the court[20] and swear that I have a poor pennyworth[21] in
the English. He is a proper man's picture, but alas, who can converse
with a dumb show?[22] How oddly he is suited![23] I think he bought his   60
doublet[24] in Italy, his round hose[25] in France, his bonnet in Germany,
and his behaviour everywhere.

NERISSA   What think you of the Scottish lord, his neighbour?

PORTIA   That he hath a neighbourly charity in him, for he borrowed
a box of the ear[26] of the Englishman and swore he would pay him   65
again when he was able. I think the Frenchman became his surety[27]
and sealed under[28] for another.

NERISSA   How like you the young German, the Duke of Saxony's
nephew?[29]

---

14 And.
15 Heraclitus of Ephesus, who lived as a recluse because he was so distressed by people's consuming
     greed and stupidity.
16 Skull.
17 He has the characteristics of every man and none of his own.
18 Thrush.
19 Dancing, i.e. 'He will dance to anyone's tune'.
20 Bear witness.
21 Not very much.
22 Pantomime, i.e. a show presented without speaking.
23 Dressed.
24 Jacket.
25 Padded-out stockings, very much in fashion at the time.
26 Clap on the ear.
27 Guarantee (that he would repay the debt), i.e. a legal term for a person who guarantees the loan of
     another in case he defaults.
28 Set his seal to.
29 Johnson raises the possibility that in naming Portia's suitors Shakespeare was alluding to
     Queen Elizabeth I's many suitors (p. 67).

PORTIA   Very vilely in the morning when he is sober, and most vilely   70
in the afternoon when he is drunk. When he is best, he is a little worse
than a man, and when he is worst, he is little better than a beast. And
the worst fall[30] that ever fell, I hope I shall make shift[31] to go without
him.

NERISSA   If he should offer[32] to choose, and choose the right cas-   75
ket,[33] you should refuse to perform your father's will if you should
refuse to accept him.

PORTIA   Therefore, for fear of the worst, I pray thee set a deep glass
of Rhenish wine[34] on the contrary casket; for if the devil be within and
that temptation without, I know he will choose it. I will do anything,   80
Nerissa, ere I will be married to a sponge.

NERISSA   You need not fear, lady, the having[35] any of these lords.
They have acquainted me with[36] their determinations, which is indeed
to return to their home and to trouble you with no more suit, unless
you may be won by some other sort[37] than your father's imposition,   85
depending on the caskets.

PORTIA   If I live to be as old as Sibylla,[38] I will die as chaste as
Diana[39] unless I be obtained by the manner of my father's will. I am
glad this parcel of wooers are so reasonable, for there is not one
among them but I dote on his very absence, and I pray God grant   90
them a fair departure.

NERISSA   Do you not remember, lady, in your father's time, a Venetian, a scholar and a soldier, that came hither in company of the
Marquis of Montferrat?

PORTIA   Yes, yes, it was Bassanio – as I think so was he called.[40]   95

NERISSA   True, madam. He of all the men that ever my foolish eyes
looked upon was the best deserving a fair lady.

PORTIA   I remember him well, and I remember him worthy of thy
praise.

Enter a SERVINGMAN.

---

30 If the worst happens.
31 Find a way.
32 Decide.
33 The word 'right' is intriguing as it could indicate that the women know what is in the caskets.
34 White wine from the German Rhine area.
35 That you will have to accept.
36 Informed me of.
37 Way.
38 The Sibyl of Cumae. In classical mythology, the god Apollo granted her as many years of life as the
     grains of sand that she could hold in her hand.
39 In classical mythology, the goddess of chastity.
40 Portia attempts to play down her initial enthusiasm; however, this corroborates what Bassanio has
     told Antonio, that he has had encouragement from Portia. Some eighteenth-century editors, such as
     Samuel Johnson, thought that Bassanio had been at Belmont earlier, with the Duke of Montferrat,
     and saw Portia while her father was yet living. Bassanio's statement, in Act 1, Scene 1, lines 162–3 –
     'Sometimes from her eyes/I did receive fair speechless messages' – indicates that there apparently
     was a previous meeting. (See Samuel Johnson, *The Plays of William Shakespeare*, London: 1765),
     I, 391, note 2.)

How now! What news?   100

SERVINGMAN   The four strangers[41] seek for you, madam, to take
their leave,[42] and there is a forerunner[43] come from a fifth, the Prince
of Morocco, who brings word the Prince his master will be here
tonight.[44]

PORTIA   If I could bid the fifth welcome with so good heart as I can 105
bid the other four farewell, I should be glad of his approach. If he have
the condition[45] of a saint and the complexion of a devil,[46] I had rather
he should shrive[47] me than wive[48] me.

Come, Nerissa; [To the SERVINGMAN] Sirrah, go before: Whiles we
shut the gate upon one wooer, another knocks at the door.   110

Exeunt.

Act 1, Scene 3, lines 32–174

A street in Venice, traditionally the Rialto bridge on which much business was
conducted in the city: Bassanio approaches Shylock for a loan of three thousand
ducats for three months on a bond for which Antonio will be responsible.
Although Antonio's credit is good, Shylock reveals his hatred of Antonio who
does not lend money at interest (thereby undercutting Shylock's potential
profits). In addition, Antonio has a history of treating Shylock contemptuously
because he is a Jew. The bond that Shylock invents states that if Antonio neg-
lects to repay the loan upon the date specified he will relinquish a pound of his
own flesh to be cut off from the area of his body that Shylock chooses. Bassanio
is distrustful of Shylock's intentions, but Antonio is confident that his ships will
return a month before the bond is due.

Act 1, Scene 3 is the first scene in the play in which the audience witnesses
Christians and Jews doing business. Shylock's dialogue with Bassanio is replete
with the urgency that Bassanio feels, as well as his uneasiness at having to ask for
the loan. Due to their unhappy shared history the interchange between Shylock
and Antonio is equally uneasy, as each fundamentally distrusts the other. One of
Shakespeare's chief intentions in writing the scene is to contrast Shylock's
views on moneylending with Antonio's. (Here, Antonio represents the Chris-

---

41 Foreigners.
42 Actually, six suitors have been discussed.
43 Messenger.
44 The director E. H. Sothern (1905) brought on Morocco's page here, and Portia's own page – a
    'Blackamoor page' – laughed at him (Edelman, p. 107, n. 103–4).
45 Character, nature.
46 Here, and elsewhere, Portia's racial prejudice emerges.
47 Grant absolution.
48 Marry. The arrival of Morocco places Portia under renewed strain as she hopes for, and waits for,
    Bassanio to arrive.

tian dislike of the practice of usury while Shylock provides a complex rationale supporting it. Many writers of Shakespeare's day, such as Thomas Wilson and Francis Bacon, participated in the controversy over usury. See **pp. 42–6**.) This scene also suggests that the conflict generated by such contrasting, strongly held views has served only to create an insidious atmosphere within the Venetian business community. In his essay 'The Jew as Renaissance Man', Peter Berek writes: 'The traditional association of Jews with money-lending and other forms of commercial enterprise makes Jews in Elizabethan England, as they have been since, suitable representations of ambivalent feelings about economic innovation and social change' **(pp. 36–7)**. In addition, Shylock is the perfect example of the self-made man, a stereotype that was just beginning to take shape as successful merchants began to rival, or surpass, the established aristocracy in terms of monetary success. Consequently, as Berek notes, Shylock is a moneylender (or 'merchant of money') within a culture that condemned moneylending but nevertheless 'watched prominent citizens grow rich on the practice' **(p. 38)**. Additionally, the playhouse owners of Shakespeare's day, who both invested in theatrical endeavours by constructing theatres and loaned money to the players, typified this new kind of capitalist (see **pp. 17–19**).

Interpreting the role of Shylock is the subject of much debate by literary critics and theatre professionals. Patrick Stewart's portrayal in a 1978 production emphasised the economic aspects of the character. For Stewart, Shylock was a man who had earned his fortune through shrewd business dealings and had – in his dress, speech and mannerisms – become assimilated into Venetian society. David Suchet, who performed the role in 1981, envisioned a Shylock who had lived a life so distinctly apart from the Christian community that he needed to both look and speak as a foreigner. As Ian McDiarmid asks: 'Where was Shakespeare's Jew from?' **(p. 122)**. Antony Sher's portrayal, of a Shylock who dressed as if he was from North Africa and seemed almost a 'creature of the desert', is characterised by James Bulman **(pp. 125–6)**.

There has been so much emphasis on Shylock and his role in the play that virtually every commentator, from the eighteenth century on, has had something different to say. In the words of Nathan Drake (1817), Shylock is 'Satanic' **(p. 73)**; for E. E. Stoll (1927), he was a stereotypical villain, in the mould of Satan and other evil characters from the tradition of the medieval morality play, and was therefore, in some way, cast as a bogeyman in a fairy tale **(pp. 75–6)**. Surprisingly, perhaps, as Nicholas Rowe commented, in 1709, Shylock had even been performed as a comic character **(pp. 64–5)**. By 1996, John Drakakis's reading of the character – which is more complicated by economic and psychological factors – interpreted Shylock as a subject onto which the Venetians can 'project a hatred which stems from the recognition of the need of his money to sustain their own society'. In this way, Drakakis reminds readers that Portia and Shylock are drawn together because 'they are both possessed of material wealth which Venice needs' **(p. 92)**.

[Bassanio is on stage with Shylock. Enter Antonio to them.]

BASSANIO   This is Signor Antonio.
SHYLOCK [*aside*]   How like a fawning[1] publican[2] he looks.
  I hate him for he is a Christian,
  But more for that in low simplicity[3]   35
  He lends out money gratis[4] and brings down
  The rate of usance[5] here with us in Venice.
  If I can catch him once upon the hip,[6]
  I will feed fat[7] the ancient grudge I bear him.
  He hates our sacred nation, and he rails,[8]   40
  Even there where merchants most do congregate,
  On me, my bargains, and my well-won thrift,[9]
  Which he calls interest.[10] Cursèd be my tribe[11]
  If I forgive him.
BASSANIO   Shylock, do you hear?[12]
SHYLOCK   I am debating of[13] my present store,[14]   45
  And by the near[15] guess of my memory
  I cannot instantly raise up the gross[16]
  Of full three thousand ducats. What of that?
  Tubal, a wealthy Hebrew of my tribe,
  Will furnish me. But soft![17] How many months   50
  Do you desire? [*To* ANTONIO] Rest you fair, good signor,
  Your worship was the last man in our mouths.
ANTONIO   Shylock, albeit I neither lend nor borrow
  By taking nor by giving of excess,[18]
  Yet to supply the ripe[19] wants of my friend   55
  I'll break a custom. [*To* BASSANIO] Is he yet possessed[20]
  How much ye would?[21]

---

1 Servile.
2 Tax collector.
3 Humble foolishness.
4 Interest free.
5 Usury, interest.
6 In a weak position (a term from wrestling).
7 Feed until fat, i.e. as an animal is fattened before slaughter.
8 Abuses.
9 Success, i.e. monetary gains.
10 Profits. The word is frequently spoken in three distinct syllables to lend it greater force.
11 An allusion to the twelve 'tribes' of Israel; but, more generally, a reference to all Jewish people.
12 Bassanio had been unsuccessful in gaining Shylock's attention several times earlier in the scene.
13 Counting. The language also suggests Shylock's conflict with Antonio.
14 Ready cash.
15 Close.
16 Entire amount.
17 'Wait a minute'.
18 i.e. interest.
19 Urgent.
20 Informed.
21 Want.

SHYLOCK	Ay, ay, three thousand ducats.[22]	
ANTONIO	And for three months.	

SHYLOCK   I had forgot; three months; [*To* BASSANIO] you told me
    so.

    Well then, your bond; and let me see. But hear you: 60
    Methoughts you said you neither lend nor borrow
    Upon advantage.[23]

ANTONIO   I do never use it.[24]

SHYLOCK   When Jacob grazed his uncle Laban's sheep –[25]
    This Jacob from our holy Abram was,
    As his wise mother wrought[26] in his behalf,   65
    The third possessor; ay, he was the third–

ANTONIO   And what of him? Did he take interest?

SHYLOCK   No, not take interest – not, as you would say,
    Directly int'rest. Mark what Jacob did:
    When Laban and himself were compromised[27]   70
    That all the eanlings[28] which were streaked and pied[29]
    Should fall as Jacob's hire,[30] the ewes being rank[31]
    In end of autumn turnèd to the rams,
    And when the work of generation was
    Between these woolly breeders in the act,   75
    The skilful shepherd peeled me certain wands,[32]
    And in the doing of the deed of kind[33]
    He stuck them up before the fulsome ewes,
    Who then conceiving did in eaning time[34]
    Fall[35] parti-coloured lambs, and those were Jacob's.   80

---

22 A considerable sum of money, and a great expense in human terms, considering that it represents
   merely a pound of a human being. In Barry Edelstein's production (1995), Shylock showed Antonio the ledger in which he had noted the sum (Edelman, p. 116, n. 57b).
23 i.e. with interest.
24 'That is not my practice'.
25 Shylock tells the story (from Genesis 27 and 30:25–43) of the clever scheme by which Jacob
   acquired a large flock of sheep. In the narrative Jacob drove stripped (multi-coloured) branches
   into the ground, and when the ewes (female sheep) saw them they produced parti-coloured lambs.
   (It was thought that offspring resembled what the mother saw at the time of conception.) According to Jacob's agreement with Laban, these sheep were his. Shylock relates the tale in order to
   rationalise the gains he makes in charging interest on loans. The debate about usury is exemplified
   in the passages from Thomas Wilson's *A Discourse upon Usury* (1572) and Francis Bacon's essay
   entitled 'Of Usury' (1625) (pp. 42–4 and pp. 44–6).
26 Devised.
27 Agreed.
28 New-born lambs.
29 Multi-coloured.
30 Should be counted as Jacob's wages.
31 Ready for mating.
32 Twigs. Michael Billington noted that Laurence Olivier 'inserted his stick with a corkscrew movement through his outstretched left hand, brilliantly summoning up both the peeling-process and
   animalistic copulation' (*The Modern Actor* (London: Hamilton, 1973), p. 84).
33 Act of breeding.
34 The time of birth.
35 Bear.

This was a way to thrive, and he was blest;
And thrift[36] is blessing, if men steal it not.[37]
ANTONIO   This was a venture, sir, that Jacob served for,
A thing not in his power to bring to pass
But swayed and fashioned by the hand of heaven.   85
Was this inserted to make interest good?[38]
Or is your gold and silver ewes and rams?
SHYLOCK   I cannot tell; I make it breed as fast.[39]
But note me, signor –
ANTONIO   Mark you this, Bassanio,
The devil can cite Scripture for his purpose.   90
An evil soul producing holy witness
Is like a villain with a smiling cheek,
A goodly apple rotten at the heart.
O, what a goodly outside falsehood hath![40]
SHYLOCK   Three thousand ducats. 'Tis a good round sum.   95
Three months from twelve; then, let me see, the rate –
ANTONIO   Well, Shylock, shall we be beholding to you?
SHYLOCK   Signor Antonio, many a time and oft[41]
In the Rialto you have rated[42] me
About my moneys and my usances.   100
Still have I borne it with a patient shrug,
For suff'rance[43] is the badge of all our tribe.
You call me misbeliever,[44] cut-throat dog,
And spit upon my Jewish gaberdine,[45]
And all for use of that which is mine own.   105
Well then, it now appears you need my help.
Go to, then.[46] You come to me and you say,
'Shylock, we would have moneys': you say so –

---

36 (1) Success, (2) monetary gain.
37 The scriptural commentary on usury as a breach of charity is explained by Peter Berek (p. 37).
38 'Was this story told to justify usury?'
39 The sterile 'breeding' of money is seen, by some commentators, as a sign of Shylock's inhumanity. Drakakis writes that 'Venice can only admit him as a demonization of its own social and economic practices' (p. 92). Some Shylocks, such as Olivier, have laughed heartily at their own joke here while others smile more humbly (Edelman, p. 118, n. 88).
40 Sinfield (pp. 95–6) interprets Antonio's hatred of Shylock's Jewishness within the context of Antonio's homosexual (i.e. 'alien') self.
41 Patrick Stewart described this speech as 'a masterly piece of controlled and brilliant irony' while other Shylocks interpret it as a 'vehement summary of past slights'. John Woodvine (1991) and David Calder (1993) 'indulged in a high level of mockery' (Edelman, p. 119, n. 98–121, and p. 120, n. 118–20).
42 Abused.
43 Forbearance.
44 Heretic. Orson Welles (1969) delivered this line as if in disbelief that anyone could come to this conclusion about an observant Jew (Edelman, p. 119, n. 103).
45 Cloak (which became associated with Jews).
46 An expression of impatience.

You, that did void your rheum[47] upon my beard
And foot[48] me as you spurn a stranger cur 110
Over your threshold, moneys is your suit.[49]
What should I say to you? Should I not say
'Hath a dog money? Is it possible
A cur can lend three thousand ducats?' Or
Shall I bend low and in a bondman's key,[50] 115
With bated breath and whisp'ring humbleness,
Say this:
'Fair sir, you spat on me on Wednesday last;
You spurned me such a day; another time
You called me dog; and for these courtesies 120
I'll lend you thus much moneys'?
ANTONIO   I am as like to call thee so again,
To spit on thee again, to spurn thee, too.
If thou wilt lend this money, lend it not
As to thy friends; for when did friendship take 125
A breed for barren metal[51] of his friend?
But lend it rather to thine enemy
Who, if he break,[52] thou mayst with better face
Exact the penalty.
SHYLOCK   Why, look you, how you storm! 130
I would be friends with you and have your love,
Forget the shames that you have stained me with,
Supply your present wants, and take no doit[53]
Of usance for my moneys; and you'll not hear me.
This is kind[54] I offer.
BASSANIO   This were kindness. 135
SHYLOCK   This kindness will I show.[55]
Go with me to a notary, seal me[56] there
Your single[57] bond, and, in a merry sport,[58]

---

47 Spit.
48 Kick.
49 Request.
50 Slave's tone of voice.
51 Offspring (interest) of barren (infertile) metal (money).
52 (1) Fails to repay, (2) becomes bankrupt.
53 Jot, small amount.
54 Kindness.
55 Henry Irving (1879) added a gesture here that drew the interest of many critics. Edelman quotes the critic writing in *The Theatre* (1 December 1879): 'the Jew touches Antonio on the heart, and, seeing the merchant recoil from him, apologises for his error by a bow in which we can perceive all the bitterness induced by the hard distinction drawn between Christian and Jew.' In the twentieth century, productions have been more invested in emphasising Shylock's amusement at the bond rather than simply his resentment of the Christians (Edelman, pp. 121–2, n. 136–44).
56 Sign for me.
57 Simple.
58 Trifle, joke.

If you repay me not on such a day,
In such a place, such sum or sums as are   140
Expressed in the condition,[59] let the forfeit
Be nominated[60] for an equal pound[61]
Of your fair flesh to be cut off and taken
In what part of your body pleaseth me.[62]

ANTONIO   Content, in faith. I'll seal to such a bond,   145
And say there is much kindness in the Jew.

BASSANIO   You shall not seal to such a bond for me.
I'll rather dwell[63] in my necessity.

ANTONIO   Why, fear not, man; I will not forfeit it.
Within these two months – that's a month before   150
This bond expires – I do expect return
Of thrice three times the value of the bond.

SHYLOCK   O father Abram, what these Christians are,
Whose own hard dealings teaches them suspect
The thoughts of others![64] [To BASSANIO] Pray you, tell me this: 155
If he should break his day,[65] what should I gain
By the exaction of the forfeiture?
A pound of man's flesh, taken from a man,
Is not so estimable, profitable neither,
As flesh of muttons, beefs, or goats.[66] I say,   160
To buy his favour, I extend this friendship.
If he will take it, so; if not, adieu.
And, for my love, I pray you wrong me not.

ANTONIO   Yes, Shylock, I will seal unto this bond.

SHYLOCK   Then meet me forthwith at the notary's.[67]   165
Give him direction for this merry bond,
And I will go and purse the ducats[68] straight,
See to my house – left in the fearful guard
Of an unthrifty knave – and presently

---

59 Written in the formal agreement.
60 Specified.
61 An equal pound. In Zhang Qi-hong's production (Chinese Youth Theatre, 1980), the director set
    this scene in a marketplace. At this moment Shylock 'cast a momentary glance to the left at a
    shopkeeper serving a customer – he is a butcher and his scales are poised' (Edelman quoting Philip
    Brockbank, p. 122, n. 142).
62 The precise terms of Shylock's bond are somewhat vague, which creates tension as the audience
    wonders what part of Antonio's body will be violated if the bond comes due. Only later does he
    decide that the pound of flesh will be cut from near Antonio's heart and this is everywhere apparent
    in the trial scene (Act 4, Scene 1, line 60ff.).
63 Remain in need.
64 In several productions ll. 153–5 have been treated as an aside.
65 Fail to pay on the date due.
66 Kim Hall discusses the ways in which the language of eating (and along with it cannibalism and
    'consuming', in all of its many manifestations) are tropes of colonial discourse (**pp. 80–2**).
67 In Trevor Nunn's *Merchant* (1999), Shylock (Henry Goodman) scribbled the notary's address on
    the back of a business card and handed it to Antonio (Edelman, p. 123, n. 165).
68 Gather the ducats, put the ducats into a purse.

I'll be with you.   *Exit.*
ANTONIO   Hie thee, gentle Jew.   170
The Hebrew will turn Christian: he grows kind.[69]
BASSANIO   I like not fair terms and a villain's mind.[70]
ANTONIO   Come on; in this there can be no dismay:
My ships come home a month before the day.[71]

                                                        Exeunt.[72]

Act 2, Scene 1, lines 1–31

Belmont, Portia's house: the Prince of Morocco declares his intention to take the casket test. Although she dislikes him, Portia puts on a polite front. However, his choice has serious consequences. As Portia warns him, if he loses he must swear never to seek another woman for a wife. Nevertheless, secure in his overconfidence Morocco agrees to accept the terms of the test. Throughout the scene Morocco has customarily been portrayed as self-involved and shallow. As such, he would have been easily dismissed by Elizabethan spectators as a stereotypical (and therefore a comical) outsider.[1]

However, beneath the humour the audience learns that, in addition to Shylock, the play will contain a variety of strangers who complicate the reading

---

69 The mention of Shylock's conversion is a foreshadowing of what will happen at the end of the trial scene (4.1); however, as Hall points out (**p. 82**), Shylock's 'kindness' is still contingent.
70 The use of the term 'villain' broadens the way in which Shylock is viewed and opens the door for E. E. Stoll's theory that Shylock is a 'comic villain' (**pp. 75–6**).
71 The overwhelming self-confidence in Antonio's final response would have been interpreted by many early spectators as justifiable based on their understanding of the fact that merchants, as the foundations of 'Christian commerce', thought of themselves as 'blessed by God' (see Alberto Tenenti, **pp. 40–2**).
72 The Folio text (1623) shows separate exits for Shylock (at 1.170) and Antonio and Bassanio (1.174). Here, as at the end of Act 5, Scene 1 (see Sinfield, **p. 95** and Robert Smallwood's commentary, **pp. 128–30**), different strategies for the exits of characters have been employed. In the nineteenth and early twentieth centuries it was common for Shylock to remain on stage while Antonio and Bassanio left. By contrast, Gordon Crosse noted in his diary that Henry Irving walked slowly in the opposite direction from Antonio and Bassanio, but before he left the stage he turned and shook his staff at them, sending 'a look of concentrated malice' in their direction. In Trevor Nunn's production (1999) Shylock 'paid for his tea and scrupulously left a tip before leaving, in pointed contrast to Bassanio and his friends' at the end of Act 1, Scene 1 (Edelman, **pp. 128–30**).

1   The many variations in contemporary actors' portrayals of Morocco range from 'dashing' to foolhardy. Additionally, some Moroccos have fallen into the trap of portraying the stereotypical black man. In the 1998 production at the new Globe, Morocco was portrayed as 'a caricature of the oversexed black man'. Edelson notes one particularly interesting portayal in a BBC Television Production, directed by Jonathan Miller in 1973. Here, Morocco wore a dark-red uniform with epaulettes, making him look 'more Spanish than Moroccan, indeed more Spanish than Arragon' while he spoke some lines like an 'Al Jolson minstrel'. The most famous actor to play Morocco was James Earl Jones, who performed the role early in his career in the 1962 production by Joseph Papp and Gladys Vaughan. He was reported to have been a more moderate Morocco than most, 'without falling into the trap of caricaturing his own race'. (See Edelman, pp. 125–7, and note 10–11a.)

of racial issues as they enter into the play. William Hazlitt (1817) stated, without qualification, that 'We do not admire the scene of the caskets: and object entirely to the Black Prince, Morocchius', although he offered no further explanation as to why he perceived that readers and spectators responded in this manner (**pp. 73–5**). In fact, it is not unusual for early commentators to discuss the casket test and to ignore Portia's suitors, except to dismiss them (as she does). However, Kim Hall suggests that the economic and social concerns of Shakespeare's time were interconnected. For her, the blurring of boundaries between cultures and races – which was encouraged by the trading intrinsic to mercantile culture – raised fears in Shakespeare's audiences that were related to 'miscegenation', i.e. intermarriage and interbreeding amongst different races. As a result, Portia's suitors, who come in pursuit of Portia and her wealth, present problems related to 'commerce and intercourse' (**p. 81**).

[*A flourish of cornets.*] *Enter* [*the Prince of*] MOROCCO, *a tawny*[2] *Moor all in white, and three or four followers accordingly;*[3] *with* PORTIA, NERISSA, *and their train.*

MOROCCO   Mislike[4] me not for my complexion,[5]
The shadowed livery[6] of the burnished sun,
To whom I am a neighbour and near bred.[7]
Bring me the fairest creature northward born,
Where Phoebus' fire[8] scarce thaws the icicles,   5
And let us make incision[9] for your love
To prove whose blood is reddest, his or mine.[10]
I tell thee, lady, this aspèct[11] of mine
Hath feared[12] the valiant; by my love, I swear
The best-regarded virgins of our clime   10
Have loved it too: I would not change this hue,
Except to steal your thoughts,[13] my gentle queen.
PORTIA   In terms of choice I am not solely led
By nice direction of a maiden's eyes.
Besides, the lott'ry of my destiny   15

2 Light-skinned (as opposed to the darker-skinned blackamoors).
3 Dressed similarly to Morocco.
4 Dislike.
5 (1) Temperament, (2) colour.
6 Dark uniform.
7 (1) Raised nearby, (2) closely related.
8 i.e. sunshine. In classical mythology Phoebus Apollo was the sun god.
9 'Cut ourselves'. Possibly an allusion to the stories of lovers who stab themselves and then write love letters in their blood.
10 Shakespeare's contemporaries associated red blood with courage and vitality.
11 Countenance.
12 Terrified.
13 Win your favour.

Bars me the right of voluntary choosing.
But if my father had not scanted[14] me,
And hedged me[15] by his wit to yield myself
His wife who wins me by that means I told you,
Yourself, renownèd Prince, then stood as fair   20
As any comer[16] I have looked on yet
For my affection.
MOROCCO   Even for that I thank you,
Therefore, I pray you, lead me to the caskets
To try my fortune. By this scimitar[17]
That slew the Sophy[18] and a Persian prince   25
That won three fields of Sultan Suleiman,[19]
I would o'erstare[20] the sternest eyes that look,
Outbrave the heart most daring on the earth,
Pluck the young sucking cubs from the she-bear,
Yea, mock the lion when a[21] roars for prey,   30
To win the lady.[22]

[*Flourish of cornets.*] *Exeunt.*

Act 2, Scene 7, lines 1–79

Belmont, Portia's house: the Prince of Morocco surveys the caskets and chooses the golden one, which contains a death's head and a scroll upon which is written a poem warning of the foolishness of being attracted by appearances alone. The Prince, disappointed and distressed, makes a swift departure, much to Portia's relief. Although the audience hears much of the casket test this is the first scene in which it is actually presented. Morocco's ostentatious language betrays the fact that he will choose the gold casket; and, in one sense, we want to interpret this as a generous gesture. After all, only gold seems good enough to house Portia's picture; and she is clearly a 'gem' in Morocco's estimation. However, that which 'many men desire' is not Portia but gold, i.e. money and personal gain. As the death's head and inscription on the scroll within the casket

14 Restricted.
15 Bound me by his wisdom.
16 (1) Has as good a chance as anyone who has come, (2) looked as fair (with a pun on fair skin) as anyone who has come.
17 Short, curved sword.
18 The Shah of Persia. Johnson comments that Shakespeare's sense of geography was erroneous here since Morocco would have had to travel 'far in order to kill the *Sophy* of Persia' (p. 67).
19 Suleiman the Great, leader of the Turks against the Persians in 1535.
20 Q2 reads 'outstare' (Mahood, p. 80).
21 Contraction for 'ha', i.e. 'he'.
22 The eighteenth-century editor, Nicholas Rowe, altered this to 'thee, lady', a reading that some modern editors prefer (Mahood, p. 81).

make clear, the person who chooses by outward appearance alone is as good as dead.

Of all of the aspects of the play that seemed to draw the attention of early critics, the casket lottery seemed to draw the most scorn. As Nicholas Rowe remarked, in 1709, it 'is a little too much remov'd from the Rules of Probability' (**p. 65**). However, more contemporary critics have been able to read the caskets within the commercial context of the play. For example, Karen Newman notes that the 'matter and mottoes of the caskets suggest commercial values, (**pp. 84–6**). Kim Hall complicates this reading by suggesting in her essay (**pp. 80–2**) that the economic and commercial worlds are so tied together that Morocco's bid for Portia's hand in marriage is viewed almost as 'foreign invasion'. She comments that Morocco

> frames his own courtship as colonial enterprise and religious pilgrimage when he chooses [a casket . . .] At the very moment in which he loses the game by making the wrong choice, Morocco raises the specter of a monetary and sexual exchange in England with the image of Portia as an angel in a golden bed [. . .] The sexual and the monetary anxieties of a Venetian state that is open to alien trade are displayed and dispelled in the casket plot, which allows Portia to avoid the threat of contact with others
>
> (**p. 82**).

Taking a different view, Joan Holmer remarks that Portia's objections to Morocco are not merely 'skin deep', and that Morocco's choice reveals his inner self. Morocco's choice demonstrates his 'superficially "golden mind"'. For Holmer, 'it is Morocco, not Portia, who cherishes outward show [. . .] his vanity regarding his own physical worthiness is clear from his celebration of his own courageous exploits' (**p. 89**).

Catherine Belsey points out the problem posed by the caskets' riddles: 'Riddles too are traditionally dangerous because they exploit the duplicity of the signifier, the secret alterity that subsists in meaning. They prevaricate, explicitly deferring and obscuring the truth. Riddles demonstrate that meaning is neither single nor transparent, that words can be used to conceal it' (**p. 91**).

[*Flourish of cornets.*] *Enter* PORTIA, *with* [*the Prince of*] MOROCCO *and both their trains.*

PORTIA   Go, draw aside the curtains and discover[1]

---

1   Reveal. There is little evidence for an actual 'discovery area' within the Elizabethan playhouse although some historians still accept the conventional wisdom that the central door between the stage and the tiring house (the area directly behind the stage where the actors were 'attired' or dressed) would have led to this space. Most modern productions seize the opportunity to place the elaborately decorated caskets on stage in full view of the audience. For Zhang Qi-hong (1980, Chinese Youth Theatre), 'the lead casket was held in the wooing scenes by a simply dressed peasant girl first seen as a silent spectator on the Rialto' while the gold casket, 'in vulgar contrast, was borne by Levantine/oriental belly dancers' (Edelman, p. 157, n. 1–2).

The several[2] caskets to this noble prince.
[*The curtains are drawn and three caskets are revealed.*]
Now make your choice.
MOROCCO   This first of gold, who this inscription bears:
'Who chooseth me shall gain what many men desire.'[3]   5
The second, silver, which this promise carries:
'Who chooseth me shall get as much as he deserves.'
This third, dull lead, with warning all as blunt:[4]
'Who chooseth me must give and hazard[5] all he hath.'
[*To* PORTIA] How shall I know if I do choose the right?   10
PORTIA   The one of them contains my picture, Prince.
If you choose that, then I am yours withal.[6]
MOROCCO   Some god direct my judgement![7] Let me see;
I will survey th'inscriptions back again.[8]
What says this leaden casket?   15
'Who chooseth me must give and hazard all he hath.'
Must give – for what? for lead? Hazard for lead?
This casket threatens. Men that hazard all
Do it in hope of fair advantages.[9]
A golden mind stoops not to shows of dross.[10]   20
I'll then nor give nor[11] hazard aught for lead.[12]
What says the silver with her virgin hue?
'Who chooseth me shall get as much as he deserves.'
As much as he deserves! Pause there, Morocco,
And weigh thy value with an even[13] hand.   25
If thou beest rated[14] by thy estimation,[15]
Thou dost deserve enough; and yet 'enough'
May not extend so far as to the lady.
And yet to be afeard of my deserving
Were but a weak disabling[16] of myself.   30

---

2 Various.
3 In Otto Schenk's 1969 production (made for Austrian/West German TV), Morocco polished the
    top of the gold casket with his sleeve before reading its inscription (Edelman, p. 157, n. 5).
4 Plain (as dull as the lead is 'blunt', i.e. dull).
5 Venture, risk.
6 With the casket.
7 The following speech is the longest in the play, reflecting all of the ongoing debate in the play
    concerning love and commerce. Nevertheless, in production it has frequently been shortened, used
    as the vehicle for humour, or both (Edelman, p. 158, n. 13–60).
8 Reading backwards, in reverse.
9 Profitable returns.
10 Impure metal, i.e. worthless rubbish.
11 'Nor . . . nor': 'neither . . . nor'.
12 Joan Plowright, playing Portia in the 1970 Jonathan Miller production, 'smiled here, making clear
    that she knew which casket had her picture' (Edelman, p. 158, n. 21).
13 (1) Steady, (2) consistent.
14 (1) Evaluated, (2) assessed.
15 Your (own) estimation.
16 Disparagement.

As much as I deserve – why, that's the lady!
I do in birth deserve her, and in fortunes,
In graces, and in qualities of breeding;
But more than these, in love I do deserve.
What if I strayed no farther, but chose here?   35
Let's see once more this saying graved[17] in gold:
'Who chooseth me shall gain what many men desire'.
Why, that's the lady! All the world desires her:
From the four corners of the earth they come
To kiss this shrine, this mortal breathing saint.[18]   40
The Hyrcanian deserts[19] and the vasty[20] wilds
Of wide Arabia are as thoroughfares[21] now
For princes to come view fair Portia.
The wat'ry kingdom, whose ambitious head
Spits in the face of heaven,[22] is no bar   45
To stop the foreign spirits,[23] but they come
As o'er a brook to see fair Portia.
One of these three contains her heavenly picture.
Is't like that lead contains her? 'Twere damnation
To think so base a thought. It were too gross   50
To rib her cerecloth in the obscure grave.[24]
Or shall I think in silver she's immured,[25]
Being ten times undervalued to tried[26] gold?
O sinful thought! Never so rich a gem
Was set in worse than gold.[27] They have in England   55
A coin that bears the figure of an angel
Stamped in gold, but that's insculped upon;[28]
But here an angel in a golden bed
Lies all within. Deliver me the key.
Here do I choose, and thrive I as I may.   60

---

17 Engraved.
18 In the 1987 production directed by Bill Alexander, Morocco kissed Portia's hand and then started
    working his way up her arm. Deborah Findley (Portia in that production) has argued that the scene
    is about sexual politics more than racial politics. Portia's revulsion can be seen as a response to
    being treated as a sexual object (Bulman, p. 136).
19 Wilderness region south of the Caspian Sea.
20 Vast.
21 Highways (made busy by Portia's suitors).
22 The ocean whose waves rise up, throwing spray (spitting) at the heavens.
23 Suitors from abroad.
24 'It would be too stupid to enclose her cerecloth (a waxed cloth used for embalming) in the obscure
    grave.' Corpses of aristocratic persons were customarily described as being 'wrapped in lead'
    during this historical period.
25 Penned in.
26 'Of less value than tested ("tried") gold'. Gold was ten times more valuable than silver.
27 Rich jewels (as Portia) are never set in baser metal than gold.
28 Engraved. An 'angel' was a coin bearing St Michael's image.

PORTIA   There, take it, Prince [*hands him the key*]; and if my form[29]
          lie there,
                    Then I am yours.
                                      [MOROCCO *unlocks the golden casket.*]
MOROCCO   O hell! What have we here?
A carrion Death,[30] within whose empty eye
There is a written scroll. I'll read the writing.

[*Reads*]   'All that glisters[31] is not gold;   65
             Often have you heard that told.
             Many a man his life hath sold
             But my outside[32] to behold.
             Gilded tombs do worms infold.
             Had you been as wise as bold,   70
             Young in limbs, in judgement old,
             Your answer had not been inscrolled.[33]
             Fare you well; your suit is cold.'[34]

Cold indeed, and labour lost.
Then farewell heat, and welcome frost!   75
Portia, adieu. I have too grieved a heart
To take a tedious[35] leave. Thus losers part.
                                      Exit [MOROCCO *with his train*].
PORTIA   A gentle riddance. Draw the curtains, go.
Let all of his complexion[36] choose me so.[37]

                                      Exeunt. [*Flourish of cornets*].

In the intervening scenes (Act 2, Scene 2–Act 2, Scene 8), Lancelot Gobbo, the
disaffected servant of Shylock, complains that his master abuses him. He
debates humorously with himself about finding a different position. In a chance

---

29 Picture.
30 Death's head, i.e. skull.
31 Glitters.
32 i.e. my shining surface.
33 Had you been experienced you would not have given the answer written on this scroll.
34 Your hopes are dead. The poem has one rhyme which makes it sound playful, but also insulting.
   The final line is certainly dismissive.
35 Lengthy.
36 (1) Temperament, (2) colour. Portia's distaste is evident. Her comment touches both Morocco's
   appearance and his character.
37 It is difficult to tell how Shakespeare's original audience would have responded to Portia's final
   comment in this scene. However, as Edelman notes: 'today this couplet is a pointer to know how a
   production does or does not confront the question of racial and religious prejudice.' Edelman also
   reminds us that 'for much of the eighteenth and nineteenth centuries Morocco was not in the play
   at all' (Edelman, pp. 160–1, n. 78–9). Johnson comments on the textual issues surrounding the
   break at the end of this scene (pp. 67–8).

meeting with Bassanio, Lancelot offers to become his servant instead, and Bassanio employs him. Also, Gratiano asks Bassanio if he can accompany him to Belmont, and Bassanio agrees on the condition that Gratiano curb his indecorous behaviour. Finally, it is revealed that Jessica (Shylock's daughter) – who is also unhappy with her father – has fallen in love with Bassanio's Christian friend, Lorenzo, and plans to elope with him on the night of a masquerade,[1] disguised as a page. Shylock goes to dinner at Bassanio's house, unaware of the plot. Before he leaves home he warns his daughter to guard the house well. Despite these admonitions, however, Jessica departs with Lorenzo, taking much of Shylock's money and other valuable possessions with her. Solanio and Salarino report that when Shylock discovers that his daughter and his possessions are missing he becomes wild with rage, shouting "My daughter! O my ducats!" They also report that there is a rumour circulating that one of Antonio's ships has been lost at sea.

Act 2, Scene 9, lines 30–83

Belmont, Portia's house: The Prince of Arragon, Portia's second suitor, arrives. He is generally cast as a foolish old man (another 'foreigner with a peculiar accent') and, as such, his quest for Portia (a young, rich heiress) would have been laughable to Shakespeare's audience. Additionally, it is no mere coincidence that the name 'Arragon' resembles the word 'arrogant'. Thinking that he 'deserves' Portia, Arragon chooses the silver casket and opens it to find a 'blinking idiot' (a mirror image of himself). The accompanying verses remind the prince that he is a vain man – silvered over, like the casket – and that his quest for the silver casket (symbolic of Portia and her estate) is all in vain.

Traditionally, many critics have passed over Arragon since he seems to be simply a further example of an unsuccessful suitor. However, Kim Hall notes that, as a Spaniard (dark skinned and foreign), Arragon is one of the train of suitors that was meant to raise fears of 'miscegenation' (racial and social intermarriage) for Shakespeare's audiences (see headnotes to Act 2, Scenes 1 and 7, and **pp. 80–2**). Joan Holmer states that 'Arragon's preoccupation with what "he deserves" looks inward to self-estimation [. . .] His [choice], like Morocco's, is a literal, not a spiritual, interpretation. Although he sounds clever, his arrogance hoodwinks any true self-knowledge [. . .] Thus, both Morocco and Arragon fail because they are worldly men who literally interpret the metals and mottos of the casket they select' **(p. 89)**. Interestingly, for Lynda E. Boose the appearance of Arragon marks a significant turning point for the

---

1   For the cultural significance of masquing and the masquerade within the Venetian setting, see Doran, **(pp. 126–7)**.

audience because it is here that a pattern begins to emerge. She reminds us that the audience is implicated in both the choices of Morocco and Arragon. The anxiety and unease raised by the play – which are never fully resolved – remind the audience that we are suitors like Morocco who choose 'what many men desire' (pp. 86–8).

At Arragon's departure a messenger announces that an envoy for a third suitor has arrived. Nerissa and Portia hope that it will prove to be Bassanio.

[*Enter* PORTIA *and the Duke of* ARRAGON *with his train.*]

ARRAGON   I will not choose what many men desire,   30
    Because I will not jump with[1] common spirits
    And rank me[2] with the barbarous multitudes.
    Why then, to thee, thou silver treasure-house;
    Tell me once more what title thou dost bear.[3]
    'Who chooseth me shall get as much as he deserves.'   35
    And well said too; for who shall go about
    To cozen[4] fortune, and be honourable
    Without the stamp of merit? Let none presume
    To wear an undeservèd dignity.
    O, that estates, degrees, and offices[5]   40
    Were not derived corruptly, and that clear honour
    Were purchased by the merit of the wearer![6]
    How many then should cover[7] that stand bare![8]
    How many be commanded that command!
    How much low peasantry would then be gleaned[9]   45
    From the true seed of honour! And how much honour
    Picked from the chaff and ruin of the times
    To be new varnished! Well, but to my choice.
    'Who chooseth me shall get as much as he deserves.'
    I will assume desert. Give me a key for this,   50
    And instantly unlock my fortunes here.

[*He opens the silver casket.*]

---

1   (1) Go along with, (2) identify with.
2   Join.
3   In the 1970 Jonathan Miller production, Arragon took a cup of tea from Portia here, added many lumps of sugar to it during the subsequent lines, then handed it back again without having drunk any of the tea (Edelman, p. 168, n. 34–48).
4   Cheat.
5   'Estates' (often used to signify positions in the social hierarchy, but probably 'lands' in this case); 'degrees' ('social positions'); 'offices' ('appointments to prestigious positions').
6   Holder of titles.
7   Keep their hat on.
8   Remove their hats (as a sign of respect).
9   Separated (and thrown away) i.e. as chaff from seed.

PORTIA   Too long a pause for that which you find there.[10]
ARRAGON   What's here?[11] The portrait of a blinking[12] idiot
Presenting me a schedule.[13] I will read it.
How much unlike art thou[14] to Portia!   55
How much unlike my hopes and my deservings!
'Who chooseth me shall have as much as he deserves.'
Did I deserve no more than a fool's head?
Is that my prize? Are my deserts no better?
PORTIA   To offend and judge are distinct offices   60
And of opposèd natures.
ARRAGON   What is here?
[He reads.]   'The fire seven times tried this;[15]
                    Seven times tried that judgement is
                    That did never choose amiss.
                    Some there be that shadows kiss;[16]   65
                    Such have but a shadow's bliss.[17]
                    There be fools alive, iwis,[18]
                    Silvered o'er,[19] and so was this.
                    Take what wife you will to bed,[20]
                    I will ever be your head.[21]   70
                    So be gone: you are sped.'[22]
Still more fool I shall appear
By the time I linger here.
With one fool's head I came to woo,
But I go away with two.   75
Sweet, adieu. I'll keep my oath,
Patiently to bear my wroth.[23]
                    [Flourish of cornets. Exeunt ARRAGON and his train.]
PORTIA   Thus hath the candle singed the moth.

---

10 Arragon is speechless. He pauses, silent, as he realises that something has gone wrong.
11 In Jonathan Miller's production (1970), Arragon realised that the 'blinking idiot's portrait' was a
    mirror in which Arragon saw himself. Other directors have used a mirror to similar effect, although
    others have called for the 'jack-in-the-box fool's head' (Edelman, p. 169, n. 53).
12 i.e. with rolling eyes.
13 Scroll.
14 The picture of the idiot.
15 Tried this: 'tested the silver casket.'
16 Embrace illusions.
17 The appearance of happiness.
18 Indeed.
19 Covered in silver (which hides the folly).
20 Johnson comments on the inconsistency in the penalties meted out to Morocco and Arragon
    (p. 68).
21 i.e. 'you will ever be an idiot'.
22 Done for. The final line – like the poem in the gold casket – is dismissive. The poetry on this scroll,
    however, is nastier in tone. Consequently, Arragon's departure is swift and bitter.
23 In Q1 the word is 'wroath', i.e. either 'wrath' ('anger') or 'ruth' ('sorrow') (Mahood, p. 106).
    Edelman notes that in some productions Portia makes fun of 'Arragon's *español* "wroth" by
    mispronouncing "moth" in the next line' (p. 170, n. 76–7).

O, these deliberate[24] fools! When they do choose,
They have the wisdom by their wit to lose.[25]   80
NERISSA   The ancient saying is no heresy,[26]
'Hanging and wiving[27] goes by destiny.'
PORTIA   Come draw the curtain, Nerissa. [. . .][28]

[*Exeunt.*]

Act 3, Scene 1, lines 40–103

A street in Venice: Salarino and Solanio, gossiping again, discuss a rumour that
another of Antonio's ships has been lost at sea. Shylock enters, distraught that
his daughter, Jessica, has eloped with Lorenzo, a Christian friend of Bassanio and
Gratiano, and has taken all of his money and jewels. In the first part of the scene,
as it is reproduced below, Shylock states that he intends to demand the pound
of flesh from Antonio if the merchant cannot meet the terms of the bond. A
messenger calls Salarino and Solanio away. Then Tubal – a friend of Shylock and
a moneylender – reveals that Antonio has lost a third ship, which will ruin him.
Shylock plans immediate legal action to ensure that he can collect his pound of
flesh.

During Act 3, Scene 2 Shylock's hatred of Antonio increases, and the audience begins to fear for Antonio as they witness, for perhaps the first time, the
full intensity of Shylock's animosity. Quite predictably, perhaps, there is widespread disagreement amongst commentators as to whether Shylock's vengeance is justified or not. Writing a guide for playgoers in 1772, John Potter
declared that Shylock is the representation of 'human Nature in her most
degenerated State'. For Potter, Shylock was the 'Hero of Villainy and Barbarity'
who could only be tolerated because it was doubtful that the character 'ever
had an Original', (**p. 70**). In 1817, however, William Hazlitt took a more
sympathetic view. For Hazlitt Shylock was 'a man no less sinned against than
sinning'. 'He becomes a half-favourite with the philosophical part of the audience, who are disposed to think that Jewish revenge is at least as good as
Christian injuries [. . .] If he carries his revenge too far, yet he has strong
grounds for "the lodged hatred he bears Antonio" [. . .] There is a strong, quick
and deep sense of justice mixed up with the gall and bitterness of his resentment' (**p. 74**).

24 Reasoning.
25 'They are just wise enough to make the wrong choice, and lose.'
26 Falsehood.
27 Marrying.
28 In Jonathan Miller's production (1970), the butler 'stared down at the leaden casket as the scene
    ended . . . reinforcing not very subtly that everyone knew which was the right casket' (Edelman,
    p. 171, n. 100).

Modern critics are equally divided on this issue, and Shylock's long speech beginning at line 46 ('Hath not a Jew eyes?') is one that remains a stumbling block for both critics and performers; and some actors, such as David Suchet, claim that they never really found the right way to deliver the speech. In terms of its content Shylock's speech is both a moving disclosure of his pain and a frightening indictment of the revenge that drives him to seek Antonio's flesh. The usual effect in the theatre is to evoke sympathy from the audience. And clearly Shylock has learned from the Christian community: 'The villainy you teach me I will execute.' Yet following this scene Shylock is cast in an increasingly unattractive manner. The audience sees him again briefly in Act 3, Scene 3, as he upbraids Antonio ('the fool who lent out money gratis'), who is being arrested by a jailer and taken away to prison for having defaulted on the bond. The next time that Shylock appears is at the trial scene – Act 4, Scene 1 – when he comes in order to claim his pound of flesh.

Act 3, Scene 1 is significant also because it is here that the audience witnesses Shylock interacting with Tubal, another representative of the Jewish community in Venice where Shakespeare portrays the Jewish community as being small. Although Tubal and Shylock appear to be friends (Shylock has hired Tubal to trace his daughter's whereabouts), Tubal, in fact, inflames Shylock's bitterness and revenge.

[*Enter* SHYLOCK, SOLANIO, *and* SALARINO.]

SALARINO   Why, I am sure, if he forfeit, thou wilt not take his flesh.   40
What's that good for?

SHYLOCK   To bait fish withal. If it will feed nothing else, it will feed my revenge. He hath disgraced me, and hindered me[1] half a million; laughed at my losses, mocked at my gains, scorned my nation, thwarted my bargains,[2] cooled my friends, heated mine enemies. And   45 what's his reason? I am a Jew. Hath not a Jew eyes? Hath not a Jew hands, organs, dimensions, senses, affections, passions; fed with the same food, hurt with the same weapons, subject to the same diseases, healed by the same means, warmed and cooled by the same winter and summer as a Christian is? If you prick us, do we not bleed? If you   50 tickle us, do we not laugh? If you poison us, do we not die? And if you wrong us, shall we not revenge? If we are like you in the rest, we will resemble you in that. If a Jew wrong a Christian, what is his humility?[3] Revenge. If a Christian wrong a Jew, what should his sufferance[4] be by Christian example? Why, revenge. The villany you teach me I   55

1   Prevented me.
2   Business deals.
3   i.e. the Christian's kindness.
4   i.e. his (the Jew's) forbearance.

will execute, and it shall go hard but I will better the instruction.

Enter a [SERVING]MAN *from* ANTONIO.

SERVINGMAN   Gentlemen, my master Antonio is at his house, and desires to speak with you both.

SALARINO   We have been up and down to seek him.   60

Enter TUBAL.[5]

SOLANIO   Here comes another of the tribe; a third cannot be matched, unless the devil himself turn Jew.

Exeunt [SALARINO *and* SOLANIO *with the* SERVINGMAN].[6]

SHYLOCK   How now, Tubal! What news from Genoa? Hast thou found my daughter?[7]

TUBAL   I often came where I did hear of her, but cannot find her.[8]   65

SHYLOCK   Why, there, there, there, there! A diamond gone, cost me two thousand ducats in Frankfurt. The curse never fell upon our nation till now; I never felt it till now. Two thousand ducats in that and other precious, precious jewels. I would my daughter were dead at my foot and the jewels in her ear! Would she were hearsed[9] at my   70 foot and the ducats in her coffin! No news of them?

[TUBAL *signs 'No'.*]

Why, so. And I know not what's spent in the search.[10] Why, thou – loss upon loss! The thief gone with so much, and so much to find the thief, and no satisfaction, no revenge, nor no ill luck stirring but what lights o'[11] my shoulders, no sighs but o' my breathing,[12] no tears but o'   75 my shedding!

TUBAL   Yes, other men have ill luck too. Antonio, as I heard in Genoa –

SHYLOCK   What, what, what? Ill luck, ill luck?

TUBAL   – hath an argosy[13] cast away,[14] coming from Tripolis.   80

SHYLOCK   I thank God, I thank God. Is it true, is it true?

TUBAL   I spoke with some of the sailors that escaped the wreck.

SHYLOCK   I thank thee, good Tubal. Good news, good news! Ha, ha! Heard in Genoa?

TUBAL   Your daughter spent in Genoa, as I heard, one night four   85 score[15] ducats.

---

5   In Greg Doran's production (1997), Salarino and Solanio spat on Tubal when he entered (Edelman, p. 178, n. 61–2).
6   Q1 reads 'Exeunt Gentlemen' (Mahood, p. 110).
7   From this comment it is clear that some time has passed since Jessica's departure.
8   Tubal's comment that Jessica was much spoken of suggests that she and Lorenzo are spending Shylock's money at a furious rate.
9   Placed in her coffin.
10 Here Tubal shows Shylock the bill.
11 Lands on.
12 i.e. 'Except the sighs that I breathe'.
13 Large merchant ship.
14 Wrecked.
15 Eighty. (A 'score' was a set of twenty.)

SHYLOCK   Thou stick'st a dagger in me. I shall never see my gold again. Four score ducats at a sitting! Four score ducats!

TUBAL   There came divers[16] of Antonio's creditors in my company[17] to Venice that swear he cannot choose but break.[18]   90

SHYLOCK   I am very glad of it. I'll plague him, I'll torture him. I am glad of it.

TUBAL   One of them showed me a ring that he had of your daughter for a monkey.

SHYLOCK   Out upon her![19] Thou torturest me, Tubal. It was my   95 turquoise. I had it of Leah[20] when I was a bachelor. I would not have given it for a wilderness of monkeys.

TUBAL   But Antonio is certainly undone.[21]

SHYLOCK   Nay, that's true, that's very true. Go, Tubal, fee me an officer.[22] Bespeak[23] him a fortnight[24] before. I will have the heart of   100 him if he forfeit, for were he out of Venice I can make what merchandise[25] I will. Go, Tubal, and meet me at our synagogue. Go, good Tubal; at our synagogue, Tubal.

Exeunt.[26]

Act 3, Scene 2, lines 40–214

Belmont, Portia's house: in a very different manner from how she has acted previously, Portia urges Bassanio to take his time in making a selection amongst the caskets, but Bassanio presses on and chooses (correctly) the lead casket, which contains Portia's picture. His friend, Gratiano, announces that he and Nerissa have likewise decided to wed. However, their mutual joy is interrupted by a letter from Antonio stating that he expects economic ruin and asking to meet with Bassanio before he must pay the forfeit of the bond. Portia offers to

16 Several.
17 Along with me.
18 Become bankrupt.
19 'Damn her!'
20 Shylock's wife (deceased before the opening of the play). This is a significant moment for any Shylock. In just two lines the passage alters the audience's sense of the character, reminding them that he once was a young man (a bachelor) with all of the optimism and innocence of youth, and that by this time in the play all of that has disappeared.
21 Ruined.
22 Hire (for me) a sheriff's officer, i.e. an arresting officer.
23 Arrange for.
24 Two weeks.
25 Bargains.
26 Many modern productions end with Shylock alone on stage. In Bill Alexander's 1987 production, Shylock (played by Antony Sher) sat in the corner of the stage, prayed in Hebrew, and rocked back and forth, 'muttering obsessively of revenge as the house lights went up' (Edelman, p. 184).

repay the loan several times over and counsels Bassanio to go to Antonio as soon as they have been married. Act 3, Scene 2, which celebrates the lovers, stands in stark contrast to the former scene exposing Shylock's hatred. It is full of music and optimism, but the song at lines 63–72 ('Tell me where is fancy bred') also warns of the dangers of choosing on the basis of appearance or other superficial criteria.

Bassanio's willingness to 'risk' his new-found love, marriage and mastership of Belmont – in order to rescue Antonio – shows his loyalty to the friend through whose generosity he was able to 'venture' for Portia in the first place. Joan Holmer comments upon this view when she writes: 'Motivated by true love that seeks to give and risk, not gain and get, that is bred in the heart or head, Bassanio avoids the straits of "eye" and "I" that proved such guilèd shores for Morocco and Arragon [. . .] Bassanio's spiritual understanding is properly based on the higher rational faculty, whose function is *sapientia* or wisdom.' Quoting the English poet John Milton she states: ' "true Love" is "judicious"' (**p. 90**). Catherine Belsey concurs: 'Bassanio is able to solve the riddle of the caskets not only because he sees through outward show, but also because he alone among the suitors recognizes the appropriate emblem of desire' (**p. 90**). However, Lynda E. Boose suggests that the dramatist had a 'comic contract' with the audience, which raised certain expectations that then had to be ful- filled at the end of the play. Most notable was the 'marriage contract' that marks the end of many of Shakespeare's romantic comedies. Thus, Jack shall have Jill. But Boose notes that this dramatic device not only 'fulfills the generic obliga- tions of comic form', the marriage of Portia and Bassanio 're-presents the ultimate wedding between the play and audience' so that the dramatic contract between playwright and audience is fulfilled (**p. 86**). The marriage between Portia and Bassanio brings with it the audience's approval, which later invites them to support Antonio (and his friend Bassanio) and, in turn, helps to distance them eventually from Shylock. Hence, the marriage takes place in the middle of the play instead of at the end, when it was frequently performed or promised. In this way, there are many 'bonds' in the play, aside from that which has been entered into by Shylock and Antonio.

Sinead Cusack describes the staging problems that the actors encountered in the 1981 production in which she performed the role of Portia. Portia was 'isolated centre-stage, under a spotlight, from the moment when she bids "Ner- issa and the rest stand all aloof." Bassanio was to circle about her in the shadows throughout her speech, likening him to Hercules and herself to "the tribute paid by howling Troy to the sea monster".' [lines 55–60] (**pp. 120–1**).

Enter BASSANIO, PORTIA, GRATIANO, [NERISSA] *and all their trains.*[1] [*The three caskets are on stage.*]

---

1   'All their trains' suggests that Portia and Bassanio are trying to impress each other.

PORTIA   Away, then! I am locked in one of them;   40
If you do love me, you will find me out.
Nerissa and the rest, stand all aloof.[2]
Let music sound while he doth make his choice;
Then if he lose he makes a swan-like end,[3]
Fading in music. That the comparison   45
May stand more proper, my eye shall be the stream
And watery deathbed for him. He may win,
What is music then? Then music is
Even as the flourish[4] when true subjects bow
To a new-crownèd monarch. Such it is   50
As are those dulcet sounds in break of day,
That creep into the dreaming bridegroom's ear
And summon him to marriage. Now he goes
With no less presence, but with much more love,
Than young Alcides[5] when he did redeem   55
The virgin tribute paid by howling Troy
To the sea monster. I stand for sacrifice.
The rest aloof are the Dardanian wives,[6]
With blearèd[7] visages come forth to view
The issue[8] of th'exploit. Go, Hercules!   60
Live thou, I live. With much much more dismay
I view the fight than thou that mak'st the fray.
[*Music begins.*] *A song the whilst* BASSANIO *comments on the caskets*
    to himself.
    Tell me where is fancy[9] bred,
    Or in the heart, or[10] in the head?
    How begot, how nourishèd?   65
        Reply, reply.[11]
    It is engendered in the eyes,[12]
    With gazing fed; and fancy dies
    In the cradle where it lies.[13]
        Let us all ring fancy's knell:[14]   70
    I'll begin it: Ding, dong, bell.

---

2 Out of the way.
3 Portia alludes to the ancient myth that the (mute) swan sings just before death.
4 Sounding of trumpets.
5 Alcides (Hercules) rescued Hesione, the daughter of the Trojan king, from sacrifice to a sea
   monster.
6 Trojan women.
7 Tear-stained.
8 Outcome.
9 Attraction.
10 'Or [. . .] or': 'either [. . .] or'.
11 Johnson questions whether this is a stage direction or a verse in the song (p. 68).
12 Q1 reads 'eye'; however, most editors alter this to 'eyes' (Mahood, p. 116).
13 Attraction grows stronger with gazing, but it has a short life.
14 Funeral bell.

ALL   Ding, dong, bell.[15]

BASSANIO   So may the outward shows be least themselves.[16]
    The world is still deceived with ornament.
    In law, what plea so tainted and corrupt   75
    But, being seasoned with a gracious voice,
    Obscures the show of evil? In religion,
    What damnèd error but some sober brow
    Will bless it and approve it with a text,
    Hiding the grossness with fair ornament?   80
    There is no vice so simple but assumes
    Some mark of virtue on his outward parts.[17]
    How many cowards, whose hearts are all as false
    As stairs of sand,[18] wear yet upon their chins
    The beards of Hercules and frowning Mars,[19]   85
    Who inward searched have livers white as milk?[20]
    And these assume but valour's excrement[21]
    To render them redoubted.[22] Look on beauty
    And you shall see 'tis purchased by the weight,
    Which therein works a miracle in nature,   90
    Making them lightest that wear most of it.[23]
    So are those crispèd,[24] snaky, golden locks
    Which maketh such wanton gambols with the wind
    Upon supposèd fairness, often known
    To be the dowry[25] of a second head,   95
    The skull that bred them in the sepulchre.
    Thus ornament is but the guilèd[26] shore
    To a most dangerous sea, the beauteous scarf
    Veiling an Indian[27] beauty; in a word,

---

15 From early texts (Q1 and F1) it is unclear who sings the first nine lines of the song; however, editors commonly ascribe it to a member of Portia's train. The last line (ascribed to 'All' in Q1) indicates that it was probably sung by a larger group of those on stage (see Mahood, p. 116, for textual specifics).

16 Not what they appear to be.

17 'No vice-ridden person is foolish enough as to not show some virtue outwardly'.

18 Q1 reads 'stayers', although most editors modernise this to 'stairs' because this is what is heard in oral delivery in the theatre. However, M. M. Mahood has suggested that the original spelling might have referred to 'stays' or ropes, as one finds in the rigging of a ship. Hence, she writes: 'a coward's support is unreliable, like an untrustworthy "stay" or rope in the rigging of a ship' (Mahood, p. 116, n. 84).

19 Hercules was the Superman of classical mythology; Mars was the god of war.

20 The Elizabethans thought that a courageous man had a liver rich with blood. A coward's liver was thought to be white.

21 Outgrowth of hair, i.e. beards.

22 Make them seem feared.

23 'Make-up [which produces "beauty"] is purchased by the ounce. It works miracles in nature but makes those who wear the most of it loose ["light"] in morals'.

24 Curled.

25 Endowment.

26 Treacherous.

27 i.e. having a dark complexion.

The seeming truth which cunning times put on   100
To entrap the wisest. Therefore, thou gaudy gold,
Hard food for Midas,[28] I will none of thee.
[*To the silver casket*]
Nor none of thee, thou pale and common drudge
'Tween man and man. But thou, thou meager[29] lead,
Which rather threaten'st than dost promise aught,[30]   105
Thy paleness moves me more than eloquence,
And here choose I. Joy be the consequence!
PORTIA [*Aside*]   How all the other passions flee to air:
As doubtful thoughts, and rash-embraced despair,
And shudd'ring fear, and green-eyed jealousy.   110
O love, be moderate, allay thy ecstasy,
In measure rain thy joy, scant[31] this excess!
I feel too much thy blessing: make it less
For fear I surfeit.
[BASSANIO *opens the leaden casket*.]
BASSANIO   What find I here?
Fair Portia's counterfeit![32] What demi-god   115
Hath come so near creation? Move these eyes?
Or whether, riding on the balls of mine,
Seem they in motion? Here are severed[33] lips
Parted with a sugar breath. So sweet a bar
Should sunder such sweet friends.[34] Here in her hairs   120
The painter plays the spider and hath woven
A golden mesh t'entrap the hearts of men
Faster than gnats in cobwebs.[35] But her eyes –
How could he see to do them? Having made one,
Methinks it should have power to steal both his   125
And leave itself unfurnished.[36] Yet look how far
The substance of my praise doth wrong this shadow
In underprizing[37] it, so far this shadow
Doth limp behind the substance. Here's the scroll,
The continent and summary of my fortune.   130
[*Reads.*]

---

28 In classical mythology everything that Midas touched turned to gold. Consequently, it was difficult
    for him to eat.
29 (1) Poor, (2) unworthy.
30 Which makes threats (rather than promises).
31 Lessen.
32 Picture.
33 Parted.
34 'Such a sweet barrier [her breath] should separate such sweet friends ["lips"]'.
35 Like the spider (which entraps gnats in cobwebs), the painter has created hair, which is like a golden
    web to catch men's hearts.
36 Not provided with a match.
37 Not indicating its true worth.

'You that choose not by the view,
Chance as fair and choose as true.[38]
Since this fortune falls to you,
Be content and seek no new.
If you be well pleased with this,   135
And hold your fortune for your bliss,
Turn you where your lady is
And claim her with a loving kiss.'
A gentle scroll. Fair lady, by your leave,
I come by note,[39] to give and to receive.[40]   140
Like one of two contending in a prize
That thinks he hath done well in people's eyes,
Hearing applause and universal shout,
Giddy in spirit, still gazing in a doubt
Whether those peals of praise be his or no,   145
So, thrice-fair lady, stand I, even so,
As doubtful whether what I see be true
Until confirmed, signed, ratified by you.[41]
PORTIA   You see me, Lord Bassanio, where I stand,
Such as I am. Though for myself alone   150
I would not be ambitious in my wish
To wish myself much better, yet for you
I would be trebled twenty times myself,
A thousand times more fair, ten thousand times
More rich, that only to stand high in your account   155
I might in virtues, beauties, livings, friends
Exceed account. But the full sum of me
Is sum of something which, to term in gross,
Is an unlessoned girl, unschooled, unpractised;
Happy[42] in this, she is not yet so old   160
But she may learn; happier than this,
She is not bred so dull but she can learn;
Happiest of all is that her gentle spirit
Commits itself to yours to be directed,
As from her lord, her governor, her king.   165
Myself and what is mine to you and yours

---

38 'May you always enjoy good fortune ["chance"] and choose as well'.
39 According to Instructions (i.e. as told) in ll. 137–8.
40 According to early texts (Q1 and F1) it is not clear where (or if) Bassanio gets his kiss, although
   l. 138 would imply that he does indeed kiss Portia at some point. Some editors think that Bassanio
   kisses Portia after 'by your leave' (l. 139), or later, after she gives him a ring at l. 171 (Mahood,
   p. 119, for textual specifics).
41 Here Bassanio's legalistic language alludes to a contract or a treaty. Newman comments that 'the
   exchange of Portia [. . .] via the caskets to Bassanio' is related to his later request to borrow money
   in order to assist Antonio.
42 Fortunate.

Is now converted.[43] But now I was the lord
Of this fair mansion, master of my servants,
Queen o'er myself; and even now, but now,
This house, these servants, and this same myself   170
Are yours, my lord's. I give them with this ring,
Which when you part from, lose, or give away,
Let it presage the ruin of your love
And be my vantage[44] to exclaim on you.
BASSANIO   Madam, you have bereft me[45] of all words.   175
Only my blood speaks[46] to you in my veins,
And there is such confusion in my powers
As after some oration fairly spoke
By a belovèd prince, there doth appear
Among the buzzing pleasèd multitude,   180
Where every something being blent together[47]
Turns to a wild of nothing, save of joy,
Expressed and not expressed. But when this ring
Parts from this finger, then parts life from hence.
O, then be bold to say Bassanio's dead!   185
NERISSA   My lord and lady, it is now our time
That have stood by and seen our wishes prosper
To cry 'Good joy, good joy, my lord and lady!'
GRATIANO   My lord Bassanio and my gentle lady,
I wish you all the joy that you can wish,   190
For I am sure you can wish none from me.
And when your honours mean to solemnize
The bargain of your faith,[48] I do beseech you
Even at that time I may be married too.
BASSANIO   With all my heart, so thou canst get a wife.   195
GRATIANO   I thank your lordship, you have got me one.
My eyes, my lord, can look as swift as yours.
You saw the mistress, I beheld the maid.
You loved, I loved; for intermission[49]
No more pertains to me, my lord, than you.   200
Your fortune stood upon the caskets there,
And so did mine too, as the matter falls;
For wooing here until I sweat again,
And swearing till my very roof was dry
With oaths of love, at last – if promise last – [50]   205

---

43 'I, and all I possess, are now yours'.
44 Opportunity.
45 Stolen (from me).
46 'I am blushing'.
47 Mixed up.
48 Contract (for your love).
49 Wasting time.
50 If she (Nerissa) keeps her promise.

I got a promise of this fair one here
To have her love, provided that your fortune
Achieved her mistress.
PORTIA   Is this true, Nerissa?
NERISSA Madam, it is, so you stand pleased withal.
BASSANIO And do you, Gratiano, mean good faith?   210
GRATIANO Yes, 'faith, my lord.
BASSANIO Our feast shall be much honoured in your marriage.
GRATIANO [*To* NERISSA] We'll play with them the first boy for a
    thousand ducats.[51] [. . .]

[*Exeunt.*]

In Act 3, Scenes 3 and 4 Antonio and the jailer speak with Shylock in the hope
that he will be merciful, but Shylock is steadfast in his intentions. Antonio is
convinced that the judge cannot disallow the forfeit because it would compromise the reputation of Venice with the foreign merchants. He is resigned to pay
the forfeit the next day. In the meantime Portia leaves her estate in the care of
Lorenzo and Jessica while she supposedly retires to a holy place to pray. Yet, in
actuality, she sends a message to her cousin, Doctor Bellario of Padua, and tells
Nerissa that they will meet their husbands in Venice disguised as a doctor of law
and his clerk.

   In Act 3, Scene 5 Lancelot jokes with Jessica and Lorenzo. Jessica refers to
Lorenzo as 'my husband' (proof that they have married) and demonstrates a
new-found confidence. It is also revealed that Lorenzo has been in search of
Lancelot who has impregnated one of Portia's servants. Predictably, Lorenzo is
critical of Lancelot for this. The scene gives Portia and Nerissa time to get to
Belmont, while the witty interchange between Lorenzo and Lancelot demonstrates that criticism is best accepted for what it is. Any attempt to deny it or
squelch it simply incites the critic more.

Act 4, Scene 1, lines 169–396

A courtroom in Venice: Portia and Nerissa, disguised as a lawyer and his clerk,
journey to Venice to defend Antonio against Shylock in court. Shylock's murderous intentions become clear when he refuses thrice the amount of the loan;
he also refuses to pay for a surgeon to minister to Antonio lest he bleed to
death during the cutting out of the pound of flesh. In an incisive moment Portia

---

51 'We'll bet with them: whoever produces the first son wins a thousand ducats'.

(acting in the guise of Balthazar) decides that Shylock can legally take his pound of flesh, but that he must not shed a drop of blood in so doing. In the middle of the scene the tables are turned on Shylock who, deserving of only his bond, must confiscate his property for plotting the death of a Venetian citizen, and who stands also potentially to lose his life. Then, in an act of 'mercy', Antonio determines that Shylock shall lose only half of his wealth to the state, with the other half to pass to his daughter, Jessica, and her husband, Lorenzo. Additionally, Antonio decides that Shylock must convert to Christianity.

The courtroom scene brings together all of the moral, social and economic issues that run through the play. Although Shylock is offered three times the money that he loaned Antonio, he refuses it because, finally, revenge is not about money. Moreover, no amount of money can offset the amount of injustice and humiliation that he thinks he has suffered. In a moment of clever insight, Portia saves the day by finding a way to invalidate Shylock's bond, an act that saves Antonio's life, his friendship with Bassanio, and the spectators who are spared having to witness bloodshed. Generally speaking, the defeat of Shylock and his outrageous bond seems to be the right decision, one on which both Christians and Jews can agree; however, what follows this decision – the meting out of 'justice' and 'mercy' – exemplifies how difficult it is to find a punishment that is both 'just' and 'merciful'. Also, the damaging face of anti-Semitism, embedded in Gratiano's jeering remarks and the confident manner in which Antonio sentences his enemy, persists throughout the scene, so much so that it is often difficult for spectators to decide whether Shylock is treated justly.

In addition to being the longest scene in the play, Act 4, Scene 1 is one of the most complex. At the centre of the action is Portia, dressed as Doctor Balthazar, who has come to defend Antonio. Amongst the many critics who have written about Portia's performance, Harley Granville-Barker was enchanted with the role of Portia, proclaiming that she 'casts a spell' upon the Venetian court. Having been set free from her father's control through her marriage to Bassanio, in Act 3, Scene 2, he writes that she becomes 'a great lady in her perfect simplicity, in her ready tact [. . .] and in her quite unconscious self-sufficiency', traits which carry through the trial scene into the final moments of the play (pp. 76–8). However, Portia's role brings with it greater complexity and, with this, a diversity of views. Sinead Cusack, who performed the role in 1981, came to the conclusion that Portia 'doesn't go into the courtroom to save Antonio (that's easy) but to save Shylock, to redeem him – she is passionate to do that' (p. 121). Leonard Tennenhouse points out that it is, in some large measure, Portia's disguise that allows her to be effective in that setting. 'To enter and exit Venice,' he writes, 'women must disguise themselves as men' (p. 83). As Juan Luis Vives comments, in his treatise The Education of a Christen Woman (1529), it is a good thing to educate women, in order to make them virtuous; however, a woman must remain in her place (pp. 49–51). Therefore, Portia's learning can only be displayed while she is disguised as a doctor of law.

Extending this to a discussion of gender and power, Karen Newman notes that 'the *Merchant* interrogates the Elizabethan sex/gender system and resists the "traffic in women," because in early modern England a woman occupying the position of a Big Man, or a lawyer in a Renaissance Venetian courtroom, or the lord of Belmont, is not the same as a man doing so. For a woman, such behavior is a form of simulation, a confusion that elides the conventional poles of sexual preference by denaturalizing gender-code behaviors; such simulation perverts authorized systems of gender and power. It is inversion with a difference' (**pp. 85–6**). Catherine Belsey remarks, furthermore, that it is Portia's disguise that allows her to challenge not only the gender system, but the economic world of Venice, which is traditionally a male enclave: 'An apparently archetypal and yet vanishing order is radically challenged by cross-dressed women who travel from Belmont to Venice.' They intervene 'in the supremely masculine and political world of law, with the effect of challenging the economic arrangements of the commercial capital of the world' (**p. 91**).

Nevertheless, while some critics argue that Portia is central to the trial scene, others warn against becoming too drawn in by Portia's seemingly high-minded generosity. Lynda E. Boose, however, points out that 'Like Antonio, Portia builds her own moral credit on Shylock [. . .] Portia actually never spends or hazards an uninsured ducat of her own; she spends Shylock's money. The "quality of mercy" identity that theater audiences have traditionally ascribed to Portia is, I suggest, possible only because of Shylock, whose threat to Christian privilege and Christian potency, both fiscal and physical, acts in this play like a lightening rod to draw all Christian fears and aggressions. Thus when audiences recall Shylock, he is imaged with the knife in his hand' (**pp. 87–8**). This side of Shylock, discussed by James Shapiro, is tied to ritual murder and to Christian superstitions associated with Jews during the early modern period; but it is also the outgrowth of a conflict in which both Antonio and Shylock are trying, in some way, to 'transform' each other. Amongst other significant points Shapiro raises the association between the flesh-bond and religious ritual: 'For Shylock to take the knife to Antonio's privy members would be to threaten circumcision (and symbolically conversion) since it is a ritual whose complex function is to separate Jew from non-Jew, and Jewish men from Jewish women' (**pp. 93–4**).

If Portia's role in the trial scene is controversial so too is Shylock's. Of course, if Portia's actions are seen to be the model of generosity, Shylock's actions seem to be the very antithesis of this. Even after he is offered three times the sum that he loaned to Antonio, Shylock claims only that he will have the terms of the bond. In this way, Joan Holmer identifies Shylock as one of those who 'choose' in the course of the play. 'Like Morocco and Arragon,' she writes, 'who literally reject the leaden chest, Shylock symbolically rejects it because he considers the true wisdom of giving and hazarding mere foolishness, insisting rather on personal gain, whether of earthly treasure or flesh. Both Morocco and Arragon ironically err exactly where they think they excel, just as Shylock does when he is undone by the letter [of the law] and strict justice.' Thus, the choices of Morocco, Arragon and Shylock share an element of selfishness, that serve as 'foils' to Bassanio's **(p. 89)**.

Still, whether readers and spectators see Portia or Shylock (or a combination of both) as the centre of the scene, they must come to some decision regarding the punishment that Antonio metes out, a punishment which robs Shylock of his remaining wealth and of his identity through a forced conversion to Christianity. While some historians speculate that, for Shakespeare's audiences, the order for religious conversion was an attempt to save his soul, modern post-Holocaust audiences are often shocked and appalled by what seem to be drastic measures. Interestingly, John Drakakis observes that, in some sense, the conversion isn't really about Shylock and his Semitism at all, but about the Christian community's perception of itself. Because Shylock is engaged in usury, 'Venice can only admit him as a demonization of its own social and economic practices, and as an obstacle [. . .] to comic closure. Only when he is coerced fully into the life of Venice by being forced to become a Christian, does he become a reconstituted subject who can then play a full patriarchal role in its affairs, transferring his wealth legitimately to his heirs, and replenishing the coffers of the state' **(p. 92)**. Thus, for Drakakis, the 'obstructive father' is transformed, although ironically, following his conversion, Shylock will be open to suffering the same anxieties as Antonio. Just before he leaves the stage Shylock states that he is 'ill', a condition that parallels Antonio's inexplicable melancholy in the first scene of the play **(p. 93)**.

Looking at the interaction between Antonio and Shylock through a different lens, Alan Sinfield comments that Shylock's punishments have to do with a culture that 'sorts out who is to control property and other human relations. Portia, Jessica and Launcelot[1] are bound as daughters and sons; Morocco and Arragon as suitors; Antonio and Bassanio as friends; Gratiano as friend or dependant; Nerissa as dependant or servant [. . .] Antonio, Shylock and even the Duke are bound by the law; and the Venetians, Shylock rather effectively remarks,[2] have no intention of freeing their slaves' **(p. 95)**.

Enter the DUKE, *the Magnificoes,*[3] ANTONIO, BASSANIO, *and* GRATIANO;
[officers and attendants of the court].
Enter [three or four with] PORTIA *[disguised as Balthazar, a Doctor of Laws].*

PORTIA   I am informèd throughly[4] of the cause.

1   Shylock's servant who abandons his master and joins Bassanio's retinue.
2   The reference is to Act 4, Scene 1, lines 90–8 in the full-text edition, a passage in which Shylock reminds the Venetian court that many citizens own slaves and will not free them, but instead will answer: 'The slaves are ours.' Similarly, Shylock argues, 'The pound of flesh which I demand of him/Is dearly bought; 'tis mine, and I will have it' (lines 99–100).
3   Dignitaries.
4   Thoroughly.

Which is the merchant here, and which the Jew?[5]   170
DUKE   Antonio and old Shylock, both stand forth.
PORTIA   Is your name Shylock?
SHYLOCK   Shylock is my name.
PORTIA   Of a strange nature is the suit you follow,
    Yet in such rule[6] that the Venetian law
    Cannot impugn you as you do proceed.
[To ANTONIO]   You stand within his danger, do you not?   175
ANTONIO   Ay, so he says.
PORTIA   Do you confess the bond?
ANTONIO   I do.
PORTIA   Then must the Jew be merciful.
SHYLOCK   On what compulsion must I? Tell me that.[7]
PORTIA   The quality of mercy is not strained.[8]   180
    It droppeth as the gentle rain from heaven
    Upon the place beneath. It is twice blest:
    It blesseth him that gives and him that takes.
    'Tis mightiest in the mightiest. It becomes
    The thronèd monarch better than his crown.   185
    His sceptre shows the force of temporal power,
    The attribute to awe and majesty,
    Wherein doth sit the dread and fear of kings;
    But mercy is above this sceptred sway.[9]
    It is enthronèd in the hearts of kings,   190
    It is an attribute to God himself,
    And earthly power doth then show likest God's
    When mercy seasons[10] justice. Therefore, Jew,
    Though justice be thy plea, consider this:
    That in the course of justice none of us   195
    Should see salvation.[11] We do pray for mercy,
    And that same prayer doth teach us all to render
    The deeds of mercy. I have spoke thus much
    To mitigate[12] the justice of thy plea,
    Which if thou follow, this strict court of Venice   200

---

5 Metaphorically speaking, there are many 'merchants' in the play, i.e. characters who risk for
   personal gain. This is emphasised by Portia's question.
6 Correct order.
7 In her review of the 1998 Globe production, Lois Potter noted that Shylock (Norbert Kentrup)
   spoke 'like a teacher politely pointing out a pupil's failure in logic' ('Shakespeare Performed', SQ,
   50 (1999), pp. 74–6 (quote from p. 76).
8 Cannot be forced, i.e. constrained. Also, 'strained', i.e. 'filtered, squeezed out'. John Barton, who
   has directed Merchant twice, described this speech as a 'spontaneous outburst triggered by Shylock's aggression to her in the court' (Gilbert, p. 125).
9 The temporal power of kings.
10 Moderates.
11 'Sin is so common that if all people received appropriate justice none should be treated with mercy'.
12 Lessen.

Must needs[13] give sentence 'gainst the merchant there.

SHYLOCK   My deeds upon my head![14] I crave the law,
The penalty and forfeit of my bond.[15]

PORTIA   Is he not able to discharge[16] the money?

BASSANIO   Yes, here I tender it for him in the court,   205
Yea, twice the sum. If that will not suffice,
I will be bound to pay it ten times o'er
On forfeit of my hands, my head, my heart.
If this will not suffice, it must appear
That malice bears down[17] truth. And, I beseech you,   210
Wrest once[18] the law to your authority.
To do a great right, do a little wrong,
And curb this cruel devil of his will.

PORTIA   It must not be. There is no power in Venice
Can alter a decree establishèd.   215
'Twill be recorded for a precedent,
And many an error by the same example
Will rush into the state. It cannot be.

SHYLOCK   A Daniel come to judgement, yea, a Daniel![19]
O wise young judge, how I do honour thee!   220

PORTIA   I pray you, let me look upon the bond.

SHYLOCK   Here 'tis, most reverend doctor, here it is.

PORTIA   Shylock, there's thrice thy money offered thee.[20]

SHYLOCK   An oath, an oath! I have an oath in heaven!
Shall I lay perjury upon my soul?   225
No, not for Venice.

PORTIA   Why, this bond is forfeit.
And lawfully by this the Jew may claim
A pound of flesh, to be by him cut off
Nearest the merchant's heart. [*To* SHYLOCK] Be merciful.
Take thrice thy money. Bid me tear the bond.   230

SHYLOCK   When it is paid according to the tenour.[21]
It doth appear you are a worthy judge;
You know the law, your exposition
Hath been most sound. I charge you by the law

---

13 Is compelled.
14 'I will be responsible for what I am doing'.
15 In some stage productions Shylock enters the scene with his scales (in order to measure out a pound of Antonio's flesh), a knife and a whetstone. Some actors – for example, Antony Sher in the 1987 RSC production at Stratford-upon-Avon – begin to sharpen the knife at this point in the scene, which creates a most unnerving sound (Bulman, pp. 129–31).
16 Repay.
17 Overwhelms.
18 Twist, for once (on this occasion).
19 Daniel was the Biblical hero who secured justice for Susannah (Apocrypha, Susannah, 42–64).
20 Henry Goodman (Shylock, 1999) tore up the cheque that Bassanio handed to him (Edelman, p. 226, n. 223).
21 The bond's wording.

Whereof you are a well-deserving pillar,   235
Proceed to judgement. By my soul I swear
There is no power in the tongue of man
To alter me. I stay here on my bond.
ANTONIO   Most heartily I do beseech the court
To give the judgement.
PORTIA   Why then, thus it is: 240
You must prepare your bosom for his knife.
SHYLOCK   O noble judge! O excellent young man!
PORTIA   For the intent and purpose of the law
Hath full relation[22] to the penalty
Which here appeareth due upon the bond.   245
SHYLOCK   'Tis very true. O wise and upright judge!
How much more elder art thou than thy looks!
PORTIA [To ANTONIO]   Therefore lay bare your bosom.
SHYLOCK   Ay, his breast.
So says the bond; doth it not, noble judge?
'Nearest his heart' – those are the very words.   250
PORTIA   It is so. Are there balance here to weigh
The flesh?[23]
SHYLOCK   I have them ready.
PORTIA   Have by some surgeon, Shylock, on your charge[24]
To stop his wounds, lest he do bleed to death.
SHYLOCK   Is it so nominated in the bond?   255
PORTIA   It is not so expressed, but what of that?
'Twere good for you do so much for charity.[25]
SHYLOCK   I cannot find it; 'tis not in the bond.[26]
PORTIA   You, merchant, have you anything to say?
ANTONIO   But little. I am armed[27] and well prepared.   260
Give me your hand, Bassanio; fare you well.
Grieve not that I am fall'n to this for you,
For herein Fortune shows herself more kind
Than is her custom; it is still her use[28]

---

22 Full supports.
23 Q1 prints ll. 251–2 as one line; however, some editors print this as two (Mahood, p. 145).
24 At your own expense. Portia's question is meant as a stalling device since her earlier appeal to
    mercy has failed; but also her stalling tactics offer many opportunities for Shylock to exhibit his
    humanity (Gilbert, p. 127).
25 David Suchet, who performed the role of Shylock in John Barton's 1981 production, commented:
    'The real suicidal time for Shylock comes when Portia pleads for charity, not mercy. Shylock knows
    about charity – by God, he does. He's lived with the lack of it. When she mentions the word
    "charity" he stops and thinks [. . .] then he says he cannot find it, it is not in the bond. From that
    moment on he goes for the kill and he knows he's finished as well' (Judith Cook, *Shakespeare's
    Players* (London: Harrap, 1983), p. 85).
26 David Calder (Shylock, 1993) held up the bond so that Antonio could see it (Edelman, p. 228,
    n. 258).
27 Mentally and spiritually fortified.
28 Always her custom.

To let the wretched man outlive his wealth,   265
To view with hollow eye and wrinkled brow
An age of poverty – from which ling'ring penance
Of such misery doth she cut me off.
Commend me to your honourable wife.
Tell her the process of Antonio's end.   270
Say how I loved you, speak me fair in death.
And when the tale is told, bid her be judge
Whether Bassanio had not once a love.[29]
Repent but you that you shall lose your friend,
And he repents not that he pays your debt;   275
For if the Jew do cut but deep enough,
I'll pay it instantly with all my heart.
BASSANIO   Antonio, I am married to a wife
Which is as dear to me as life itself;
But life itself, my wife, and all the world   280
Are not with me esteemed above thy life.
I would lose all, ay, sacrifice them all
Here to this devil, to deliver you.
PORTIA   Your wife would give you little thanks for that,
If she were by to hear you make the offer.   285
GRATIANO   I have a wife who, I protest, I love.
I would she were in heaven, so she could
Entreat some power to change this currish Jew.
NERISSA   'Tis well you offer it behind her back;
The wish would make else an unquiet house.   290
SHYLOCK   These be the Christian husbands! I have a daughter:
Would any of the stock of Barabbas[30]
Had been her husband rather than a Christian! –
We trifle time.[31] I pray thee, pursue sentence.[32]
PORTIA   A pound of that same merchant's flesh is thine.   295
The court awards it, and the law doth give it.
SHYLOCK   Most rightful judge![33]
PORTIA   And you must cut this flesh from off his breast.
The law allows it, and the court awards it.

---

29 The homoerotic overtones that many directors and critics identify in the relationship between
    Antonio and Bassanio have been carried through to this point (and even beyond) in many produc-
    tions. In Trevor Nunn's 1999 production, lines 271–3 were 'accompanied by an embrace more
    passionate than any other in the play, Bassanio burying his head in his lover's shoulder, and
    Antonio stroking the hair and neck of his young friend' (Bulman, p. 130).
30 The thief who was let go in place of Jesus.
31 Waste.
32 Move ahead with the sentencing.
33 Here are six beats of silence as Portia tries desperately to decide what to do next.

SHYLOCK   Most learnèd judge! A sentence! [*To* ANTONIO] Come,
    Prepare!³⁴   300
PORTIA   Tarry a little; there is something else.
    This bond doth give thee here no jot³⁵ of blood;
    The words expressly are 'a pound of flesh'.
    Take then thy bond. Take thou thy pound of flesh.³⁶
    But in the cutting it, if thou dost shed   305
    One drop of Christian blood, thy lands and goods
    Are by the laws of Venice confiscate
    Unto the state of Venice.
GRATIANO   O upright judge!
    Mark, Jew. O learnèd judge!³⁷
SHYLOCK   Is that the law?
PORTIA   Thyself shalt see the Act;   310
    For as thou urgest³⁸ justice, be assured
    Thou shalt have justice, more than thou desir'st.³⁹
GRATIANO   O learnèd judge! Mark, Jew – a learnèd judge!
SHYLOCK   I take this offer, then. Pay the bond thrice
    And let the Christian go.
BASSANIO   Here is the money.   315
PORTIA   Soft!
    The Jew shall have all justice. Soft! No haste!⁴⁰
    He shall have nothing but the penalty.
GRATIANO   O Jew! An upright⁴¹ judge, a learnèd judge!
PORTIA   Therefore prepare thee to cut off the flesh.   320
    Shed thou no blood, nor cut thou less nor more
    But just a pound of flesh. If thou tak'st more
    Or less than a just pound, be it but so much
    As makes it light or heavy in the substance⁴²
    Or the division of the twentieth part   325
    Of one poor scruple – nay, if the scale do turn
    But in the estimation of a hair,⁴³
    Thou diest, and all thy goods are confiscate.
GRATIANO   A second Daniel, a Daniel, Jew!

---

34 In Bill Alexander's production (1987), Shylock donned a *tallith* at this point in the scene and began
    to chant a Hebraic song of sacrifice (Edelman, p. 231, n. 300).
35 Drop.
36 As Portia interprets the bond she carefully turns its legal rhetoric back on Shylock.
37 Miriam Gilbert remarks: 'Indeed, in productions without lots of extras, Gratiano functions as a
    one man jeering section. Mark Lockyer, in 1993, lost all restraint, and seemed so wild that one
    started imagining a character who had taken drugs before coming to court; even Bassanio was
    startled and Salerio and Solanio had to quiet him down' (Gilbert, p. 121).
38 Demand.
39 Q1 prints 'desirst' (Mahood, p. 147).
40 Q1 prints ll. 316–17 as one line.
41 Honest.
42 In weight.
43 As little as the weight of a hair.

Now, infidel, I have you on the hip.[44]   330
PORTIA   Why doth the Jew pause? Take thy forfeiture.
SHYLOCK   Give me my principal,[45] and let me go.[46]
BASSANIO   I have it ready for thee. Here it is.[47]
PORTIA   He hath refused it in the open court.
    He shall have merely justice and his bond.   335
GRATIANO   A Daniel, still say I, a second Daniel!
    I thank thee, Jew, for teaching me that word.
SHYLOCK   Shall I not have barely my principal?
PORTIA   Thou shalt have nothing but the forfeiture
    To be so taken at thy peril, Jew.   340
SHYLOCK   Why then, the devil give him good of it![48]
    I'll stay no longer question.[49]
PORTIA   Tarry, Jew,
    The law hath yet another hold on you.
    It is enacted[50] in the laws of Venice,
    If it be proved against an alien[51]   345
    That by direct or indirect attempts
    He seek the life of any citizen,
    The party[52] 'gainst the which he doth contrive[53]
    Shall seize one half his goods; the other half
    Comes to the privy coffer[54] of the state,   350
    And the offender's life lies in the mercy
    Of the Duke only, 'gainst all other voice – [55]
    In which predicament I say thou stand'st;
    For it appears by manifest proceeding[56]
    That indirectly, and directly too,   355
    Thou hast contrived against the very life
    Of the defendant, and thou hast incurred
    The danger formerly by me rehearsed.[57]
    Down, therefore, and beg mercy of the Duke.

44 At his mercy (a wrestling term).
45 The sum of the original loan.
46 In one of Booth's nineteenth-century productions there was a struggle amongst Bassanio, Gratianio
    and Antonio over a bag of money (Edelman, p. 234, n. 332).
47 The money is, of course, Portia's, making Bassanio 'twice a borrower' since he has already bor-
    rowed money from Antonio.
48 In Otto Schenk's 1969 production (Austrian/West German Television), 'the courtroom spectators
    riotously manhandled Shylock and scrambled for coins on the floor' (Edelman, p. 234, n. 341–2).
49 To argue.
50 Decreed.
51 An outsider. Having construed Shylock as an 'alien' she can then demand that he be punished as a
    Jew who must convert to Christianity.
52 Person.
53 Plot.
54 Treasury.
55 Regardless of what others say. (The Duke has sole authority to pronounce sentence.)
56 Obviously, from what has occurred.
57 Stated.

GRATIANO   Beg that thou mayst have leave to hang thyself!   360
   And yet, thy wealth being forfeit to the state,
   Thou hast not left the value of a cord;
   Therefore thou must be hanged at the state's charge.
DUKE [To SHYLOCK]   That thou shalt see the difference of our
   spirit,
   I pardon thee thy life before thou ask it.   365
   For half thy wealth, it is Antonio's.
   The other half comes to the general state,
   Which humbleness may drive unto a fine.[58]
PORTIA   Ay, for the state, not for Antonio.[59]
SHYLOCK   Nay, take my life and all! Pardon not that!   370
   You take my house when you do take the prop
   That doth sustain my house; you take my life
   When you do take the means whereby I live.
PORTIA   What mercy can you render him, Antonio?
GRATIANO   A halter, gratis.[60] Nothing else, for God's sake!   375
ANTONIO   So please my lord the Duke and all the court
   To quit[61] the fine for one half of his goods,
   I am content, so he will let me have
   The other half in use,[62] to render it
   Upon his death unto the gentleman   380
   That lately stole his daughter.[63]
   Two things provided more: that for this favour
   He presently become a Christian;
   The other, that he do record a gift
   Here in the court, of all he dies possessed   385
   Unto his son Lorenzo and his daughter.
DUKE   He shall do this, or else I do recant[64]
   The pardon that I late pronouncèd here.
PORTIA   Art thou contented, Jew? What dost thou say?
SHYLOCK   I am content.
PORTIA [To NERISSA]   Clerk, draw a deed of gift.   390
SHYLOCK   I pray you, give me leave to go from hence.
   I am not well. Send the deed after me,
   And I will sign it.
DUKE   Get thee gone, but do it.

---

58 The general use of the state, which – if you are humble – could be reduced to a simple fine.
59 i.e. the money intended for Antonio will not be reduced.
60 'Halter, gratis', i.e. a 'hangman's noose, free of charge'.
61 Remit.
62 In trust.
63 Johnson proposes a reading of the terms that Antonio stipulates (p. 68).
64 Withdraw.

GRATIANO [*To* SHYLOCK]   In christ'ning shalt thou have two
    godfathers.[65]
Had I been judge, thou shouldst have had ten more –   395
To bring thee to the gallows, not the font.

Exit [SHYLOCK[66]].

> There follows an interaction amongst Bassanio, Gratiano and their disguised
> wives who demand of them their rings as payment for their legal services. The
> men, at first, protest, but eventually give them over to the judge and his clerk.

[Exeunt omnes.]

Act 5, Scene 1, lines 161–307

> Belmont, Portia's house: as the scene opens Jessica and Lorenzo, already on
> stage, are enjoying the evening when Portia with Nerissa, and Bassanio with
> Gratiano arrive. The women pretend to be angry that their rings have been
> given away, but Portia eventually discloses the truth. She also reveals that all
> three of Antonio's ships have come to port safely. Antonio, who has been a
> 'broker' for the relationship between Portia and Bassanio by lending his wealth,
> again brings the lovers together. In addition to its comic overtones, the last
> word of the play – 'ring' – unites the characters, both literally and metaphoric-
> ally. The circle of friends and lovers in Belmont have come together through
> marriage to create a larger and stronger union; and also, they are a new 'ring' in
> the sense that they constitute the new ruling elite of the social and commercial
> world that they inhabit.
>
> The final scene of the play has traditionally been said to draw the stray ends
> together, fulfilling the 'comic contract' (as Lynda E. Boose puts it) with the audi-
> ence. When Sinead Cusack performed the role of Portia she felt that it became
> another kind of 'trial scene'. She took it to be 'another painful trial scene' (in her
> own words) because 'it is, after all, Portia herself who wins the ring back from
> Bassanio. She wins both ways, and is in a wonderful position to know the

65 In the Christian faith a godfather guides the spiritual education of a baptised child. 'Godfathers'
    also jokingly referred to a jury (a body of twelve men).
66 Shylock's exit has been performed very differently by different actors, and in the 1998 new Globe
    production, Norbert Kentrup (Shylock) was hissed off the stage. As Miriam Gilbert notes, some
    productions have 'read the exit in terms of humiliation' while in others Shylock has exited in a
    'businesslike' manner. Philip Voss slipped on the coins and had difficulty standing up. In some
    productions the Christians are openly antagonistic right to Shylock's exit. Gilbert mentions one
    production in which Gratiano snatched the yarmulke from Shylock's head, and Bassanio and
    Gratiano pushed him out of the court (see Gilbert, pp. 140–3). Q1 prints only 'Exit', omitting
    'Shylock' (Mahood, p. 150).

whole truth about Bassanio in the courtroom, and is therefore in a position to show him something as well as to forgive him' (**pp. 121–2**). Therefore, there are really three 'trial' scenes in the play, including the casket test and the courtroom scene (Act 4, Scene 1). And, as Cusack implies, the mercy that seems oddly absent in the previous scene returns in the final moments of the play.

Commentators have written extensively on the exchange of rings that is the centre of both the re-ordering and the humour of Act 5, Scene 1. Many note that when Portia returns the ring to Bassanio (lines 254–5), she gives it first to Antonio who then hands the ring to Bassanio. Moreover, Portia makes a point of the fact that, in the future, Antonio will be Bassanio's 'surety' (legal guarantor). Additionally, some critics – for instance, Karen Newman and Lynda E. Boose – are concerned with the way in which the rings, as symbols, travel from hand to hand in the course of the play. In a play in which there are so many 'merchants' and so many 'trades', the ultimate 'broker' might be Portia, Boose suggests, 'who can best lay claim to being the signified "merchant" of the play's ambiguous title'. Moreover, Boose asserts, Portia (as the play's 'chief banker' and a woman) 'acquires control over any remaining male debts [. . .] But through the sexual innuendos of the ring game, it likewise becomes clear that Portia's bid implicitly promises Bassanio and Gratiano [. . .] a return interest that neither Antonio nor Shylock can offer as creditors [. . .] in the "act of generation," Portia, we might say, can offer stock options', i.e. in the form of heirs (**pp. 86–8**). Yet, as Newman notes, by putting the ring on the hand of Doctor Balthazar, 'Bassanio opens his marriage to forces of disorder, to bisexuality, equality between the sexes, and linguistic equivalence in opposition to the decorous world of Renaissance marriage represented by the love pledges in Act III. ii. Bassanio gives his ring to an "unruly woman," that is, to a woman who steps outside her role and functions as subservient, a woman who dresses like a man' (**p. 85**). For Newman, as well as for Alan Sinfield, Portia's behaviour exposes the male homosocial bond (**p. 96**); but, as Catherine Belsey points out, 'homosexual acts were perceived as less dangerous to men than heterosexual love, because it was association with women which was effeminating' (**p. 91**).

For some critics the end of the play presents a closed circle – literally and metaphorically – as the rings are returned to the correct 'hands' and as the friendship circle widens sufficiently to include Antonio who is a stranger to Belmont and to Portia. But Leonard Tennenhouse expresses discomfort with the resolution of the play as Shakespeare has constructed it; yet the play seems not to be able to end 'well' whether it were to end in Venice or in Belmont. The play cannot end in Venice, as Tennenhouse states, because the locale 'is so firmly rooted in mercantilism that no amount of artistry can wish these economic realities away'. Yet when all is said and done, Tennenhouse comments: 'something seems to have gone wrong with the ending [. . .] The translation of the meaning of the bond, the humor of the ring plot resolution, and the isolation of Antonio are disturbing [. . .] Despite its contrast to Venice [. . .] Belmont becomes in the fifth act a less lyrical, less benevolent world – a world of sexual contest, threatened betrayals, and rivalrous competition' (p. 83).

The end of the play is therefore awkward both because Antonio is expected to 'share' Bassanio with Portia, and also because there are three of them and Antonio is the only character left without a partner. This raises many questions for directors in planning the last moments of a production when the characters are actually exiting the stage. As Robert Smallwood notes (see pp. 128–30), the last word of the first quarto (1600) is simply 'Exeunt', which offers little guidance. Nonetheless, whether Antonio exits with Bassanio and Portia (as in some productions) or whether he remains alone as the stage lights dim (as in other productions), there is a significant difference in what the audience perceives. If Antonio returns, alone, to the melancholy that overwhelmed him at the beginning of the play it would seem that the end of the play offers less of a new beginning for Antonio than for the other characters who, as newly-weds, have their lives before them. However, if Antonio exits between Portia and Bassanio, as is sometimes the case, then he appears to be 'brokering' the relationship still, and the audience is left to wonder whether he won't continue to do so, perhaps for ever. If the latter is the case, then the audience is prompted to ask a further question: is there any romantic love in Shakespeare's world, even in a mythical place like Belmont, that is not somehow 'brokered' by commercial transactions? Of course, most readers and spectators would prefer to answer 'no'; eternal optimism seems in order when we are reading or watching a play that is classified as a 'romantic comedy'. Still, when Portia says, in her last lines, 'It is almost morning/and yet I am sure you are not satisfied/Of these events at full', some directors have positioned Portia on the stage so that she appears to be addressing the audience's discontent as well as the discontent of the other characters on the stage.

Some critics, such as Lynda E. Boose, would argue that spectators watching a comedy enter into a 'comic contract', and, therefore, they want to be 'satisfied' at the end of the play. With the players they enter into a contract (a 'bond' of sorts), from which they hope to gain 'interest'. For Shakespeare and his contemporaries the process was no different, except that he and his fellow actors were, self-consciously, the traders and the merchants who owned the playhouses and made a living from it. Boose notes that, at a certain point – like Bassanio's ring – the play becomes 'transferred' to the hands of the audience and the spectators end up in a 'marriage' with Portia and Bassanio (along with the playwright and his play). So, by extension, did the actors who performed *The Merchant of Venice* in Shakespeare's time. The 'marriage' of actor and audience was integral to the commercial world of the early modern theatre.

Enter PORTIA *and* NERISSA [*dressed as themselves. To them,* ANTONIO, BASSANIO *and* GRATIANO. GRATIANO *frantically tries to explain why he has given away his ring.*]

GRATIANO [*To* NERISSA]   Now by this hand, I gave it to a youth,
  A kind of boy, a little scrubbèd[1] boy,
  No higher than thyself, the judge's clerk,
  A prating[2] boy, that begged it as a fee.
  I could not for my heart deny it him.   165
PORTIA   You were to blame, I must be plain with you,
  To part so slightly with your wife's first gift,
  A thing stuck on with oaths upon your finger
  And so riveted with faith unto your flesh.
  I gave my love a ring and made him swear   170
  Never to part with it; and here he stands.
  I dare be sworn for him he would not leave[3] it,
  Nor pluck it from his finger for the wealth
  That the world masters. Now, in faith, Gratiano,
  You give your wife too unkind a cause of grief.   175
  An[4] 'twere to me, I should be mad at it.
BASSANIO [*aside*]   Why, I were best to cut my left hand off
  And swear I lost the ring defending it.
GRATIANO   My Lord Bassanio gave his ring away
  Unto the judge that begged it, and indeed   180
  Deserved it, too; and then the boy, his clerk,
  That took some pains[5] in writing, he begged mine,
  And neither man nor master would take aught
  But the two rings.
PORTIA [*to* BASSANIO]   What ring gave you, my lord?
  Not that, I hope, which you received of me.   185
BASSANIO   If I could add a lie unto a fault,
  I would deny it; but you see my finger
  Hath not the ring upon it. It is gone.
PORTIA   Even so void is your false heart of truth.
  By heaven, I will ne'er come in your bed   190
  Until I see the ring.
NERISSA [*to* GRATIANO]   Nor I in yours
  Till I again see mine.
BASSANIO   Sweet Portia,
  If you did know to whom I gave the ring,
  If you did know for whom I gave the ring.
  And would conceive for what I gave the ring,   195
  And how unwillingly I left the ring,
  When naught would be accepted but the ring,
  You would abate the strength of your displeasure.

1   Stunted.
2   Chattering.
3   Part with.
4   And.
5   Effort, care.

PORTIA   If you had known the virtue[6] of the ring,
   Or half her worthiness that gave the ring,   200
   Or your own honour to contain the ring,[7]
   You would not then have parted with the ring.
   What man is there so much unreasonable,
   If you had pleased to have defended it
   With any terms of zeal,[8] wanted the modesty   205
   To urge the thing held as a ceremony?[9]
   Nerissa teaches me what to believe:
   I'll die for't but some woman had the ring!
BASSANIO   No, by my honour, madam, by my soul,
   No woman had it, but a civil doctor,[10]   210
   Which did refuse three thousand ducats of me
   And begged the ring, the which I did deny him
   And suffered him to go displeased away –
   Even he that had held up[11] the very life
   Of my dear friend. What should I say, sweet lady?   215
   I was enforced to send it after him.
   I was beset with shame and courtesy.
   My honour would not let ingratitude
   So much besmear[12] it. Pardon me, good lady,
   For by these blessèd candles of the night,[13]   220
   Had you been there I think you would have begged
   The ring of me to give the worthy doctor.
PORTIA   Let not that doctor e'er come near my house.
   Since he hath got the jewel that I loved,
   And that which you did swear to keep for me,   225
   I will become as liberal as you.
   I'll not deny him anything I have,
   No, not my body nor my husband's bed.
   Know him I shall, I am well sure of it.
   Lie not a night from home. Watch me like Argus.[14]   230
   If you do not, if I be left alone,
   Now, by mine honour, which is yet mine own,
   I'll have that doctor for my bedfellow.
NERISSA   And I his clerk. Therefore be well advised

---

6 Power.
7 i.e. it was a matter of honour to keep the ring.
8 Determination.
9 Would have lacked good manners, so as to insist that the ring was an important symbol, something sacred.
10 Doctor of civil law.
11 Preserved.
12 Stain.
13 Stars.
14 Argus was a creature, in classical mythology, with one hundred eyes who guarded Io, daughter of the river god.

How you do leave me to mine own protection. 235

GRATIANO Well, do you so. Let not me take[15] him, then.
For if I do, I'll mar the young clerk's pen.[16]

ANTONIO I am th'unhappy subject of these quarrels.

PORTIA Sir, grieve not you. You are welcome notwithstanding.

BASSANIO Portia, forgive me this enforcèd wrong, 240
And in the hearing of these many friends,
I swear to thee, even by thine own fair eyes,
Wherein I see myself –

PORTIA   Mark you but that?
In both my eyes he doubly sees himself,
In each eye one. Swear by your double self, 245
And there's an oath of credit![17]

BASSANIO   Nay, but hear me.
Pardon this fault, and by my soul I swear
I never more will break an oath with thee.

ANTONIO I once did lend my body for his wealth[18]
Which, but for him that had your husband's ring, 250
Had quite miscarried. I dare be bound again,
My soul upon the forfeit,[19] that your lord
Will never more break faith advisedly.[20]

PORTIA Then you shall be his surety.[21] Give him this
[She gives the ring to ANTONIO][22]
And bid him keep it better than the other. 255

ANTONIO Here, Lord Bassanio; swear to keep this ring. [He hands
the ring to BASSANIO]

BASSANIO By heaven, it is the same I gave the doctor!

PORTIA I had it of him. Pardon me, Bassanio,
For by this ring the doctor lay with me.

NERISSA And pardon me, my gentle Gratiano; 260
For that same scrubbèd boy, the doctor's clerk,
In lieu of[23] this last night did lie with me.

GRATIANO Why, this is like the mending of highways
In summer where the ways are fair enough!
What, are we cuckolds[24] ere we have deserved it? 265

---

15 Catch.
16 'I'll harm the young clerk's quill pen' (also, figuratively, penis).
17 Believable vow. (Portia is being sarcastic.)
18 (1) Well-being, (2) material reward. Johnson offers a reading of 'wealth' that is 'opposite to *adversity* or *calamity*' (p. 69).
19 Risking to forfeit his soul. (Previously Bassanio pledged his body.)
20 Intentionally.
21 Security.
22 As has been noted in the headnote, and in Newman's analysis (which follows the movement of Portia's ring in order to interrogate Elizabethan structures of 'figural and sexual exchange' (p. 85), Portia gives the ring first to Antonio who then passes it to Bassanio.
23 In return for.
24 Men whose wives are unfaithful.

PORTIA   Speak not so grossly.[25] You are all amazed.
Here is a letter. Read it at your leisure.
It comes from Padua, from Bellario.
There you shall find that Portia was the doctor,
Nerissa there her clerk. Lorenzo here   270
Shall witness I set forth as soon as you
And even but now returned; I have not yet
Entered my house. Antonio, you are welcome,
And I have better news in store for you
Than you expect. Unseal this letter soon.   275
There you shall find three of your argosies[26]
Are richly come to harbour suddenly.
You shall not know by what strange accident
I chancèd on this letter.
ANTONIO [*Reads the letter*]   I am dumb![27]
BASSANIO   Were you the doctor and I knew you not?   280
GRATIANO   Were you the clerk that is to make me cuckold?
NERISSA   Ay, but the clerk that never means to do it,
Unless he live until he be a man.
BASSANIO   Sweet doctor, you shall be my bedfellow.
When I am absent, then lie with my wife.   285
ANTONIO   Sweet lady, you have given me life and living,
For here I read for certain that my ships
Are safely come to road.[28]
PORTIA   How now, Lorenzo!
My clerk hath some good comforts too for you.
NERISSA   Ay, and I'll give them him without a fee.   290
There do I give to you and Jessica
From the rich Jew, a special deed of gift,[29]
After his death, of all he dies possessed of.
LORENZO   Fair ladies, you drop manna[30] in the way
Of starvèd people.
PORTIA   It is almost morning,   295
And yet I am sure you are not satisfied
Of these events at full.[31] Let us go in,
And charge us there upon inter'gatories,[32]
And we will answer all things faithfully.

---

25 Coarsely, rudely.
26 Merchant ships.
27 Struck dumb, i.e. silenced.
28 Anchorage.
29 A legal document conveying property from one person to another.
30 Food, miraculously discovered by the Israelites during the Exodus, which was – they thought – sent from heaven (Exodus 16:14–15).
31 In detail.
32 Witnesses, under oath, were required to answer a set of questions called 'interrogatories'.

GRATIANO   Let it be so. The first inter'gatory   300
        That my Nerissa shall be sworn on is
        Whether till the next night she had rather stay
        Or go to bed now, being two hours to day.
        But were the day come, I should wish it dark
        Till I were couching[33] with the doctor's clerk.   305
        Well, while I live I'll fear no other thing
        So sore as keeping safe Nerissa's ring.[34]

                                                            Exeunt.[35]

---

33 Going to bed.
34 Literally, 'while I live I'll guard nothing so much as Nerissa's ring', i.e. jewellery (with a bawdy pun on 'ring' as 'vulva').
35 In his essay on the significance of directorial decisions in Shakespearean productions, Robert Smallwood discusses the many different ways in which directors have set up the actors' final exit from the stage, and the ways in which these have shaped, in a vital manner, the audience's last impressions of the play (pp. 128–30).

4

Further Reading

Further Reading

Recommended Editions

The First Quarto of *The Merchant of Venice* appeared in 1600, and is designated by editors as 'Q1'. It is difficult to know what the source of this text was; however, it appears to be a good text, and some editors have concluded that it was printed from an authorial draft of the play. The text reproduced in this book is based on Q1. A second quarto (Q2) was printed in 1619 (though it was falsely dated '1600'), which was probably taken from the text of Q1. Then in 1623, seven years after Shakespeare's death, a complete collection of his plays appeared for the first time in a large format volume, intended for purchase by individuals who owned private libraries, or as an expensive gift. This well-known collection – which was compiled by John Heminges and Henry Condell, two of Shakespeare's friends and fellow actors – is referred to as the First Folio (F1). It was clearly treasured in its own time, and down through the ages. As a result, roughly two hundred copies of the Folio have survived.[1] The stage directions in F1 suggest that theatrical sources were consulted in the preparation of the text. Readers who wish to see what the original Folio looks like should consult a photographic facsimile, for instance *The First Folio of Shakespeare* prepared by Charlton Hinman, with a new introduction by Peter W. M. Blayney (New York.: W. W. Norton, 1996), or its earlier manifestation (prepared by Hinman alone and published in 1968).

The First Quarto (1600) can be consulted in an old spelling, modern-type edition edited by Annabel Patterson, *The Most Excellent Historie of The Merchant of Venice* (London: Prentice Hall/Harvester Wheatsheaf, 1995). Readers who wish to see a photographic facsimile of the First Quarto, owned by the Huntington Library, should consult Michael J. B. Allen and Kenneth Muir, eds, *Shakespeare's Plays in Quarto* (Berkeley, Calif.: University of California Press, 1981), pp. 449–86. Excellent modernised editions, all based on Q1, which offer the full text of the play are:

---

1   This statistic was obtained from a recent count done by Anthony James West, *The Shakespeare First Folio: the History of the Book* (Oxford: Oxford University Press, 2001), vol. 1, p. viii. West lists 228 copies as currently being extant.

A. R. Braunmuller, ed., *The Merchant of Venice* (New York: Penguin, 2000).

Jay L. Halio, ed., *The Merchant of Venice* (New York: Oxford University Press, 1993).

M. M. Mahood, ed., *The Merchant of Venice* (Cambridge: Cambridge University Press, 1987).

Barbara Mowat and Paul Werstine, eds, *The Merchant of Venice* (New York: Washington Square Press, 1992).

Historical Background

Branca, Cittore, ed., *Merchant Writers of the Italian Renaissance from Boccaccio to Machiavelli* (New York: Marsilio Publishers, 1999). A collection of stories and detailed descriptions of everyday life created by businessmen whose dedication to finance was entwined with the moral and philosophical sense that the Italian city states would eventually become the greatest economic and cultural force in early modern Europe.

Chojnacki, Stanley, *Women and Men in Renaissance Venice* (Baltimore, Md.: Johns Hopkins University Press, 2000). The twelve essays in this excellent collection cover marriage regulation, dowries, kinship ties, adolescence and gender, husband–wife relations and patrician bachelors.

Curiel, Roberta and Bernard Dov Cooperman, *The Venetian Ghetto* (New York: Rizzolli International Publications, 1990). A fascinating cultural history of the Venetian ghetto, featuring an erudite, informative narrative and many captivating photographs of local landmarks.

Davis, Robert C. and Benjamin Ravid, *The Jews of Early Modern Europe* (Baltimore, Md.: Johns Hopkins University Press, 2001). This collection contains the most up-to-date thinking on the Jews in early modern Venice. The essays cover predictable areas of interest, such as economics, politics and cultural history, as well as women's studies, religious studies and musicology.

Divitiis, Gigliola Pagano de, *English Merchants in Seventeenth-century Italy* (Cambridge: Cambridge University Press, 1990). The author traces the takeover of Mediterranean trade by English merchants and mercantile practices up through the seventeenth century.

Dotson, John E., *Merchant Culture in Fourteenth Century Venice* (Binghamton, NY: Medieval & Renaissance Texts & Studies, 1994). A careful study of the well-known *Zibaldone da Canal*, an early notebook that offers a detailed picture of merchant life in Venice.

Katz, David S., *The Jews in the History of England, 1485–1850* (Oxford: Oxford University Press, 1994). Katz provides an excellent overview of the issues and incidents that shaped the history of the Jews in England. His bibliography (pp. 391–432) includes a useful list of manuscript and modern secondary sources, as well as citations of early printed books.

Lane, Frederic C., *Venice: A Maritime Republic* (Baltimore, Md.: Johns Hopkins University Press, 1973). Lane's comprehensive history is the standard reference work on Venice.

Pullan, Brian, 'The Occupation and Investments of the Venetian Nobility in the Middle and Late Sixteenth Century', in *Renaissance Venice*, ed. J. R. Hale (Totowa, NJ: Rowman and Littlefield, 1973), pp. 379–408. An informative historical description and analysis of the financial interests and habits of the Venetians.

Wills, Garry, *Venice: Lion City* (New York: Simon & Schuster, 2001). Wills surveys fifteenth- and sixteenth-century Venice to demonstrate that it was, in reality, a ruthless imperial city noted for its shrewd business acumen, rather than a city of decadence.

Literary Criticism

Barber, C. L., *Shakespeare's Festive Comedy* (Princeton, NJ: Princeton University Press, 1959). One of the traditional sources for the discussion of Shakespearean comedy, including *The Merchant*, as a dramatic genre.

Cartelli, Thomas, 'Shakespeare's *Merchant*, Marlowe's *Jew*: The Problem of Cultural Difference', *Shakespeare Studies*, 20 (1988), 255–60. Cartelli argues that Marlowe's *The Jew of Malta* influenced not only Shakespeare's play, but that the critical response to it has also indirectly shaped the tradition of critical response to *The Merchant*.

Danson, Lawrence, *The Harmonies of The Merchant of Venice* (New Haven, Conn.: Yale University Press, 1978). Danson focuses on the emblem of the circle as the play's most dominant symbol. From this the central contrasts of the play – Venice/Belmont, justice/mercy, Jew/Christian – which appear at first to be a series of complex contrasts 'interlock into a concordant whole'.

Gross, John, *Shylock* (New York: Simon & Schuster, 1992). Gross examines the origins and evolution of the Shylock character within Shakespeare's play, and then discusses the many interpreters of Shylock's character – in Britain and America – up to World War II. The final section of the book covers a more extensive geographical, socio-political and cultural range of interpretations.

Hutson, Lorna, *The Usurer's Daughter: Male Friendship and Fictions of Women in Sixteenth-century England* (London: Routledge, 1994), pp. 224–38. In the epilogue to Hutson's book, the author discusses the ways in which *The Merchant* measures up to the paradigm that she explores regarding the anxieties created by male friendship. Within this context she also comments on *The Merchant* vis-à-vis Shakespeare's source story *Il Pecorone*.

Jardine, Lisa, 'Cultural Confusion and Shakespeare's Learned Heroine: These Old Paradoxes', *Shakespeare Quarterly*, 38 (1987), 1–18. Jardine discusses Renaissance society's ambivalence about the place of women and demonstrates how Portia's skilful use of the law produces a 'confused response' within the audience and *The Merchant*.

Novy, Marianne, 'Sex, Reciprocity and Self-sacrifice in *The Merchant of Venice*' in *Human Sexuality in the Middle Ages and Renaissance*, ed. Douglas Radcliffe-Umstead (Pittsburgh, Pa.: University of Pittsburgh Press, 1978), pp. 153–66. Novy asserts that *The Merchant* exemplifies the divided attitude between self-promotion (Shylock) and asceticism (Antonio). Portia, who both gives and receives money and love, serves as a bridge between medieval attitudes and the newly emerging Renaissance attitudes.

Shapiro, Michael, 'Duplication in *The Merchant of Venice*' in *Gender in Play on the Shakespearean Stage* (Ann Arbor, Mich.: University of Michigan Press, 1994), pp. 97–113. Shapiro concentrates on Shakespeare's use of a specific dramatic device – the cross-dressing motif – concluding that 'in adding a second and a third woman in cross-gender disguise . . . Shakespeare transcended the simple duplications of farce, but used repetitions to achieve more sophisticated kinds of cross-referencing' (p. 97).

Production History

Bulman, James C., *The Merchant of Venice* (Manchester: Manchester University Press, 1991). Bulman's overview concentrates on key productions from Henry Irving through to the production in 1987 by the Royal Shakespeare Company.

Dessen, Alan C., 'The Elizabethan Stage Jew and Christian Example: Gerontus, Barabas, and Shylock', *Modern Language Quarterly*, 35 (1974), 231–45. An examination of Shakespeare's character in the context of other stage Jews of his time.

Edelman, Charles, ed., *The Merchant of Venice* (Cambridge: Cambridge University Press, 2002). An edition of the play that pays special attention to production history, both in its introduction and in its annotations.

Gilbert, Miriam, *The Merchant of Venice* (London: Thomson Learning, 2002). Gilbert surveys and analyses the most significant productions of the play performed by the Royal Shakespeare Company between 1947 and 1997.

Hankey, Julie, 'Victorian Portias: Shakespeare's Borderline Heroine', *Shakespeare Quarterly*, 45, 4 (1994), 426–48. The article examines 'the status of Shakespeare's women not in Shakespeare's time but in the afterlife of his plays'.

Lelyveld, Toby, *Shylock on the Stage* (London: Routledge & Kegan Paul, 1961). Lelyveld offers the most detailed account of the production history of *The Merchant of Venice*, with specific attention to the character of Shylock, from the late sixteenth century through to the early twentieth century.

Oz, Avraham, 'Transformations of Authenticity: *The Merchant of Venice* in Israel', *Jahrbuch Deautsche Shakespeare Gesellschaft West*, 1983, pp. 156–68. A description and analysis of productions of *The Merchant* in Israel, in which a heroic portrayal of Shylock is often used as a touchstone in the making of a national Jewish identity.

Salgado, Gamini, *Eyewitnesses of Shakespeare: First-hand Accounts of Performances, 1590–1890* (New York: Barnes and Noble Books, 1975), pp. 127–43. The book reproduces several first-hand accounts of key performances between the mid–1750s and 1879, including reports of performances by Charles Macklin, Edmund Kean, Charles Kean and Ellen Terry.

Adaptations

Armour, Richard, *Twisted Tales from Shakespeare* (New York: McGraw-Hill, 1957), pp. 108–24. Armour's version of *The Merchant of Venice* is a witty retelling of the plot, full of humorous puns.

Castelnuovo-Tedesco, Mario, *The Merchant of Venice*, Italian translation by the composer (Milan: Ricordi, 1966), 28pp. The libretto of Castelnuovo-Tedesco's opera, performed first in 1961.

Cournos, John, 'Shylock's Choice' in *Imagist Anthology 1930* (London: Chatto & Windus, 1930), pp. 34–42. An interesting one-act play which presents a conversation between Shylock and Tubal on the night before the trial of Antonio. Shylock imagines that he first menaces Antonio with his knife and then flings it away, offering him mercy. In this version of the story Shylock's final revenge will be the fact that Antonio will ultimately owe his life to him.

Dean, Winton, 'Shakespeare and Opera' in Phyllis Hartnoll, ed., *Shakespeare in Music* (London: Macmillan, 1964), pp. 89–175. Winton Dean discusses operas based on *The Merchant*, including those by Pinsuti (1873), Taubman (*Porzia*, 1916), Adrian Beecham (1922), Hahn (1935) and Castelnuovo-Tedesco (1961).

Dias, Walter, *Voices from Shakespeareana: Dramatic Autobiographies* (New Delhi: S. Chand, 1978). Dias's collection contains dramatic monologues by Portia, Shylock and Jessica, all of whom are aware of what scholars and critics are saying about them. Each explains his or her part in Shakespeare's play, filling in background. Each monologue represents an interesting, substantive interpretation of the character.

Ervine, St John, *The Lady of Belmont* (New York: Macmillan, 1924). A five-act play beginning ten years after the trial scene, in which events are complicated when Bassanio, a profligate adulterer, has an affair with Shylock's daughter, Jessica. In the last part of the play Shylock ends up lending money to Portia, since Bassanio has spent virtually every penny of her money, and she asks Shylock for his forgiveness.

Granville, George, Lord Lansdowne, *The Jew of Venice* (London: Cornmarket, 1969). A facsimile of the popular Restoration adaptation, published originally in 1701. A discussion of the play can be found in Hazleton Spencer, *Shakespeare Improved* (Cambridge, Mass.: Harvard University Press, 1927), pp. 338–44.

Gurney, A. R., *Overtime: A Modern Sequel to 'The Merchant of Venice'* (New York: Dramatists Play Service, Inc., 1996). Gurney's play, a sequel set in contemporary times, premièred at the Old Globe Theatre in San Diego, California (July 1995). It was later produced in New York by Manhattan Theatre Club (5 March 1996).

Ibn-Zahav, Ari, *Jessica, My Daughter* (New York: Crown Publishers, 1948). This novel, based on Shakespeare's play, focuses on Jessica.

Lewisohn, Ludwig *The Last Days of Shylock* (New York: Harper & Brothers, 1931). This novel seeks to explain the events from Shylock's tragic past that shape his actions in Shakespeare's play. The second part of the novel, beginning with Shylock's baptism, consists of Shylock's escape to Constantinople where he is taken in by the Sultan's treasurer, Joseph Nassi, a Spanish Jew. At the end there is a chance encounter between Jessica and Shylock, who is finally reunited with his daughter and his grandchildren.

Rubenstein, Harold, *Shylock's End and Other Plays* (London: Gollancz, 1971). *Shylock's End* (pp. 75–104) purports to be a dream-play in one act, which begins several years after the trial when Lorenzo comes to Shylock to borrow 3000 ducats.

Wesker, Arnold, *The Merchant* (London: Methuen, 1983). Wesker's two-act play begins with the friendship between Antonio and Shylock, from which context Antonio borrows the money that Bassanio needs in order to court Portia. Shylock proposes the flesh-bond in order to make fun of the rigidity of Venetian law, but the play takes a serious twist at the end when Venetian justice deprives Shylock of all he owns. The play exists in many other editions and collections. For commentary on Wesker's play, see Ann-Mari Hedbäck, 'The Scheme of Things in Arnold Wesker's *The Merchant*', *Studia Neophilologica*, 51 (1979), 233–44.

Films

The Merchant of Venice starring Sir Laurence Olivier and Joan Plowright, 1973, directed by Jonathan Miller for BBC TV (available on tape cassettes from major video distributors).

Other recent film versions include two productions sponsored by BBC TV. The first, directed by Cedric Messina, was produced in 1972, starring Frank Finlay and Maggie Smith. The second production, directed by Jack Gold in 1980, starred Warren Mitchell and Gemma Jones. (These are not currently available to the general public.)

The National Theatre production, on stage in 1999, was made into a film later on and aired in the USA by PBS on 8 October 2001 (sponsored by Exxon Mobil Masterpiece Theatre). The production, set in 1930s Venice, was directed by Trevor Nunn and starred Henry Goodman (Shylock) and Derbhle Crotty (Portia).

The most recent film version of the play is *The Maori Merchant of Venice*, released in New Zealand on 17 February 2002, and directed by Don Selwyn. This translation was created by Pei Te Hurinui Jones. It stars Waihoroi Shortland (Shylock) and Ngarimu Daniels (Portia).

Sound Recordings

Australia: ABC FM Radio (Sydney), 1988, cassette tape (90 mins).

CBC11/Canada: Canadian Broadcasting Corporation, 2 CDs (120 mins), with Peter Hutt, Donald Carrier, Lucy Peacock, Paul Soles (part of the Bell Canada/ Shaw Festival reading series for CBC Radio).

UK: two-cassette tape recording done in 1963 (140 minutes), with Hugh Griffith (Shylock) and Dorothy Tutin (Portia). Caedmon Audio (Shakespeare Recording Society Production).

UK: two-cassette tape recording done in 1998 (2 hrs, 30 mins), with Bill Nighy (Antonio), Trevor Peacock (Shylock), Haydn Gwynne (Portia) and others (Arkangel Audiobooks (ARK08)/Arkangel Complete Shakespeare); unabridged text.

UK: two-CD set released in 2000 (2 hrs), with Warren Mitchell (Shylock), Gemma Jones (Portia), Martin Jarvis (Antonio) and Samuel West (Bassanio). BBC radio production.

USA: two-CD sound recording (148 mins) of the 1938–9 Mercury Theatre Production, starring Orson Welles (Pearl's Plays and Poets Series).

Index

Kortner, Fritz 106, 107
Krauss, Werner 106

Laban, parable of 40, 48, 153n
Lamb, Charles and Mary 108, 109
Langley, Francis 18, 23
Lanham, Henry 17, 18, 22
Lopez, Roderigo 16–17
Lyceum Theatre 111

Macklin, Charles 99
McDiarmid, Ian 102, 119, 122–3
Macready, William Charles 100
Mahood, M. M. 138
Maori film version 117
Marrano see Jews
Marlowe, Christopher: The Jew of Malta
    23, 28–9, 135
marriage: irreligious 48; parental authority
    and 20, 48; for wealth 3, 48, 60, 61,
    81
Marxist interpretation 79–80, 91–3
Matthews, Brander 58
mercantilism: and Christian virtue 12–13,
    38–40, 40–2; mercantile culture 1, 3,
    12–13, 80–2, 83, 158
Merchant of Venice: adaptations 56, 108,
    109, 203–4; Arragon, Duke of 62, 88,
    89, 90, 95, 137, 164, 165, 171, 179,
    180; casket test 55, 58–9, 62, 64–5, 74,
    77, 85, 88–90, 91, 109, 119, 120–1,
    134, 146, 147, 158, 159, 160, 164, 179;
    'choosing' 62, 88–90, 160, 164, 170,
    171, 179; classification (as comedy,
    tragedy, fable, fairy tale) 2, 57, 58, 70–1,
    72, 75–6, 77, 99, 116; colonialism and
    60; as a comedy 2; court performances
    99; critical history 55–63; design
    elements 110–11, 126–7; disguise 49, 60,
    83, 91, 127, 178; early criticism 56–7,
    64–78; fairy-tale aspects 77–8; film
    versions 117–19, 204; flesh–bond plot
    19, 55, 63, 134, 150, 167, 168, 179,
    189; Gratiano 21, 47, 59, 60, 75, 76, 95,
    134, 137, 164, 167, 170, 178, 180, 188,
    189; Jessica 21, 47, 59, 60, 74, 83, 94,
    95, 101, 116, 122, 127, 129, 164, 167,
    177, 188; laceration 63, 93–4, 179;
    Lancelot 95, 103, 134, 163, 177;
    Lorenzo 21, 59, 74, 127, 129, 167, 177,
188; mercy 20, 58, 65, 74, 84, 121, 178,
    179, 189; modern criticism 57–63,
    79–96; Morocco, Prince of 60, 62, 68,
    74, 82, 88, 89, 90, 95, 96, 137, 157, 158,
    159, 160, 165, 171, 179, 180; Nerissa
    20, 21, 47, 59, 60, 67, 74, 78, 91, 95,
    108, 121, 129, 134, 135, 137, 146, 165,
    170, 177; printing of 2, 24, 26, 55;
    revenge 65, 74, 75, 76, 105, 133, 167;
    riddles 59, 62, 91, 160; rings, ring plot
    20, 61, 84–6, 87, 91, 122, 188, 190;
    ritual murder 63, 93–4, 179; setting
    7–12, 59, 60, 82–4, 85, 90, 111, 117,
    140, 189–90; sexuality 63, 80–2, 85–6,
    94, 95–6, 141, 158, 160, 179, 189; sound
    recordings 204–5; sources 69, 134–5;
    suitors to Portia (in general) 61, 67,
    88–90, 90–1, 95, 134, 158; text and
    textual issues 56, 66, 67–8, 114, 129,
    135, 140, 166n, 173n, 175n, 199; title
    page 55; translations 1, 109; trial scene
    49, 62, 63, 65, 72, 74, 75–6, 82, 94, 100,
    121, 177–88, 189; Tubal 167–8;
    Venetians (in the play) 95, 117, 127–8;
    see also stage history, television
Miller, Jonathan 101, 107, 145n, 161n,
    165n, 166n
Miln Company 109
Milton, John 90, 171
miscegenation 81, 171
Mitchell, Warren 117
money lending see usury
More, Sir Thomas 49
Morris, Jan 9, 32–4
Morrison, Scott 118
Munday, Antony 135
Murray, Gilbert 76
Murry, John Middleton 58
Muru, Selwyn 118

National Theatre 102
new historicist interpretation 80–2
Newman, Karen 61, 84–6, 146, 160, 179,
    189
Nicholls, Anthony 127
Nunn, Trevor 128, 145n, 156n, 184n

Olivier, Sir Laurence 102, 114, 117, 125,
    153n, 154n
Olivier, Richard 103

eBooks – at www.eBookstore.tandf.co.uk

A library at your fingertips!

eBooks are electronic versions of printed books. You can store them on your PC/laptop or browse them online.

They have advantages for anyone needing rapid access to a wide variety of published, copyright information.

eBooks can help your research by enabling you to bookmark chapters, annotate text and use instant searches to find specific words or phrases. Several eBook files would fit on even a small laptop or PDA.

NEW: Save money by eSubscribing: cheap, online access to any eBook for as long as you need it.

Annual subscription packages

We now offer special low-cost bulk subscriptions to packages of eBooks in certain subject areas. These are available to libraries or to individuals.

For more information please contact webmaster.ebooks@tandf.co.uk

We're continually developing the eBook concept, so keep up to date by visiting the website.

www.eBookstore.tandf.co.uk